PHP
Essentials

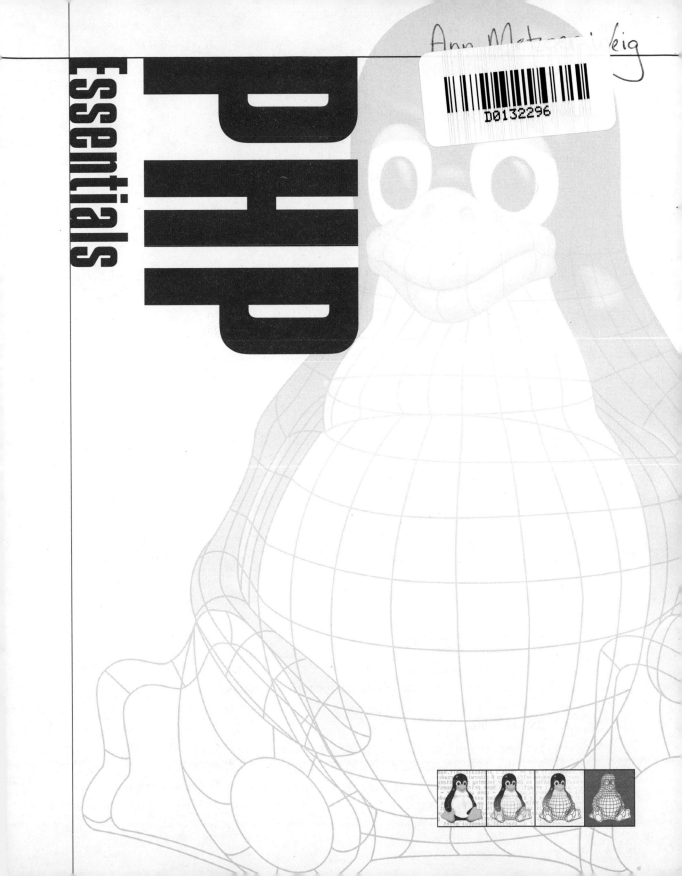

Send Us Your Comments

To comment on this book or any other PRIMA TECH title, visit our reader response page on the Web at **www.prima-tech.com/comments**.

How to Order

For information on quantity discounts, contact the publisher: Prima Publishing, P.O. Box 1260BK, Rocklin, CA 95677-1260; (916) 787-7000. On your letterhead include information concerning the intended use of the books and the number of books you wish to purchase. For individual orders, turn to the back of this book for more information.

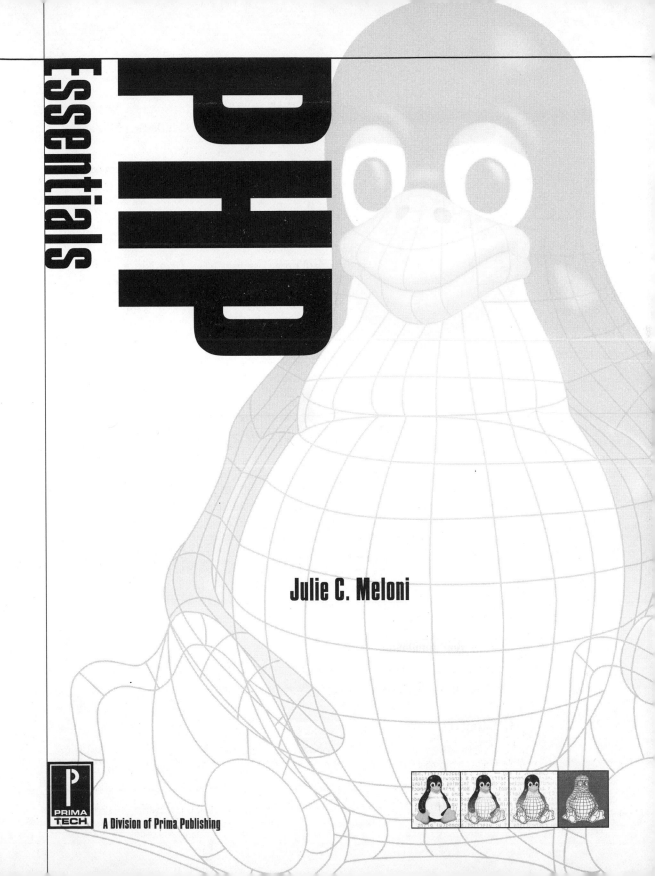

PHP Essentials

Julie C. Meloni

A Division of Prima Publishing

A Division of Prima Publishing

Prima Publishing and colophon are registered trademarks of Prima Communications, Inc. PRIMA TECH is a trademark of Prima Communications, Inc., Roseville, California 95661.

PHP was written by the PHP Development Team, and released under the GNU General Public License (GPL).

Important: Prima Publishing cannot provide software support. Please contact the appropriate software manufacturer's technical support line or Web site for assistance.

ISBN: 0-7615-2729-X

Library of Congress Catalog Card Number: 99-069005

Printed in the United States of America

00 01 02 03 04 II 10 9 8 7 6 5 4 3 2

Publisher
Stacy L. Hiquet

Marketing Manager
Judi Taylor

Associate Marketing Manager
Jody Kennen

Managing Editor
Sandy Doell

Acquisitions Editor
Lynette Quinn

Project Editor
Estelle Manticas

Editorial Assistant
Cathleen D. Snyder

Technical Reviewer
Gianluca Baldo

Copy Editor
Gayle Johnson

Interior Layout
Scribe Tribe

Cover Design
Prima Design Team

Indexer
Sherry Massey

To the person who once told me
"You might want to look into this Web thing."
Who knew?

Acknowledgments

Hats off to Rasmus Lerdorf and the core developers on the PHP and Zend teams, specifically Stig Bakken, Shane Caraveo, Andi Gutmans, Zeev Suraski and Jim Winstead. Without their tireless dedication to the development of the language, this book wouldn't be necessary.

Additional tip of the brim to all the developers who answer questions on the mailing lists, point new users in the right direction, and maintain PHP resource sites…these are getting too numerous to name individually, and I wouldn't want to try! You know who you are — keep up the good work.

Kudos to everyone at Prima, especially Lynette Quinn and Estelle Manticas, who certainly know how to deal with a neurotic author.

Enormous thanks to everyone at i2i Interactive for their ongoing support and patience, with a special thank-you to my boss, for everything…especially the job.

Finally, thanks to my parents. While they don't really understand what it is that I do for a living, they did buy me a Commodore 64, a TRS-80, and a subscription to BYTE when I was a kid, so this is pretty much all their fault.

Julie Meloni is the Technical Director for i2i Interactive, a multimedia company located in usually-sunny Campbell, CA. She's been developing Web-based applications since the Web first saw the light of day, and remembers the excitement surrounding the first GUI Web browser.

She wholeheartedly believes that Linux is the OS of the present, not just the future, and feels guilty for once working at Sun Microsystems. She would like to list all the activities she likes to do in her spare time, but she hasn't had any spare time in five years, so that would be a short list.

About the Author

Contents at a Glance

Chapter 1:
Getting Started with PHP 1

Chapter 2:
Basic PHP Techniques 25

Chapter 3:
Working with Databases 69

Chapter 4:
Creating and Populating Database Tables 107

Chapter 5:
User Authentication 133

Chapter 6:
User Tracking and Session Management 149

Chapter 7:
Advanced PHP Techniques:
Web-Based Database Administration 165

Chapter 8:
Advanced PHP Techniques: e-Commerce 219

Appendix A:
Essential PHP Language Reference 287

Appendix B:
Getting Support 347

Index 351

Contents

Introduction xix

Chapter 1:
Getting Started with PHP   1

A Brief History of PHP 2
What Does PHP Do? 3
   The Future of PHP 3
   Is PHP Right for Me? 4
   A Note Regarding Open Source Development 4
Installing a Web Server 5
   Downloading and Installing Apache 6
      Apache on Windows 6
      Apache on UNIX 7
   Downloading and Installing Xitami 11
      Xitami on Windows 11
      Xitami on UNIX 13
   Downloading and Installing Microsoft IIS 14
   Downloading and Installing WebTen 14
Downloading and Installing PHP3 15
   Installing PHP3 on Windows 15
      Configuring Apache to Use PHP3 16
      Configuring Xitami to Use PHP3 17
      Configuring IIS to Use PHP3 17
   Installing PHP3 on UNIX 18
      Configuring Apache to Use PHP3 19
      Configuring Xitami to Use PHP3 20
   Testing Your PHP Installation 20
Installing a Database 21
   Downloading MySQL 22
      Installing and Configuring MySQL for Windows 22

Installing and Configuring MySQL for UNIX 22

Using PHP4 ....**23**

Chapter 2:
Basic PHP Techniques   25

An HTML Refresher **26**

HTML Tags *26*

Block-Level Tags 27

Text-Level Tags 28

Creating a Valid HTML Document *28*

Understanding HTML Tables 29

Understanding HTML Forms 30

Commenting Your Code 33

Your First PHP Script **34**

All About Variables *36*

PHP Variables 36

HTML Form Variables 43

HTTP Environment Variables 49

Displaying Dynamic Content *51*

Redirecting to a New Location 51

Displaying Browser-Specific Code 55

Sending E-Mail *58*

Reading and Writing Data Files *64*

Writing Data Files 64

Reading Data Files 66

Chapter 3:
Working with Databases   69

Basic Database Theory **70**

The Importance of Unique Identifiers *71*

What About Relationships? *72*

Basic SQL **74**

CREATE *74*

ALTER *75*

DROP *76*

INSERT *76*

UPDATE *77*

SELECT *78*

DELETE *79*

Establishing a Database Connection with PHP **80**

Connecting to Informix Databases *81*

Connecting to Microsoft SQL Server *83*

Connecting to an mSQL Database *86*

Connecting to a MySQL Database *90*

Connecting to an Oracle Database *93*

Connecting to a PostgreSQL Database *97*

Connecting to a Sybase Database *100*

Making ODBC Connections *103*

Chapter 4:
Creating and Populating Database Tables 107

Create a Database Table **108**

Step 1: Basic Table Definition *108*

Step 2: Field Definitions *110*

Step 3: Connect to MySQL and Create the Table *116*

Inserting Data **121**

Select and Display Data **128**

Chapter 5:
User Authentication 133

Basic HTTP Authentication **134**

Configuring HTTP Authentication on Apache *135*

Creating the Users and Groups Files 135

Configuring the Web Server 136

Working with PHP Authentication Variables 137

Database-Driven Authentication **139**

Using PHP Authentication Variables to Validate Users 139

Using HTML Forms to Validate Users 141

Limit by IP Address **146**

Chapter 6:
User Tracking and Session Management   149

Cookies **150**

Setting Cookies 151

Reading Cookies 152

PHP4 Session Handling **154**

Understanding Session Variables 155

Starting a Session and Registering Variables 156

Managing User Preferences with Sessions 157

A Word of Advice 164

Chapter 7:
Advanced PHP Techniques:
Web-Based Database Administration   165

Planning Your Product Catalog **166**

Developing an Administration Menu 169

Adding Records to the Product Catalog 173

Modifying Records in the Product Catalog 186

Deleting Records from the Product Catalog 208

Chapter 8:
Advanced PHP Techniques: e-Commerce   219

Data Encryption, or Safe and Secure Shopping **220**

A Brief Glance at Data Encryption 220

Using PGP 222

Using GNUPG 229

Creating a Shopping System 235

Displaying Your Product Catalog 236

Tracking Your Users' Shopping Carts 255

Counting the Cart Items 259

Checkout Time! 262

Sending Secure Orders Via E-Mail 274

More Advanced Techniques 285

Appendix A:
Essential PHP Language Reference 287

Appendix B:
Getting Support 347

Index 351

I wanted to write the kind of book that you could hold on your lap without bruising yourself. I wanted to write a book that anyone could learn something from, not just someone with a degree in computer science. Ultimately, I wanted to write a book that someone could take off the shelf, skim through, and say, "Hey, this PHP thing looks like a neat language, and it's ever-so-easy to learn!"

If you've been programming with PHP since the beginning of time, there's probably not much you can get out of this book, except to hand it to your boss and say, "Look! Another book on what a wonderful language this is. Can we please stop using ASP/Cold Fusion/Java/Perl/C++ and migrate to PHP now?" But if you've just dabbled with PHP or have never seen a PHP script, this is the book for you. Whether you're a first-time programmer or you have a few years of Web application development under your belt, you'll find something useful here. I hope what you'll find is a simple "learn-by-example" path to developing highly successful Web sites.

Unlike the Web itself, this book is fairly linear. You'll start by installing the software needed to use PHP, and then you'll gradually move into "Hello World!" scripts and eventually create shopping carts and other database-driven applications.

If you have an account with an Internet Service Provider that has enabled the use of PHP for all users on the server, you can skip ahead to Chapter 2. But since you can install freely-available Web servers, PHP, and a database or two on your own machine with a little poking and prodding along the way, I recommend doing so. It's a great way to learn the "guts" of what you're doing (and it looks good on a résumé!).

For More Stuff

This book has its own Web site (that figures, doesn't it?), at http://www.thickbook.com/. At this site you can download all of the code samples in this book, as well as all of the samples I didn't include, such as examples geared toward alternative database types. You can also use the site to alert me to bugs and other problems you have with the examples. Although they have been tested many times, one errant semicolon or quotation mark can cause the dreaded parse error.

Also, please use the Web site to tell me about examples you wish I had included. I'll do my best to keep the "Tutorials" section filled with new and exciting topics not covered in this book.

A Brief History of PHP

What Does PHP Do?

Installing a Web Server

Downloading and Installing PHP3

Installing a Database

Using PHP4

So, what's all the hoopla about "fip"? First, it's not "fip"—it's P-H-P, from its original name: "Personal Home Page Tools." PHP is a server-side scripting language. When your Web browser accesses an URL, it is making a request to a Web server. If you are requesting a PHP page, something like http://www.yourcompany.com/home.php, the Web server wakes up the PHP parsing engine and says, "Hey! You've got to do something before I send a result back to this person's Web browser." The PHP parsing engine runs through the PHP code found in `home.php` and returns the resulting output. This output is passed back to the Web server as the HTML code in the document, which in turn is passed on to your browser, which displays it to you.

A Brief History of PHP

In 1994, an incredibly forward-thinking man named Rasmus Lerdorf developed a set of tools that used a parsing engine to interpret a few macros here and there. They were not extravagant: a guest book, a counter, and some other "home page" elements that were cool when the Web was in its infancy. He eventually combined these tools with a form interpretation (FI) package he had written, added some database support, and released what was known as PHP/FI.

Then, in the spirit of Open Source software development, developers all over the world began contributing to PHP/FI. By 1997, more than 50,000 Web sites were using PHP/FI to accomplish different tasks—connecting to a database, displaying dynamic content, and so on.

At that point, the development process really started becoming a team effort. With primary assistance from developers Zeev Suraski and Andi Gutmans, the version 3.0 parser was created. The final release of PHP3 occurred in June of 1998, when it was upgraded to include support for multiple platforms (it's not just for Linux anymore!) and Web servers, numerous databases, and SNMP (Simple Network Management Protocol) and IMAP (Internet Message Access Protocol).

So where are we now? While I'm writing this paragraph just two weeks before the end of 1999, the rapid growth and popularity of PHP are apparent:

- PHP3 is in use on over one million Web servers.
- PHP3 ships with the Red Hat Linux distribution.

- The PHP Development Team is close to releasing a non-beta version of PHP4, featuring a super-fast engine called Zend.

In fact, PHP4 is so close to being released that I'll detail some of the features of this new version later in this book. Code or features that are specific to PHP4 are indicated with the New Feature icon.

What Does PHP Do?

PHP does anything you want, except sit on its head and spin. Actually, with a little on-the-fly image manipulation and Dynamic HTML, it can probably do that, too.

According to the PHP Manual, "The goal of the language is to allow Web developers to write dynamically generated pages quickly."

Here are some common uses of PHP:

- Perform system functions: create, open, read from, write to, and close files on your system; execute system commands; create directories; and modify permissions.
- Gather data from forms: save the data to a file, send data via e-mail, return manipulated data to the user.
- Access databases and generate content on-the-fly, or create a Web interface for adding, deleting, and modifying elements within your database.
- Set cookies and access cookie variables.
- Use PHP user authentication to restrict access to sections of your Web site.
- Create images on-the-fly.
- Encrypt data.

The Future of PHP

The future of PHP has arrived, with the beta release of PHP4 and the Zend engine (created by Zend Technologies). The final version of PHP4 is scheduled for release during the first quarter of 2000, and all signs point to a successful launch.

It is important to note that PHP4 will be nearly 100 percent backward-compatible with PHP3. This means that with a few minor (and obscure) exceptions, all of the code in this book, as well as any other PHP3 code, will work flawlessly using PHP4/Zend.

Here are some PHP4 highlights, besides the "it's really fast!" feature:

- The Zend Engine (http://www.zend.com/) has increased performance and additional support for objects.
- Server Abstraction Layer
- Built-in session handling

Is PHP Right for Me?

Only you can decide if PHP should be your language of choice, whether you're developing sites for personal or commercial use on a small or large scale. I can only tell you that in the commercial realm, I've worked with all of the popular server-side scripting languages—Active Server Pages (ASP), ColdFusion, Java Server Pages (JSP), Perl, and PHP—on numerous platforms and various Web servers, with various degrees of success. PHP is the right choice for me: it's flexible, fast, and simplistic in its requirements yet powerful in its output.

Before deciding whether to use PHP in a large-scale or commercial environment, consider your answers to these questions:

- Can you say with absolute certainty that you will always use the same Web server hardware and software? If not, look for something cross-platform and available for multiple Web servers: PHP.
- Will you always have the exact same development team, comprised entirely of ASP (or ColdFusion) developers? Or will you use whoever is available, thus necessitating a language that is easy to learn and syntactically similar to C and Perl? If you have reason to believe that your ASP or ColdFusion developers might drop off the face of the earth, don't use those tools; use PHP.
- Are memory and server load an issue? If so, don't use bloated third-party software that leaks precious memory; use PHP.

A Note Regarding Open Source Development

Open Source software must follow these criteria (they are available in detail at http://www.opensource.org/):

- Free redistribution
- Source code. The program must include source code and must allow distribution in source code as well as compiled form.
- Derived works. The license must allow modifications and derived works.
- Integrity of the author's source code

- No discrimination against persons or groups
- No discrimination against fields of endeavor
- Distribution of license
- License must not be specific to a product
- License must not contaminate other software

PHP is a fine example of Open Source development and distribution. Other examples include the following:

- **Apache.** The Web Server of choice for more than 4.8 million Web sites
- **Linux.** The operating system of choice for more people than Microsoft would like you to think
- **BIND.** The software providing Domain Name Services to the Internet—all of it
- **Sendmail.** The most widely-used software for transporting e-mail from sender to recipient

Synonymous with "Open Source" is "volunteerism." Developers contributing to Open Source software don't directly make money from doing so. The cost of equipment, connectivity, tools, and, most importantly, brainpower is absorbed directly by the volunteer developer, so that you and I have a freely (and widely) available piece of software.

With that in mind, if you or your company would like to help fund development of PHP, please visit the Funding page at http://www.php.net/funding.php3 for addresses and information.

A portion of the royalties from this book will be sent to the PHP Team, so tell your friends and fellow soon-to-be PHP developers!

Installing a Web Server

Now the fun begins! It's time to install a Web server, PHP, and a database on your own machine. The following instructional sections require Internet access in order to download the various software bundles.

You can find a complete list of popular Web servers at the ServerWatch Web site (http://www.serverwatch.com/). The Web servers discussed in this section were chosen because of their status as freeware or demoware, as well as their immediate availability via download. Only the most basic installation and configurations are documented here. I cannot stress enough that you must read the documentation that is distributed with each Web server in order to fine-tune and optimize the Web server you choose.

I use Apache both at home and at work, on Windows 98 and Linux machines; if I were asked for a recommendation, Apache would be it. However, you should visit the ServerWatch Web site for each of the servers listed here and choose the software that best fits your own criteria.

Downloading and Installing Apache

Apache is a freeware Web server, available for numerous flavors of UNIX as well as for Windows 95/98/NT. The Apache Web site is at http://www.apache.org/. I suggest you read the product information found there before deciding whether Apache is right for you.

Apache on Windows

If you are a Windows user and you decide Apache is right for you, head to http://www.apache.org/ and download the latest version of the Windows binary file (the one with the *.exe extension). This file is precompiled and ready to install. It's a 2.9MB file, so grab a cup of coffee first.

Once you have the executable file on your hard drive, run it by double-clicking it or typing its location in the Run dialog box under the Start menu.

You will be asked for the following:

- The Apache installation directory. The default is `C:\Program Files\Apache Group\Apache\`, but you can change this to `C:\Apache\` or anything else you want.
- The name that will appear on the Start menu. The default is Apache Web Server.
- The installation type: typical, minimum, or custom.

Make the selections appropriate to your installation, and continue. The Apache installation program will place a default set of configuration files in the `conf` directory, under the installation directory (for example, `C:\Program Files\Apache Group\Apache\conf\`). The default configuration files will contain the custom information—such as directory locations—you indicated during the installation process. No additional configuration will be necessary for a basic installation of Apache on Windows. If you modify the configuration files, you must restart Apache for the changes to take effect. Be sure to back up your original files!

In addition to other system directories, the installation program will create the default document root, htdocs. The document root of a Web server is the directory that holds your HTML documents.

Next, try to run Apache. There are two options: running Apache as a Windows NT Service, or running Apache from a console window (the only option available for Windows 95/98 users). To install and run Apache as a Windows NT Service, do the following:

1. Select Install Apache as Service (NT only) from the Start menu.

2. After installation is complete, start the service named Apache by opening the Services window in the Control Panel, selecting Apache, and clicking the Start button.

3. The Apache Web server will continue to run in the background and will automatically start whenever your machine starts.

4. To stop Apache when it is running as a service, you can issue the NET STOP APACHE command from the command line, or you can go to the Services window in the Control Panel, select Apache, and click the Stop button.

To run Apache from a console window, do the following:

1. Select Start Apache or Start Apache as a Console App from the Apache folder on the Start menu. A console window will open, and Apache will run. Keep this window open!

2. To stop Apache, select Shutdown Apache Console App from the Apache folder on the Start menu, or close the window manually (although this is an ungraceful way to shut down Apache). Read the Apache documentation for additional instructions on signaling Apache from the command line.

Now that Apache is installed and running, open your Web browser and type http://127.0.0.1/.

You should see the Welcome to Apache! page, containing links to the Apache Web site and the Apache manual. If you do not see the Welcome page, or if your installation fails at any point, read the Apache documentation and the Apache FAQ to attempt to pinpoint your problem, and then try again.

Apache on UNIX

If you use any flavor of UNIX and you decide that Apache is right for you, head to http://www.apache.org/ to begin the download process. You have two options: downloading the precompiled binary, or downloading the source files and compiling Apache yourself.

To install precompiled binaries, go to the distribution directory at http://www.apache.org/dist/ and select a binary distribution for your operating system. If you're using Linux, you'll want to get a file from the Linux directory; if you're using Solaris, you'll want to get a file from the Solaris directory; and so forth.

Once you have downloaded the zipped tar file, place it in an accessible directory (such as /usr/local/) and unzip it using the following command:

```
gunzip [filename].gz
```

This command will create a *.tar file. To unpack it, use this command:

```
tar -xvf [filename].tar
```

This command will create the /usr/local/apache_[version]/ directory, with the following subdirectories: cgi-bin, conf, htdocs, icons, and src. Each subdirectory comes complete with other goodies.

In addition to the system directories, the default document root was created: htdocs. The document root of a Web server is the directory that holds your HTML documents. You should have a binary file called httpd in the src directory. This is good; it's the file that makes Apache go.

The next step is to edit the configuration files, if necessary. If you look in the conf subdirectory of your Apache installation, you will find three generic configuration files: srm.conf-dist, access.conf-dist, and httpd.conf-dist. Copy these files to srm.conf, access.conf, and httpd.conf, and make the following modifications in httpd.conf to produce a basic Web server configuration:

1. Modify the ServerRoot entry so that it points to the top-level Apache directory.
2. Modify the ServerAdmin entry so that it matches your e-mail address (or the e-mail address of another system administrator).
3. Modify the ServerName entry so that it matches the name of the Web server.
4. Modify the DocumentRoot entry so that it points to the directory in which your HTML files are kept.

These modifications are the only changes necessary for a basic installation of Apache on UNIX. Anytime you modify the configuration files you must restart Apache for the changes to take effect. Be sure to back up your original files!

Now, try to run Apache by running httpd:

```
/usr/local/apache_[version]/httpd
```

The `httpd` program will look for the `httpd.conf` file in the `/usr/local/apache/conf/` directory by default. Should your `httpd.conf` file be located somewhere else, you can specify the location by issuing the following start command instead:

```
/usr/local/apache_[version]/httpd -f /path/to/conf/httpd.conf
```

where `/path/to/` is replaced by your custom path to the Apache configuration files.

After the start command is issued, you will return to the command prompt without any errors, and the server will be running. You can also start Apache by using the `apachectl` script, usually located in the `/usr/local/apache_[version]/bin/` directory: `./apachectl start`

Now that Apache is installed and running, open your Web browser and type http://127.0.0.1/.

You should see the Welcome to Apache! page containing links to the Apache Web site and the Apache manual. If you do not see the Welcome page, or if your installation fails at any point, read the Apache documentation and the Apache FAQ to pinpoint your problem, and then try again. To stop Apache at any time, send the kill signal:

```
kill -TERM 'cat /path/to/logs/httpd.pid'
```

where `/path/to/` is replaced by your custom path to the Apache log files. Alternately, you can use the `apachectl` script, located in the `/usr/local/apache_[version]/bin/` directory: `./apachectl stop`

To compile the Apache Source Code, go to the distribution directory at http://www.apache.org/dist/ and grab the gzipped version of the Apache server that you want; place it in an accessible directory (such as `/usr/local/`) and unzip it using the following command:

```
gunzip [filename].gz
```

This command will create a `*.tar` file. To unpack it, use this command:

```
tar -xvf [filename].tar
```

This command will create the `/usr/local/apache_[version]/` directory, with the following subdirectories: `cgi-bin`, `conf`, `htdocs`, `icons`, and `src`. Each has its own subdirectories filled with goodies. In addition to the system directories, the default document root was created: `htdocs`. The document root of a Web server is the directory that holds your HTML documents.

The next step is to compile the source:

1. Change directories to the `src` subdirectory: `cd /usr/local/apache_[version]/src/`
2. Run the configuration script: `Configure`
3. After the configuration utility returns you to the prompt, type `Make`

If the Make command is successful, you will have the `httpd` binary file in your `src` directory. This is good: `httpd` is the file that makes Apache go. If your compilation fails at any point, visit the Apache Web site at http://www.apache.org/ for additional instructions and frequently asked questions.

After compiling the `httpd` binary, the next step is to edit the configuration files. If you look in the `conf` subdirectory of your Apache installation, you will find three generic configuration files: `srm.conf-dist`, `access.conf-dist`, and `httpd.conf-dist`. Copy these files to `srm.conf`, `access.conf`, and `httpd.conf`, and make the following modifications in `httpd.conf` to produce a basic Web server configuration:

1. Modify the ServerRoot entry so that it points to the top-level Apache directory.
2. Modify the ServerAdmin entry so that it matches your e-mail address (or the e-mail address of another system administrator).
3. Modify the ServerName entry so that it matches the name of the Web server.
4. Modify the DocumentRoot entry so that it points to the directory in which your HTML files are kept.

These modifications are the only changes necessary for a basic installation of Apache on UNIX. Anytime you modify the configuration files you must restart Apache for the changes to take effect. Be sure to back up your original files!

Now, try to run Apache by running `httpd`:

```
/usr/local/apache_[version]/httpd
```

The `httpd` program will look for the `httpd.conf` file in the `/usr/local/apache/conf/` directory by default. Should your `httpd.conf` file be located somewhere else, you can specify the location by issuing this start command instead:

```
/usr/local/apache_[version]/httpd -f /path/to/conf/httpd.conf
```

where `/path/to/` is replaced by your custom path to the Apache configuration files.

After the start command is issued, your will return to the command prompt without any errors, and the server will be running. You can also start Apache by using

the `apachectl` script, located in the `/usr/local/apache_[version]/bin/` directory:
`./apachectl start`

Now that Apache is installed and running, open your Web browser and type http://127.0.0.1/.

You should see the Welcome to Apache! page, containing links to the Apache Web site and the Apache manual. If you do not see the Welcome page, or if your installation fails at any point, read the Apache documentation and the Apache FAQ to pinpoint your problem, and then try again. To stop Apache at any time, send the kill signal:

`kill -TERM 'cat /path/to/logs/httpd.pid'`

where `/path/to/` is replaced by your custom path to the Apache log files. Alternately, you can use the `apachectl` script, located in the `/usr/local/apache_[version]/bin/` directory: `./apachectl stop`

Downloading and Installing Xitami

Xitami is a freeware Web server that is available for Windows 95/98/NT, OS/2, and flavors of UNIX. Although I have never used Xitami in a production environment, numerous people have done so without incident. My installation and configuration of Xitami with PHP have been successful on the Windows platform, and although I haven't tried it on the UNIX side of things, I have no reason to believe it would not perform as documented. The Xitami Web site is at http://www.xitami.com/. I suggest you read the product information found there before deciding if Xitami is right for you.

Xitami on Windows

If you are a Windows user and you decide Xitami is right for you, head to http://www.xitami.com/ and download the latest version of the Windows binary file (the one with the *.exe extension). This file is precompiled and ready to install. It's a relatively tiny file, less than 1MB!

Once you have the executable file on your hard drive, run it by double-clicking it or typing its location in the Run dialog box under the Start menu. You will be asked for the following:

- The Xitami installation directory. The default is `C:\Xitami`, but you can change this to `C:\Program Files\Xitami\` or anything else you want.
- The name that will appear on the Start menu

- An Administration username and password
- The installation type

Make the selections appropriate to your installation, and continue. The Xitami installation program will place a default configuration file (`xitami.cfg`) in the installation directory. In addition to other system directories, the installation program will create the default document root, `webpages`. The document root of a Web server is the directory that holds your HTML documents.

Next, try to run Xitami. There are two options: running Xitami as a Windows NT Service, or running Xitami from the Start menu.

To install and run Xitami as a Windows NT Service, do the following:

1. Download the NT Service Package from the Xitami Web site.
2. Run the NT Service Package. The program will prompt you for an installation directory and will install Xitami as an NT service.
3. After installation is complete, start the service named Xitami by opening the Services window in the Control Panel, selecting Xitami, and clicking the Start button.
4. The Xitami Web server will continue to run in the background and will automatically start whenever your machine starts.
5. To stop Xitami when it is running as a service, go to the Services window in the Control Panel, select Xitami, and click the Stop button.

To run Xitami from the Start menu, follow these steps:

1. Select Xitami Web Server - Windows from the Xitami folder on the Start menu.
2. The Xitami icon will appear in your system tray, and the Xitami Web server will be running.
3. To stop Apache, right-click the Xitami icon in the system tray and select Terminate.

Now that Xitami is installed and running, open your Web browser and type http://127.0.0.1/.

You should see the Welcome to Xitami! page, containing links to the Xitami Web site and the Xitami manual and FAQ list. If you do not see the Welcome page, or if your installation fails at any point, read the Xitami documentation and the Xitami FAQ to pinpoint your problem, and then try again.

Xitami on UNIX

Installing Xitami on a UNIX machine requires you to compile the source code. According to the Xitami Web site, compilation of Xitami has been reported as successful for the following operating systems:

- Linux
- IBM RS/6000 AIX
- HP/UX
- Digital UNIX (OSF/1)
- SunOS and Solaris
- SCO UNIXWare and OpenServer
- SGI Irix
- FreeBSD, BSD/OS, NetBSD

If your operating system is one of these, or if you are confident in your building skills, download and install the appropriate zipped tar file from http://www.xitami.com/.

Place the file in an accessible directory (such as /usr/local/) and unzip it:

```
gunzip [filename].gz
```

This command will create a *.tar file. To unpack it, use this command:

```
tar -xvf [filename].tar
```

You now should have an Xitami directory in /usr/local/ (or wherever you placed the file) containing the full source code, the build script (xibuild), and other directories full of goodies, such as the Xitami manual.

To run the xibuild script, which compiles Xitami and installs the executable program in the appropriate directory, type the following commands at the prompt:

```
chmod +x xibuild
./xibuild
```

Run the Xitami executable, and then open your Web browser and type http://127.0.0.1/.

You should see the Welcome to Xitami! page, containing links to the Xitami Web site and the Xitami manual and FAQ list. If you do not see the Welcome page, or if your installation fails at any point, read the Xitami documentation and the Xitami FAQ to pinpoint your problem, and then try again.

Downloading and Installing Microsoft IIS

Microsoft Corporation's Internet Information Server (IIS) runs on Windows NT and is included in NT Service Pack 4. It can also be downloaded for free at http://www.microsoft.com/ or purchased on CD-ROM for $99. Beware of the download option: IIS is 75MB. That's more than 25 times the size of Apache, and almost 100 times the size of Xitami.

I don't recommend using IIS, not only because of the sheer size of the software, but also due to the memory requirements and just a personal disdain of the products. However, 2.1 million Web sites use IIS or some type of Microsoft Web server, and ultimately the choice of Web server is yours. I suggest you read the product information found at the Microsoft Web site before deciding if IIS is right for you.

If you choose IIS, the installation is quite simple: run the executable file by double-clicking it or typing its location in the Run dialog box under the Start menu.

The Installation Wizard will prompt you to make system-specific selections, such as directory locations. Make the selections appropriate to your installation, and continue. Restart your machine if necessary. After restarting your machine and verifying that IIS is running as an NT service, open your Web browser and type http://127.0.0.1/.

You should see a Welcome page, indicating a successful installation. If you do not see the Welcome page, or if your installation fails at any point, read the IIS documentation to pinpoint your problem, and then try again.

Downloading and Installing WebTen

WebTen is an Apache-based Web server for the Macintosh (it requires OS 9 or above) that is made by Tenon Intersystems. Currently it is the only Web server for the Macintosh that includes support for PHP.

You can download and try WebTen free for 14 days, after which time it costs $495. I suggest you read the product information found at the WebTen/Tenon Intersystems Web site (http://www.webten.com/) before deciding if WebTen is right for you.

After downloading the installation file, double-click the Installer application file to begin the installation process. Follow the installation steps, which will extract and install the WebTen files. After installation is complete, create an alias to the WebTen application and place it in the Startup Items folder of your System folder. This will ensure that WebTen automatically launches when you start your machine.

Try to connect to the WebTen Web server by opening your Web browser and typing http://127.0.0.1/.

You should see a default installation page containing information about the WebTen server. If you do not see a default page, or if your installation fails at any point, read the WebTen documentation to pinpoint your problem, and then try again.

Downloading and Installing PHP3

The installation process for PHP is so simple that it makes me giddy. There are two methods for running PHP with a Web server: as a module or as a CGI extension. If you're not running Apache or WebTen, the option has been chosen for you: you can only run PHP as a module when running one of those two Web servers, so all others use the CGI version.

Running PHP as a module means that the PHP engine is compiled into the Web server. Running PHP as a CGI extension is a bit slower, because the PHP engine must start as an external process each time a request is made. When PHP runs as a module, it's all one fluid motion as far as the Web server is concerned—no external processes are started. However, installing PHP as a module requires a recompilation of the Web server, so it's a bit more difficult than just plopping in a binary file and moving along.

To get you up and running as soon as possible, the following instructions detail the installation of PHP as a CGI extension. You can find the instructions for recompiling the Apache Web server and using PHP as a module in the PHP Manual, always at http://www.php.net/manual/.

If running Windows or UNIX, point your Web browser to http://www.php.net/ (the home of everything PHP) and go to the Downloads section. Download either the compressed tar file of PHP3 source code (for UNIX) or the executable file (for Windows). If you're on a Macintosh and using WebTen, PHP3 was installed during your original server installation, so you can skip ahead to Chapter 2.

Installing PHP3 on Windows

To install PHP on a Windows machine, follow the installation instructions given in this section. If your installation fails at any point, your path to a solution should be as follows:

1. Reread the PHP INSTALL file.
2. Read the PHP FAQ at http://www.php.net/.

3. Reread the PHP FAQ at http://www.php.net/.

4. Check the mailing list archives. (A list can be found at http://www.php.net/support.php3.)

5. Send a well-phrased question to the very helpful folks on the PHP mailing list; send a text-only e-mail (no HTML formatting!) to php3@lists.php.net. Be sure to include as much information, errors, warnings, and so forth as possible.

After downloading the PHP distribution file for Windows, extract the contents to a directory such as `C:\PHP3\` (or another directory of your choice).

Next, locate the `php3-dist.ini` file in your `C:\PHP3\` directory. Copy that file to your `C:\Windows\ or c:\winnt\` directory, and rename it `php3.ini`.

Make the following changes to the `php3.ini` file:

1. Verify that the value of `php-install-dir` is the directory you created when you extracted the files, such as `C:\PHP3\`.

2. Change the value of `extension_dir` to point to the installation directory, or anywhere else you might have placed the `*.dll` files beginning with `php3`.

3. Change the value of `doc_root` to point to the document root of your Web server, such as `C:\apache\htdocs\` or `C:\wwwroot\`.

4. Select the PHP modules you'd like to have loaded when PHP runs, such as database connectivity or encryption modules. For each module you want to use, uncomment its line (remove the preceding `;`) in the `php3.ini` file.

Configuring Apache to Use PHP3

Configuring Apache requires that you edit the `httpd.conf` file, located in your Apache configuration (`conf`) directory. The goal of the configuration is to tell Apache what to do with files ending with `.php3`, `.phtml`, `.php`, or anything else you use to indicate a PHP file. You'll be telling Apache to execute an application in order to do something with those files—in this case, to run the `php.exe` program to parse the PHP code.

Add the following lines to the file:

```
ScriptAlias /php3/ "c:/path-to-php-dir/"
AddType application/x-httpd-php3 .php3 .phtml
Action application/x-httpd-php3 "/php3/php.exe"
```

In the ScriptAlias line, use `"C:/PHP3/"` if that is the location of your PHP directory.

These modifications to the `httpd.conf` file produce a generic, working configuration of Apache with PHP.

> Use forward slashes instead of backslashes in path statements in your Apache configuration file. For example, `"C:\PHP3\"` becomes `"C:/PHP3/"`.

If you want to use additional file extensions to indicate PHP files, such as `.php`, add the extension to the list in the AddType line.

Configuring Xitami to Use PHP3

Configuring Xitami requires that you edit the `xitami.cfg` file, located in the `C:\Xitami\` directory (or wherever you installed Xitami). The goal of the configuration is to tell Xitami what to do with files ending with `.php3`, `.phtml`, `.php`, or anything else you use to indicate a PHP file. You'll be telling Xitami to execute an application in order to do something with those files—in this case, running the `php.exe` program to parse the PHP code.

Add the following lines to the file:

```
[Filter]
.php3=c:\path\to\php.exe
.phtml=c:\path\to\php.exe


[Mime]
php3=application/x-httpd-php3
phtml=application/x-httpd-php3
```

These modifications to the `xitami.cfg` file produce a generic, working configuration of Xitami with PHP.

In the Filter block, use `C:\PHP3\php.exe` if that is the location of your PHP directory and executable file.

If you want to use additional file extensions to indicate PHP files, such as `.php`, add another line in the Mime block as well as the Filter block, using `php` in place of `php3` or `phtml`.

Configuring IIS to Use PHP3

Use the Microsoft Management Console to configure IIS for use with PHP. The goal of the configuration is to tell IIS what to do with files ending with `.php3`,

`.phtml`, `.php`, or anything else you use to indicate a PHP file. You'll be telling IIS to execute an application in order to do something with those files—in this case, running the `php.exe` program to parse the PHP code.

Follow these steps in the Microsoft Management Console:

1. Select a Web site or the starting point directory of an application.
2. Right-click to select the Properties tab.
3. Click Home Directory, Virtual Directory, or Directory, as appropriate to your installation.
4. Click Configuration, and then click App Mappings.
5. Click Add, and in the Executable box, type the following: `C:\path-to-php-dir\php.exe %s %s`. For example, if PHP was installed in `C:\PHP3\`, the command would be `C:\PHP3\php.exe %s %s`.
6. In the Extension box, type the file name extension to associate with PHP scripts, such as `.php3`, `.phtml`, or `.php`. You can add only one extension at a time, so repeat this step as necessary.
7. Restart IIS.

Installing PHP3 on UNIX

To install PHP on a UNIX machine, follow the installation instructions given here. If your installation fails at any point, your path to a solution should be the following:

1. Reread the PHP INSTALL file.
2. Read the PHP FAQ at http://www.php.net/.
3. Reread the PHP FAQ at http://www.php.net/.
4. Check the mailing list archives. (A list can be found at http://www.php.net/support.php3.)
5. Send a well-phrased question to the very helpful folks on the PHP mailing list; send a text-only e-mail (no HTML formatting!) to `php3@lists.php.net`. Be sure to include as much information, errors, warnings, and so forth as possible.

Once you have downloaded the zipped tar file, place it in an accessible directory (such as `/usr/local/`) and then unzip it:

```
gunzip [filename].gz
```

This command will create a `*.tar` file. To unpack it, use this command:

```
tar -xvf [filename].tar
```

This command will create the `/usr/local/php/` directory, containing various source, setup, and configuration files. The default installation will create PHP as a CGI extension, so start by running the setup script:

1. Type `./setup` at the command prompt.
2. You will be prompted for the answers to many configuration questions. The most important question is about type. You don't want to compile it as a module, but you *do* want to compile it as a CGI extension.
3. To build the CGI executable, type `make` at the command prompt.
4. To test your build, type `make test` at the command prompt.
5. Take the newly-created `php` binary file and place it in your Web server's `cgi-bin` directory.
6. Copy the file called `php3.ini-dist` into your `cgi-bin` directory, and rename it `php3.ini`.

If you have questions at any time during the build process, or if you want to edit your `php3.ini` file but you don't know how to do so, point your Web browser to the PHP Manual at http://www.php.net/manual/ or to the PHP FAQ (also at www.php.net). I recommend taking the time at some point to understand the numerous configuration options.

Configuring Apache to Use PHP3

Configuring Apache requires that you edit the `httpd.conf` file, located in your Apache configuration (`conf`) directory. The goal of the configuration is to tell Apache what to do with files ending with `.php3`, `.phtml`, `.php`, or anything else you use to indicate a PHP file. You'll be telling Apache to execute an application in order to do something with those files—in this case, running the `php` binary (now located in the `cgi-bin` directory) to parse the PHP code.

Add the following lines to the file:

```
AddType application/x-httpd-php3 .php3 .phtml
Action application/x-httpd-php3 /cgi-bin/php
```

These modifications to the `httpd.conf` file produce a generic, working configuration of Apache with PHP.

If you want to use additional file extensions to indicate PHP files, such as `.php`, add the extension to the list in the AddType line.

Configuring Xitami to Use PHP3

Configuring Xitami requires that you edit the `xitami.cfg` file, located in the `/usr/local/xitami` directory (or wherever you installed Xitami). The goal of the configuration is to tell Xitami what to do with files ending with `.php3`, `.phtml`, `.php`, or anything else you use to indicate a PHP file. You'll be telling Xitami to execute an application in order to do something with those files—in this case, running the `php` binary program to parse the PHP code.

Add the following lines to the file:

```
[Filter]
.php3=/path/to/phpb
.phtml=/path/to/php


[Mime]
php3=application/x-httpd-php3
phtml=application/x-httpd-php3
```

These modifications to the `xitami.cfg` file produce a generic, working configuration of Xitami with PHP.

In the Filter block, use `/usr/local/bin/xitami/cgi-bin/` if that is the location of your PHP directory and binary file.

If you want to use additional file extensions to indicate PHP files, such as `.php`, add another line in the Mime block as well as the Filter block, using `php` in place of `php3` or `phtml`.

Testing Your PHP Installation

It's time to see if your hard work has paid off, or if I'm a lousy teacher. If my instructions have led you far afield, please visit this book's Web site at http://www.thickbook.com/ and tell me about it. I'll make sure that the instructions are better in the next version. I'll also do my best to help you with your current installation issues so that you can use this book for something more than a doorstop.

To test your installation:

1. Verify that your Web server is running.
2. Create a text file called `test.php` and type the following: `<?php echo "Hello World!  I'm using PHP!"; ?>`
3. Save the file and place it in your Web server's document root. Open your Web browser to http://127.0.0.1/test.php

You should see the following in your browser window:

Hello World! I'm using PHP!

If you don't, double-check your installation. If you have followed the basic installation and configuration instructions, any issues you might have will likely be in the PHP FAQ, in the Installation section. You can also use the feedback forms at http://www.thickbook.com/ to let me know that you are having problems with the instructions or sample code in this book, and I'll help you out as much as I can.

Anytime you have a PHP-related question, the path to a solution should be the following:

1. Read the PHP FAQ at http://www.php.net/.
2. Reread the PHP FAQ at http://www.php.net/.
3. Check the mailing list archives. (A list can be found at http://www.php.net/support.php3.)
4. Send a well-phrased question to the very helpful folks on the PHP mailing list. Send a text-only e-mail (no HTML formatting!) to php3@lists.php.net. Be sure to include as much information, errors, warnings, and so forth as possible.

While this chapter did not cover the build and configuration of PHP as a server module, the installation instructions in the PHP Manual are very easy to follow.

Installing a Database

One of the selling points of PHP is its ability to interface with numerous databases. This ability makes PHP a logical choice for generating database-driven dynamic content and developing e-commerce applications, project and document management applications, and virtually any other application you can imagine that might use a database.

Although the choice of a database is your own personal decision, I use MySQL because it is multithreaded, multiplatform, very powerful, and essentially free. Visit the MySQL Web site at http://www.mysql.com/ to read more about this database and see some benchmark results. If you decide to use another database, the PHP functions for database connectivity are located in Chapter 3, "Working with Databases." However, this book's examples of database usage in the context of application development use MySQL as the database.

Downloading MySQL

To download MySQL, go to http://www.mysql.com/ and head to the Downloads section. A few words about licensing: MySQL is free for normal usage on non-Microsoft platforms. If you're using the Windows version, you can download it for free, but you should pay for a $200 license after 30 days. When compared to the less-powerful Microsoft SQL Server (around $2,000) and the extremely large and expensive Oracle database, MySQL is a steal at $200. Plus, the SQL tutorial included in the MySQL documentation is more than worth the licensing fee.

Licensing requirements tend to change, so always check the MySQL Web site for an accurate account of their licensing policies.

Installing and Configuring MySQL for Windows

To install MySQL for Windows, go to the Downloads area of the MySQL Web site, and download the Windows installation file (the one with a *.zip extension).

Next, unzip the contents into a temporary directory, such as `C:\temp\`.

Run the setup.exe program from `C:\temp\` by double-clicking the file or by typing the location in the Run dialog box. The MySQL installer will place the MySQL files into `C:\mysql\` by default. To run MySQL, do the following:

1. Open a DOS console and type `cd C:\mysql\bin\`
2. Type `mysqld` to start the MySQL server process in the background.
3. Type `mysqladmin -h` to start the administrative interface and display the help text. Use the commands listed to create a database and grant yourself a username and password.

If you have any problems during MySQL administration, consult the documentation included with your installation.

Installing and Configuring MySQL for UNIX

To install MySQL on the UNIX platform, go to the Downloads area of the MySQL Web site and download the binary distribution specific to your platform.

Next, place the zipped tar file in a directory such as `/usr/local/`. Unzip and unpack this file by typing

```
gunzip [filename].tar.gz
tar -xvf [filename].tar
```

These commands will create a `/usr/local/mysql_[version]/` directory structure containing the MySQL binaries.

To run MySQL, do the following:

1. Navigate to the MySQL scripts directory by typing `cd /usr/local/ mysql_[version]/scripts/`

2. Type `mysql_install_db` to create an initial database.

3. Type `cd /usr/local/mysql_[version]/bin/`

4. Type `safe_mysqld &` to start the MySQL server process.

5. Type `mysqladmin version` to see that MySQL server is indeed running.

If you have any problems during MySQL administration, consult the documentation included with your installation.

Using PHP4

As of this writing, PHP4 is currently in beta for Windows and UNIX platforms. You can download and install PHP4 using the source or binary distributions found at http://www.php.net/version4/, which also contains PHP4 installation instructions. Similar instructions can also be found in the "Tutorials" section at http://www.thickbook.com/.

Chapter 2: Basic PHP Techniques

An HTML Refresher

Your First PHP Script

Before delving directly into PHP scripting, it's important to get a handle on basic HTML techniques. Since PHP is embedded within HTML, or perhaps the script itself generates marked-up text, knowing the fundamental structure of HTML will help you to avoid potential problems with your script output. For example, if your PHP script is generating a table layout, and that table does not render on-screen, don't jump to the assumption that there's a problem with your PHP code. Most likely, the problem is a missing table tag!

An HTML Refresher

Hypertext Markup Language, or HTML, isn't a programming language in the same vein as C++ or Java. Instead, it is as its name implies, a markup language. You take a simple ASCII text file and "mark up" that text by putting text in brackets around other text. Now put that page on a Web server and then request it in your Web browser by typing its URL, such as http://www.yourserver.com/yourpage.html. Your Web browser makes a request to the Web server, and the Web server responds with the file. This transaction essentially says "Please take the file called `yourpage.html` that exists on this machine, and send it to my Web browser."

Your Web browser then "renders" the document, taking the file, looking at the text in funny brackets, and following the directions they contain. These directions tell the Web browser how the information displayed on the page should appear: bold, italicized, blue, with line breaks, and so on.

HTML Tags

The "text in funny brackets" are HTML tags. These tags define elements of the document: titles, headings, paragraphs, lists, and so on. Without tags, the Web browser has no way to determine how to display the elements.

Tags begin with a left-angle bracket (<) and end with a right-angle bracket (>). Additionally, tags are usually in pairs: the opening tag and the closing tag. Here's an example:

- `<HTML>` The opening tag, which tells the browser that everything from that point forward is HTML.

- `</HTML>` The closing tag, which tells the browser that the HTML document should end at that point. Note the / before the tag name, defining it as a closing tag.

Certain HTML tags can contain *attributes*, or additional information included in the tag, such as alignment directives:

```
<P align=center>This is a centered paragraph.</P>
```

The attribute `align=center` tells the browser to center the paragraph.

There are two main types of HTML tags: block-level and text-level. An HTML document contains one or more block-level elements, or text surrounded by block-level tags.

Block-Level Tags

Block-level tags, such as the logical division tag (`<DIV></DIV>`), contain block-level elements. Block-level elements can contain other block-level elements, as well as text-level elements. For example, a logical division can contain a paragraph, and the paragraph can contain emphasized text:

```
<DIV>
    <P>This paragraph introduces the next paragraph.</P>
    <P>This paragraph contains <em>very</em> useful information.</P>
    <P>Both paragraphs are within a logical division.</P>
</DIV>
```

Here are some examples of block-level tags:

- `<H1></H1>`, `<H2></H2>`, `<H3></H3>`, `<H4></H4>`, `<H5></H5>`, `<H6></H6>` The level heading tags. The level 1 heading (`<H1></H1>`) appears more prominently than other level heading tags, followed by `<H2></H2>` and `<H3></H3>`, through `<H6></H6>`. Use level heading tags in a hierarchical order: level 2 after level 1, level 3 after level 2, and so on.

- `<BLOCKQUOTE></BLOCKQUOTE>` Used when quoting large blocks of text from another document.

- `<UL></UL>` The unordered list. Unordered list items, indicated with the `<LI>` tag, are preceded with a bullet symbol.

- `<OL></OL>` The ordered list. Ordered list items, indicated with the `<LI>` tag, are preceded with a number.

- `<TABLE></TABLE>` Create a table when surrounding the `<TH></TH>` and `<TD></TD>` text-level tags.

- `<TR></TR>` These tags insert a table row within a `<TABLE>` element. Table rows contain `<TH></TH>` and `<TD></TD>` elements.
- `<TH></TH>` These tags insert a table header cell within a `<TR>` element.
- `<TD></TD>` These tags insert a table data cell within a `<TR>` element.

Text-Level Tags

Text-level tags are applied to specific text within block-level elements. For example, a paragraph can contain emphasized text and a hypertext link, both examples of text-level elements:

```
<P>This paragraph contains a link to a <em>very</em> interesting <a href="http://
www.yourserver.com/story.html">story</a>.</P>
```

Here are some examples of text-level tags:

- `<STRONG></STRONG>` Strongly emphasized text.
- `<IMG>` Displays an image. No closing tag is necessary.
- `<BR>` Inserts a line break. No closing tag is necessary.

Creating a Valid HTML Document

HTML documents have a specific structure that should be followed to avoid display problems. Understanding the structure of an HTML document is especially important when integrating it with PHP code, because in some instances PHP code must exist before certain HTML elements. For example, when creating browser cookies, the PHP code used to create and send the cookie must exist before any text, line breaks, or other HTML is sent to the browser.

The following steps will create a structurally sound HTML document:

1. Define the document type according to the HTML standard it follows.
2. Open the `<HTML>` tag, stating that the information that follows is in HTML.
3. Open the `<HEAD>` tag. This area contains the title of your document, as well as other document information. With the exception of the document title, none of the information in the `<HEAD>` element is displayed by the browser.
4. Insert the title of the document within the `<TITLE></TITLE>` tag pair.
5. Insert any `<META>` information. Examples of `<META>` information include document descriptions and expiration dates.

6. Insert any `<LINK>` information. Examples of `<LINK>` information include the e-mail address of the document's author and the location of the associated style sheet.

7. Insert the closing `<HEAD>` tag: `</HEAD>`

8. Open the `<BODY>` tag. This area contains all of the information displayed by the browser. Only one `<BODY>` element exists in each document.

9. Insert your content, in HTML format.

10. Insert the closing `<BODY>` tag: `</BODY>`

11. Insert the closing `<HTML>` tag: `</HTML>`

Following these steps produces a valid HTML document, something like this:

```
<!DOCTYPE HTML PUBLIC "-//W3C//DTD HTML 3.2//EN">
<HTML>
<HEAD>
<TITLE>Your Title</TITLE>
<META NAME="description" CONTENT="My first document">
<LINK REV="made" HREF="mailto:you@yourserver.com">
</HEAD>
<BODY>
<P>All of your content goes here!</P>
</BODY>
</HTML>
```

Understanding valid HTML document structure is the first step in creating error-free PHP scripts. The next two sections provide an overview of HTML tables and forms. For a selection of in-depth HTML tutorials, visit the "Links" section at http://www.thickbook.com/.

Understanding HTML Tables

HTML tables follow a structure as strict as the overall HTML document structure. One miscue, such as a missing closing tag, can cause great debugging headaches. Many programmers have examined their code for hours, calling in reinforcements to help them debug the mystery of the non-displaying pages, only to discover that they failed to insert the `</TABLE>` tag to close the table. This is known as "smack the forehead" syndrome. Repeat the mantra "Close all table tags" and you probably won't suffer from "smack the forehead" syndrome.

A simple table contains one row and two columns. The row starts with a `<TR>` tag and ends with a `</TR>` closing tag. Within the `<TR>` tag are the `<TD>` opening tag, followed by the data for that cell and the `</TD>` closing tag. Each `<TD></TD>` tag pair represents a column, so if you have two columns, you'll need two tag pairs. For example:

```
<TABLE>
<TR>
    <TD>Cell 1</TD>
    <TD>Cell 2</TD>
</TR>
</TABLE>
```

The browser will display this code like this:

Cell 1   Cell 2

To place a column heading above each column, use the `<TH></TH>` tag pair. For example:

```
<TABLE>
<TR>
    <TH>Heading 1</TH>
    <TH>Heading 2</TH>
</TR>
<TR>
    <TD>Cell 1</TD>
    <TD>Cell 2</TD>
</TR>
</TABLE>
```

Table headings are usually displayed in bold text. The browser will display this code like this:

Heading 1   Heading 2
Cell 1   Cell 2

HTML tables can be as complex or as simple as you need them to be, including being nested within one another. The more complex the table code, the greater the chance for rendering errors. If you remember to close all open table tags, including row and data tags, the likelihood of these errors will certainly decrease.

Understanding HTML Forms

This section explains the display and internal elements of an HTML form. Later in this chapter you'll learn how to make functional forms using PHP scripts, but first, the basics. Committing form basics to memory will alleviate script-debugging headaches, just like remembering to close all table tags!

Forms begin with an opening <FORM> tag and end with the closing </FORM> tag. The form's method and action are defined in the opening <FORM> tag, like this:

```
<FORM METHOD="POST" ACTION="go.php">
```

Two methods exist for sending forms:

- GET The default method. Sends input to a script via a URL. The GET method has a limit to the amount of data that can be sent, so if you plan to send a large amount, use POST.
- POST Sends input in the body of the submission, allowing for larger form submissions.

The action is the name of the script receiving the input.

After defining the method and action, you need a way to get data to your script: input elements.

There are three input element tags—<INPUT>, <TEXTAREA>, and <SELECT>—and there are several types within those elements. Here are the common types:

- **Text fields.** An input field with a size indicated in the SIZE attribute and a maximum length indicated in the MAXLENGTH attribute. Here's a 20-character text field named "Field1" with a character limit of 50 characters:

  ```
  <input type="text" name="Field1" size=20 maxlength=50>
  ```

- **Password fields.** Similar to text fields, except each typed character is displayed as an asterisk (*). Here's an example of a 20-character password field named "Pass1" with a character limit of 50 characters:

  ```
  <input type="password" name="Pass1" size=20 maxlength=50>
  ```

- **Radio buttons.** A radio button exists in a group. Each member of the group has the same name but different values. Only one of the group can be checked—for example, a button with the value "yes" or a button with the value "no". Additionally, you can specify that one of the values is checked by default. Here's an example of a radio button group named "like_coffee", with "yes" and "no" as available answers:

  ```
  <input type="radio" name="like_coffee" value="yes" checked> yes
  <input type="radio" name="like_coffee" value="no"> no
  ```

  If "yes" stays selected, the script will receive like_coffee=yes.

- **Checkboxes.** Like radio buttons, checkboxes exist in a group. Each member of the group has the same name but different values. However, multiple checkboxes in each group can be selected. Additionally, you can specify that one or more of the values is checked by default. Here's an example of a checkbox group named "drink," with "coffee," "tea," "water," and "soda" as available answers:

```
<input type="checkbox" name="drink" value="coffee" checked> coffee
<input type="checkbox" name="drink" value="tea"> tea
<input type="checkbox" name="drink" value="water"> water
<input type="checkbox" name="drink" value="soda"> soda
```

If "coffee" stays selected, and the user also checks the "water" checkbox, the script will receive `drink=coffee` and `drink=water`.

- **Text areas.** These are displayed as a box with a width indicated by the number of COLS and a height indicated by the number of ROWS. Text areas must have a closing </TEXTAREA> tag. Here's an example of a text area named "message" with a width of 20 characters and a height of 5 characters:

```
<textarea name="message" cols=20 rows=5></textarea>
```

- **List boxes/drop-down list boxes.** These input types begin with the <SELECT> tag, contain one or more <OPTION> tags, and must end with the closing </SELECT> tag. The SIZE attribute indicates the number of <OPTION> elements displayed. If SIZE=1, a drop-down list will appear; otherwise, the user will see a scrollable list box. If the MULTIPLE attribute is present within a list box, the user can select more than one <OPTION> from the list. <OPTION>s have unique values. The default <OPTION> is set using the SELECTED attribute. Here's a drop-down list named "year," with "2000" as the default selection from the options of 1999, 2000, and 2001:

```
<select name="year" size="1">
<option value="1999">1999</option>
<option value="2000" selected>2000</option>
<option value="2001">2001</option>
</select>
```

When you create forms, the NAME attributes of your input elements must all be unique. These element names become the variables interpreted by your scripts. If you first send a variable called "my_name" with a value of "Joe," and then you send a variable named "my_name" with a value of "coffee," the script will overwrite the former value with the latter. From that point forward, according to the script, your name is "coffee" and not "Joe."

The final element of a form is crucial: it's the button that submits it to the script! Submit buttons can be the default gray 3D form buttons with text, or you can use images.

For a gray 3D button that displays SUBMIT, use this:

```
<INPUT TYPE="submit" NAME="submitme" VALUE="SUBMIT">
```

The VALUE attribute contains the text that appears on the face of the button. If you wanted this button to say "Send Form", the code would look like this:

```
<INPUT TYPE="submit" NAME="submitme" VALUE="Send Form">
```

To use an image as a submission button, use this:

```
<INPUT TYPE="image" NAME="submitme" SRC="button_image.gif" alt="Submit Me" border=0>
```

When the user clicks the form submission button, the input field names and their associated values are sent to the script specified as the form's ACTION.

Commenting Your Code

Commenting your code is a good habit to have. Entering comments in HTML documents helps you (and others who might have to edit your document later) keep track of areas of large documents. Commenting also allows you to write notes to yourself during the development process.

HTML comments are ignored by the browser and are contained within <!-- and --> tags. For example, the following comment reminds you that the code following it contains your logo graphic:

```
<!-- logo graphic goes here -->
```

Similarly, PHP comments are ignored by the parsing engine. PHP comments are usually preceded by double slashes, like this:

```
// this is a comment in PHP code
```

Other types of commenting can be used in PHP files, such as:

```
# This is shell-style style comment
```

and

```
/* This begins a C-style comment that runs
onto two lines */
```

HTML and PHP comments are used extensively throughout this book to explain blocks of code. Get used to reading comments, and try to pick up the habit of using them. Writing clean, bug-free code with comments and white space will make you popular among your developer peers, because they won't have to work hard to figure out what your code is trying to do.

Your First PHP Script

In a PHP document, PHP code coexists with HTML, whether it is embedded within the HTML or the code itself determines the HTML output. When a Web browser requests a PHP document, the document first goes through the PHP engine, which executes the PHP code and prints the results in place of the PHP code. The Web server then sends this document, now consisting only of HTML, to the Web browser, which displays it to the user. This method of code execution is called *server-side*. Code executed by the browser, such as JavaScript, is called *client-side*.

To combine PHP code with HTML, the PHP code must be *escaped*, or set apart, from the HTML. The following method is the default configuration of the PHP engine:

```
<?php
// PHP code goes here.
?>
```

The PHP engine will consider anything within the `<?php` opening tag and the `?>` closing tag as PHP code. You can also escape your PHP code by using the `<?` opening tag and the `?>` closing tag, or by using the `<SCRIPT Language=php>` opening tag and the `</SCRIPT>` closing tag.

Now it's time to write that first script. Your first PHP script will display "Hello World! I'm using PHP!" in the browser window.

First, open your favorite text editor and create a simple text file called `first.php`. In this text file, type the following code:

```
<!DOCTYPE HTML PUBLIC "-//W3C//DTD HTML 3.2//EN">
<HTML>
<HEAD>
<TITLE>My First PHP Script</TITLE>
</HEAD>
<BODY>
    <?php
        echo "<P>Hello World! I'm using PHP!</P>\n";
?>
</BODY>
</HTML>
```

Save this file and place it on your Web server. Now access it with your browser at its URL, http://www.yourserver.com/first.php.

In your browser window, you should see this:

Hello World! I'm using PHP!

If you use your browser to view the source of the document, you should see this:

```
<!DOCTYPE HTML PUBLIC "-//W3C//DTD HTML 3.2//EN">
<HTML>
<HEAD>
<TITLE>My First PHP Script</TITLE>
</HEAD>
<BODY>
    <P>Hello World! I'm using PHP!</P>
</BODY>
</HTML>
```

Take a look at the command issued in the PHP code. It contains three elements: the command (echo), the string (<P>Hello World...), and the instruction terminator (;).

Familiarize yourself now with echo, because it will likely be your most often-used command. The echo() function is used to output information—in this case, to print <P>Hello World! I'm using PHP!</P> in the HTML file.

Within the string, note the newline character ("\n"). This optional character ensures that the echoed content won't be printed all in one line in your HTML source file. Although the newline character makes no difference to the Web browser, it is useful when you are viewing your source code.

The instruction terminator, also known as the semicolon, is absolutely required. If you do not end your command with a semicolon, the PHP code will not be parsed properly by the PHP engine, and ugly errors will occur. For example, this code:

```
<?php
    echo "<P>Hello World! I'm using PHP!</P>\n"
    echo "<P>This is another message.</P>";
?>
```

produces this nasty error:

```
Parse error: parse error, expecting "," or ";" in /home/devbox/dev-www/phptest/
error.php on line 9
```

Avoid this error at all costs: remember to terminate commands with a semicolon!

All About Variables

Very simply put, variables represent data. If you want your script to hold onto a specific piece of information, first create a variable and then assign a literal value to it using the equal sign (=).

For example, the variable "username" holds the literal value "joe" when appearing in your script as

```
$username = "joe";
```

Variable names begin with the dollar sign ($) and are followed by a concise, meaningful name. The variable name cannot begin with a numeric character, but it can contain numbers and the underscore character (_). Additionally, variable names are case-sensitive, meaning that $YOURVAR and $yourvar are two different variables.

Creating meaningful variable names is another step to lessening headaches while coding. If your script deals with name and password values, don't create a variable called $n for the name and $p for the password—those are not meaningful names. If you pick up that script weeks later, you might think that $n is the variable for "number" rather than "name" and that $p stands for "page" rather than "password."

This section describes several kinds of variables. Some variables change values as your script runs, and others are assigned values outside of your PHP script—such as HTML forms.

PHP Variables

You will create two main types of variables in your PHP code: scalar and arrays. Scalar variables contain only one value at a time, while arrays contain a list of values or another array (thus producing a multi-dimensional array). Within variables, their associated values can be of different types, such as these:

- **Integers.** Whole numbers (numbers without decimals). Examples are 1, 345, and 9922786. You can also use octal and hexadecimal notation: the octal "0123" is decimal 83 and the hexadecimal "0x12" is decimal 18.

- **Floating-point numbers ("floats" or "doubles").** Numbers with decimals. Examples are 1.5, 87.3446, and 0.88889992.

- **Strings.** Text and/or numeric information, specified within double quotes (" ") or single quotes (' ').

As you begin your PHP script, plan your variables and variable names carefully, and use comments in your code to remind you of the assignments you have made.

Operators

Values are assigned to variables using different types of operators. A list of common operators and operator types follows. For a complete list, see the "Operators" section in Appendix A, "The PHP Language."

Assignment Operators

You've already seen an assignment operator at work: the equal sign (=) in `$username = "joe"` is the basic assignment operator.

> The single equal sign does not mean "equal to." Instead, the single equal sign always means "is assigned to." The double equal sign (==) means "equal to." Commit this to memory to alleviate debugging headaches.

NOTE

Other assignment operators include +=, -=, and .=:

```
$ex += 1;      // Assigns the value of ($ex + 1) to $ex.
               // If $ex = 2, then the value of ($ex += 1) is 3.
$ex -= 1;      // Assigns the value of ($ex - 1) to $ex.
               // If $ex = 2, then the value of ($ex -= 1) is 1.
$ex .= "coffee";    // Concatenates (adds to) a string. If $ex = "I like "
                    // then the value of ($ex .= "coffee") is "I like coffee".
```

Arithmetic Operators

Even if you've never written a line of code in your life, you already know most of the arithmetic operators—they're basic math!

- \+ addition
- \- subtraction
- * multiplication
- / division
- % modulus, or "remainder"

In the following examples, `$a = 5` and `$b = 4`.

```
$c = $a + $b;      // $c = 9
$c = $a - $b;      // $c = 1
$c = $a * $b;      // $c = 20
$c = $a / $b;      // $c = 1.25
$c = $a % $b;      // $c = 1
```

You don't have to limit mathematical operations to variables—you can use hard-coded numbers as well. For example:

```
$c = 3 + 4;     // $c = 7
$c = 8 * 4;     // $c = 32
$c = $a * 10;   // $c = 50
```

Comparison Operators

It should come as no surprise that comparison operators compare two values. As with the arithmetic operators, you already know most of the comparison operators:

    ==   equal to

    !=   not equal to

    >   greater than

    <   less than

    >=   greater than or equal to

    <=   less than or equal to

In the following examples, `$a = 5` and `$b = 4`.

- Is `$a == $b`? No; 5 does not equal 4. The comparison is FALSE.
- Is `$a != $b`? Yes; 5 does not equal 4. The comparison is TRUE.
- Is `$a > $b`? Yes; 5 is greater than 4. The comparison is TRUE.
- Is `$a < $b`? No; 5 is not less than 4. The comparison is FALSE.
- Is `$a >= $b`? Yes; although 5 does not equal 4, 5 is greater than 4. The comparison is TRUE.
- Is `$a <= $b`? No; 5 does not equal 4, and 5 is not less than 4. The comparison is FALSE.

Comparison operators are often used in conjunction with control statements (`if...else`, `while`) to perform a specific task based on the validity of expressions. For example, if you are writing a number-guessing program, and you want your script to print "That's the right number!" when a successful guess is made, you might include this code:

```
// secret number 5
if ($guess == "5") {
    echo "That's the right number!";
} else {
    echo "Sorry. Bad guess.";
}
```

Logical Operators

Logical operators, like comparison operators, are often found within `if...else` and `while` control statements. These operators allow your script to determine the status of conditions and, in the context of your `if...else` or `while` statements, execute certain code based on which conditions are true and which are false.

A common logical operator is `||`, meaning `OR`. The following example shows the evaluation of two variables and the result of the statement. In this example, I really want to drink coffee. I have two options, `$drink1` and `$drink2`. If either of my options is "coffee", I will be happy. Otherwise, I'll still need caffeine.

```
$drink1 = "coffee";
$drink2 = "milk";
    if (($drink1 == "coffee") || ($drink2 == "coffee")) {
        echo "I'm happy!";
    } else {
        echo "I still need caffeine.";
    }
```

In this example, because the value of the `$drink1` variable is "coffee," the logical OR comparison of `$drink1` and `$drink2` is TRUE, and the script returns "I'm happy!".

Other logical operators include AND (`&&`) and NOT (`!`).

Using PHP Variables: A Calculation Script

You now have a fundamental knowledge of variables and operators—enough to create a PHP script that does some sort of variable calculation and displays results. To begin, open your favorite text editor, create a file called `calc01.php`, and set up the HTML "shell" around your script:

```
<!DOCTYPE HTML PUBLIC "-//W3C//DTD HTML 3.2//EN">
<HTML>
<HEAD>
<TITLE>Calculate Values</TITLE>
</HEAD>
<BODY>
    <?php
        // PHP code goes here.
    ?>
</BODY>
</HTML>
```

In the following examples, replace the `<?php ... ?>` block with the code provided.

Initially, this script will use hard-coded values. In the following sections, you'll learn how to use values from outside your PHP script.

The `calc01.php` script will calculate an order for coffee beans. We know only the following information:

- The price of one bag of beans is $10.00, including shipping.
- Sales tax is 8.25%.
- Joe wants four bags.

Begin the script by creating variables for your known information and assigning values to those variables:

```php
<?php
    $price = 10.00;
    $sales_tax = .0825;
    $quantity = 4;
?>
```

You know that to find the subtotal of an order, you multiply the price of the item by the quantity ordered. You've just found another variable: `$sub_total`.

```php
<?php
    $price = 10.00;
    $sales_tax = .0825;
    $quantity = 4;
    $sub_total = $price * $quantity;
?>
```

You also know that the grand total of an order is the subtotal of the order plus the sales tax amount. The sales tax amount is determined by multiplying the sales tax by the subtotal of the order. You now know all of your remaining variables: `$sales_tax_amount` and `$grand_total`.

```php
<?php
    $price = 10.00;
    $sales_tax = .0825;
```

```php
    $quantity = 4;
    $sub_total = $price * $quantity;
    $sales_tax_amount = $sub_total * $sales_tax;
    $grand_total = $sub_total + $sales_tax_amount;
?>
```

Now that you have all the numbers, display the results in the browser window. Display the value of a variable with the echo command, just as if you were displaying a normal text string: `echo "$variablename";`

```php
<?php
    $price = 10.00;
    $sales_tax = .0825;
    $quantity = 4;
    $sub_total = $price * $quantity;
    $sales_tax_amount = $sub_total * $sales_tax;
    $grand_total = $sub_total + $sales_tax_amount;
    echo "<P>You ordered $quantity bags of coffee.</p>";
    echo "<P>Bags of coffee are $price each.</p>";
    echo "<P>Your subtotal is $sub_total.</p>";
    echo "<P>Sales tax is $sales_tax in this location.</p>";
    echo "<P>$sales_tax_amount has been added to your order.</p>";
    echo "<P>You owe $grand_total for your coffee.</p>";
?>
```

Save this file and place it on your Web server. Now access it with your browser at its URL, http://www.yourserver.com/calc01.php.

In your browser window, you should see this:

> You ordered 4 bags of coffee.
>
> Bags of coffee are 10 each.
>
> Your subtotal is 40.
>
> Sales tax is 0.0825 in this location.
>
> $3.3 has been added to your order.
>
> You owe 43.3 for your coffee.

While these calculations are correct, the results could use a little formatting help: placing a dollar sign before the amount, displaying the sales tax as a percentage, and showing the amount with two decimal places.

To print a dollar sign, place a backslash (\) before it. Dollar signs must be "escaped," or delineated, in this way because dollar signs are also used to indicate the presence of a variable. In your script, use

```
echo "<P>Bags of coffee are \$$price each.</p>";
```

to print a dollar sign before the value of $price. The result will look like this:

> Bags of coffee are $10 each.

Add the escaped dollar sign to other echo statements containing dollar amounts.

To get the percentage value of $sales_tax, first create a new variable called $sales_tax_pct. Then transform the value 0.0825 into 8.25 by multiplying 0.0825 by 100:

```
$sales_tax_pct = $sales_tax * 100;
```

The variable $sales_tax_pct now contains the value 8.25. Rewrite the echo statement to include the new variable and the percent sign:

```
echo "<P>Sales tax is $sales_tax_pct% in this location.</p>";
```

Here's the result:

> Sales tax is 8.25% in this location.

The final bit of formatting, ensuring that the dollar amount prints to two decimal places, involves the use of the sprintf() function. This function takes two arguments: the formatting argument and the name of the value to be formatted. The following code takes the value of $price, formats it by creating a floating-point number with two decimal places, and puts the value (10.00) into a new variable called $fmt_price:

```
$fmt_price = sprintf("%0.2f",$price);
```

Repeat this process for the other monetary values in the script: $sub_total and $grand_total:

```
$fmt_price = sprintf("%0.2f",$price);
$fmt_sub_total = sprintf("%0.2f",$sub_total);
$fmt_sales_tax_amount = sprintf("%0.2f",$sales_tax_amount);
$fmt_grand_total = sprintf("%0.2f",$grand_total);
```

In your echo statements, replace the old variables with the newly formatted variables. Your script should look something like this:

```
<?php
    $price = 10.00;
    $sales_tax = .0825;
```

```
    $quantity = 4;
    $sub_total = $price * $quantity;
    $sales_tax_amount = $sub_total * $sales_tax;
    $sales_tax_pct = $sales_tax * 100;
    $grand_total = $sub_total + $sales_tax_amount;
    $fmt_price = sprintf("%0.2f",$price);
    $fmt_sub_total = sprintf("%0.2f",$sub_total);
    $fmt_sales_tax_amount = sprintf("%0.2f",$sales_tax_amount);
    $fmt_grand_total = sprintf("%0.2f",$grand_total);
    echo "<P>You ordered $quantity bags of coffee.</p>";
    echo "<P>Bags of coffee are \$$fmt_price each.</p>";
    echo "<P>Your subtotal is \$$fmt_sub_total.</p>";
    echo "<P>Sales tax is $sales_tax_pct% in this location.</p>";
    echo "<P>\$$fmt_sales_tax_amount has been added to your order.</p>";
    echo "<P>You owe \$$fmt_grand_total for your coffee.</p>";
?>
```

Name this version of the script `calc02.php`, place it on your Web server, and access it with your browser at its URL, http://www.yourserver.com/calc02.php. In your browser window, you should now see this:

> You ordered 4 bags of coffee.
>
> Bags of coffee are $10.00 each.
>
> Your subtotal is $40.00.
>
> Sales tax is 8.25% in this location.
>
> $3.30 has been added to your order.
>
> You owe $43.30 for your coffee.

In the next section, you'll learn how to use variables from outside your PHP script—namely, from HTML forms—to create a coffee bean calculator.

HTML Form Variables

HTML forms always have three elements: a method, an action, and a submit button. Clicking the submit button in an HTML form causes variables to be passed to the script specified in the form ACTION via the specified METHOD. In this example, clicking the Calculate button would pass form variables to a script called `docalc.php` using the POST method:

```
<FORM method="POST" action="docalc.php">
    <INPUT type="submit" value="Calculate">
</FORM>
```

Variables passed from a form to a PHP script are placed in the global associative array $HTTP_POST_VARS or $HTTP_GET_VARS (depending on the form method) and are automatically made available to the script.

> Enabling variable tracking, or placing variables in global arrays, is an option configured when the PHP engine is installed on the server. If you are unsure whether variable tracking is turned on, you can add the line `<?php_track_vars?>` to the beginning of your script.

For example, the following form has one input text field and therefore passes one variable to the goform.php script:

```
<FORM method="POST" action="goform.php">
    <P>Name: <INPUT type="text" name="your_name" size=10></P>
    <INPUT type="submit" value="Submit">
</FORM>
```

Upon submission, the script goform.php receives a variable called $your_name, with a value of whatever the user typed in the form field. Variables are named according to the name attribute of the input field.

Here are some examples:

- The information typed in the following text field is placed in a variable called $phone_number:

  ```
  <INPUT type="text" name="phone_number" size=20>
  ```

- When the following radio button is enabled, the script receives a variable called $like_coffee with a value of "Y".

  ```
  <INPUT type="radio" name="like_coffee" value="Y">
  ```

- The value selected from the following drop-down list box is sent to the script in a variable called $year:

  ```
  <SELECT name="year" size=1>
      <OPTION value="1999">1999</OPTION>
      <OPTION value="2000">2000</OPTION>
      <OPTION value="2001">2001</OPTION>
  </SELECT>
  ```

Putting a Form to Work

In this section, you'll use your knowledge of HTML forms and basic PHP scripting to develop an interactive coffee bean calculator. Before you create the form, recall some hard-coded variables from the calc02.php script earlier in this chapter: $price and $quantity. To make the script interactive, you just create a form that allows the user to specify the values of these variables.

To begin, open your favorite text editor, create a file called show_calculate.html, and set up an HTML "shell":

```
<!DOCTYPE HTML PUBLIC "-//W3C//DTD HTML 3.2//EN">
<HTML>
<HEAD>
<TITLE>Bean Counter Form</TITLE>
</HEAD>
<BODY>
    <!-- your HTML form will go here -->
</BODY>
</HTML>
```

To create the form code, assume that your PHP script will be called do_calculate.php and that your form will use the POST method:

```
<FORM method="POST" action="do_calculate.php">
```

Next, create two simple text fields to capture the values for $price and $quantity:

```
<P>Enter the price per bag of coffee beans: $ <INPUT type="text" name="price"
size=10 maxlength=10></P>
```

Use the MAXLENGTH attribute to set a maximum number of characters entered in the text field, including spaces.

```
<P>How many bags would you like? <INPUT type="text" name="quantity" size=10
maxlength=10></P>
```

Finally, add a submit button:

```
<INPUT type="submit" value="Submit">
```

Don't forget the closing </FORM> tag!

Your HTML source code should look something like this:

```
<!DOCTYPE HTML PUBLIC "-//W3C//DTD HTML 3.2//EN">
<HTML>
```

```
<HEAD>
<TITLE>Bean Counter Form</TITLE>
</HEAD>
<BODY>
<FORM method="POST" action="do_calculate.php">
<P>Enter the price per bag of coffee beans: <INPUT type="text" name="price" size=10
maxlength=10></P>
<P>How many bags would you like? <INPUT type="text" name="quantity" size=10
maxlength=10></P>
<INPUT type="submit" value="Submit">
</FORM>
</BODY>
</HTML>
```

Place this file on your Web server, and access it with your browser at its URL, http://www.yourserver.com/show_calculate.html. In your browser window, you should see what is shown in Figure 2.1.

Now that you have a form all set to send two variables to a script, it's time to create the script. You'll be making a few modifications to the calc02.php script, so rename it do_calculate.php and open it in your favorite text editor.

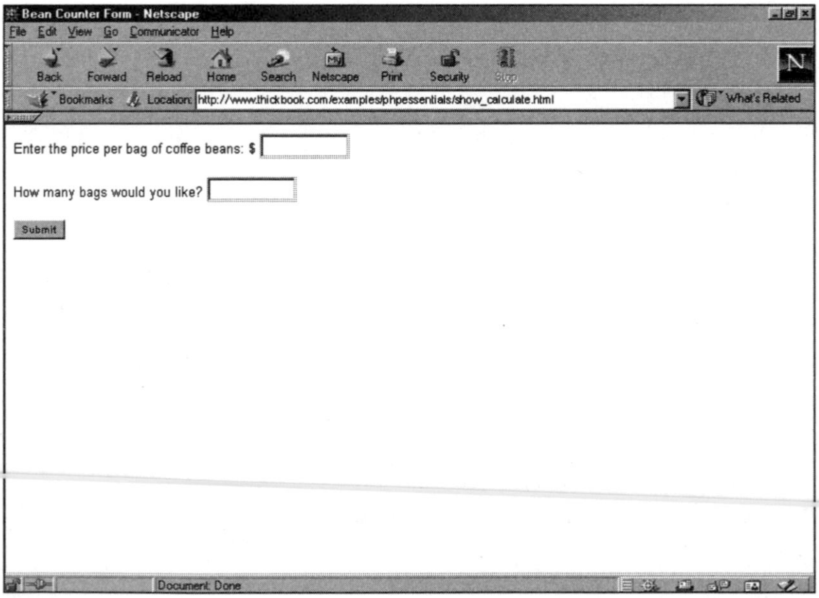

Figure 2.1   *Bean Counter form*

Make the following modifications:

1. Change the TITLE of the document to Bean Counter Results.
2. Add the directive `<?php_track_vars?>` at the top of your PHP code to ensure that variable tracking is in effect.
3. Delete the value assignment statements for `$price` and `$quantity`.

Place this file on your Web server and open the Bean Counter Form in your browser. Enter 10.00 in the first field and 4 in the second field, and then click the Submit button. You should see the same results as in the `calc02.php` script:

> You ordered 4 bags of coffee.
>
> Bags of coffee are $10.00 each.
>
> Your subtotal is $40.00.
>
> Sales tax is 8.25% in this location.
>
> $3.30 has been added to your order.
>
> You owe $43.30 for your coffee.

Try entering different values to see how the calculations turn out. Buying one bag of coffee at $14.25 should produce a grand total of $15.43, for example.

You can take the Bean Counter a step further by adding drop-down lists to your form and using conditional statements within your script to assign values to the variables sent from the form.

First, create a drop-down list of coffee types. Your form will pass the type of beans in a variable called $beans.

```
<P>Select a bean type:</P>
<SELECT name="beans" size="1">
    <OPTION value="Ethiopian Harrar">Ethiopian Harrar - $14.25</OPTION>
    <OPTION value="Kona">Kona - $16.25</OPTION>
    <OPTION value="Sumatra">Sumatra - $13.00</OPTION>
</SELECT>
```

Next, create a drop-down list of quantities:

```
<P>How many bags would you like?</P>
<SELECT name="quantity" size="1">
    <OPTION value="1">1</OPTION>
    <OPTION value="2">2</OPTION>
    <OPTION value="3">3</OPTION>
    <OPTION value="4">4</OPTION>
```

```
    <OPTION value="5">5</OPTION>
</SELECT>
```

Place this file on your Web server and access it with your browser at its URL, http://www.yourserver.com/show_calculate.html. In your browser window, you should see what is shown in Figure 2.2.

Now you will make a few more modifications to the do_calculate.php script, including setting up the pricing assignments for the variable $beans. Open the script in your favorite text editor and add the following:

```
// set up the pricing assignments
if ($beans == "Ethiopian Harrar") {
    $price = 14.25;
} else if ($beans == "Kona") {
    $price = 16.25;
} else if ($beans == "Sumatra") {
    $price = 13.00;
}
```

Previously, the user entered a number in a text field associated with the variable $price. In the new version, the user selects a bean type and the script assigns a value to the variable $price, based on the value of $beans.

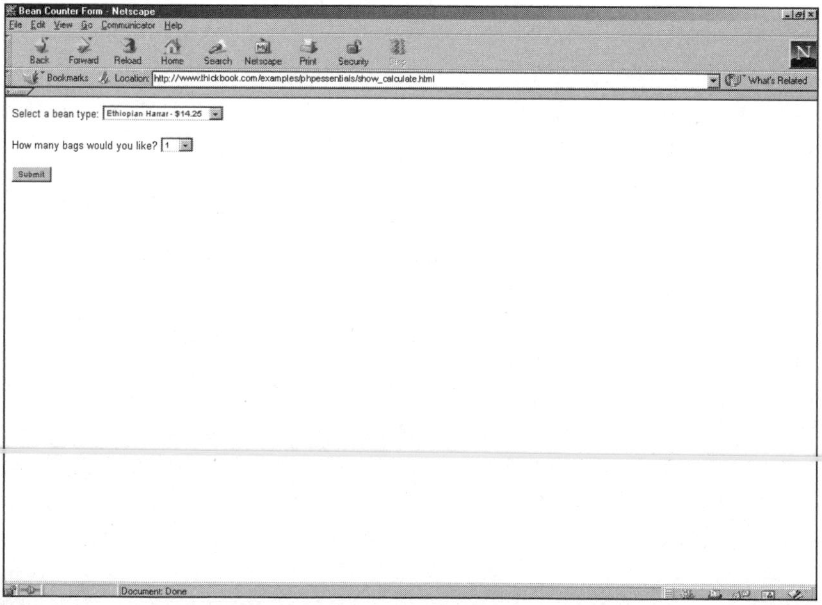

Figure 2.2   Bean Counter form, using pull-down menus

Using comparison operators, the script first checks to see if the value of $beans is equal to the string "Ethiopian Harrar." If it is not, the script jumps to the next statement, to see if the value of $beans is "Kona." If it still hasn't found a match, the script tries the last statement, to see if the value of $beans is "Sumatra." Since you are offering only three choices to the user, and the default value of the drop-down list is "Ethiopian Harrar," if you use the form interface you are assured of a match somewhere along the line.

Make two more modifications to the PHP script, to return the selected bean type to the user instead of the generic term "coffee":

```
echo "<P>You ordered $quantity bags of $beans.</P>";
```

and

```
echo "<P>Bags of $beans are \$$fmt_price each.</P>";
```

Save the file and place it on your Web server, and then open the Bean Counter Form in your browser. Select Kona from the bean type drop-down list and 2 from the quantity drop-down list, and then click the Submit button. You should see the following results:

> You ordered 2 bags of Kona.
>
> Bags of Kona are $16.25 each.
>
> Your subtotal is $32.50.
>
> Sales tax is 8.25% in this location.
>
> $2.68 has been added to your order.
>
> You owe $35.18 for your coffee.

Try entering different values to see how the calculations turn out. Try buying five bags of Ethiopian Harrar, and see how expensive it is ($77.13)!

HTTP Environment Variables

When a Web browser makes a request of a Web server, it sends along with the request a list of extra variables. These are called *environment variables,* and they can be very useful for displaying dynamic content or authorizing users.

Additionally, the phpinfo() function displays a wealth of information about the version of PHP that you are running and your Web server software, in addition to the basic HTTP environment. Create a file called phpinfo.php, containing only the following lines:

```
<?php
    phpinfo();
?>
```

To view a list of your environment variables and their values, place this file on your server and access it with your browser at its URL, http://www.yourserver.com/phpinfo.php.

In this section, you'll learn how to use two environment variables: REMOTE_ADDR and HTTP_USER_AGENT. For a list of HTTP environment variables and their descriptions, visit http://hoohoo.ncsa.uiuc.edu/cgi/env.html.

By default, environment variables are available to PHP scripts as $VAR_NAME. For example, the REMOTE_ADDR environment variable is already contained as $REMOTE_ADDR. However, to be absolutely sure that you're reading the correct value, use the getenv() function to assign a value to a variable of your choice. For example, the following code explicitly places the value of the environment variable REMOTE_ADDR into a variable called $remote_address:

```
$remote_address = getenv("REMOTE_ADDR");
```

REMOTE_ADDR

The REMOTE_ADDR environment variable contains the IP address of the machine making the request. Create a script called remote_address.php, containing the following code:

```php
<?php
    $remote_address = getenv("REMOTE_ADDR");
    echo "Your IP address is $remote_address.";
?>
```

Save this file and place it on your server, and then access it with your browser at its URL, http://www.yourserver.com/remote_address.php.

You should see "Your IP address is [some number]" on your screen. For example, I see "Your IP address is 209.244.209.209." This IP address is the address currently assigned to my computer by my Internet Service Provider.

In Chapter 5, "User Authentication," you'll learn how to use the REMOTE_ADDR environment variable as a form of user authentication by limiting the display of your Web site content to users accessing it from a specific domain or range of IP addresses.

HTTP_USER_AGENT

The HTTP_USER_AGENT variable contains the browser type, browser version, language encoding, and platform. For example:

```
Mozilla/4.61 - (Win98; I)
```

refers to the Netscape (Mozilla) browser, version 4.61, in English, on the Windows 98 platform.

Here are some other `HTTP_USER_AGENT` values, for my own browser library:

```
Mozilla/4.0 (compatible; MSIE 5.0; Windows 98)
```

This value refers to Microsoft Internet Explorer (MSIE) version 5.0 on Windows 98. Sometimes you will see MSIE return an `HTTP_USER_AGENT` value that looks like a Netscape value, until you notice that the value says it's "compatible" and is actually "MSIE 5.0."

I am one of those die-hard Lynx users. Don't count out the text-only browsers! A Lynx `HTTP_USER_AGENT` value looks like this:

```
Lynx/2.8rel.3 libwww-FM/2.14
```

Find your own `HTTP_USER_AGENT` value by creating a script called `browser_type.php`, containing the following code:

```php
<?php
    $browser_type = getenv("HTTP_USER_AGENT");
    echo "You are using $browser_type.";
?>
```

Save this file and place it on your server, and then access it with your browser at its URL, http://www.yourserver.com/browser_type.php.

You should see "You are using [some browser type]" on your screen. For example, I see "You are using Mozilla/4.51 – (X11; I; Linux 2.2.12 i586)." This is true, for at this very moment, I am using Netscape Communicator 4.51 on my Linux machine.

In the next section, you'll learn how to display specific content based on the browser accessing your Web site.

Displaying Dynamic Content

The Web is a dynamic environment, always changing and growing by leaps and bounds, so why not use your programming skills to display dynamic content? You can create a customized user environment by displaying specific content based on values sent through an HTML form, the type of browser being used, or (as you'll learn in later chapters) variables stored in cookies.

Redirecting to a New Location

Automatically redirecting a user to a new URL means that your script has to send an HTTP header to the browser before any other information, indicating a new location. Many types of HTTP headers exist, from those indicating the character encoding and expiration date of the document to those that send the 404 - File Not Found error message. If you would like to learn more than anyone should ever know about headers, feel free to read the current HTTP 1.1 specification at http://www.w3.org/Protocols/rfc2068/rfc2068.

The format for sending an HTTP header from a PHP script is

```
header(string);
```

where `string` is the header text, in quotations. For example, use this code to print a redirection header that will send the browser to the PHP site:

```
<?php
header("Location: http://www.php.net/");
exit;
?>
```

Use the `exit` statement to ensure that the script does not continue to run.

Take the redirection script one step further, and add an HTML form with a drop-down list box as a front end to the redirection routine. Depending on the values sent by the form, the script redirects the browser to any of a number of URLs.

To begin, open your favorite text editor, create a file called `show_menu.html`, and set up an HTML "shell."

Next, create the form code, assuming that your PHP script will be called `do_redirect.php` and your form will use the `POST` method:

```
<FORM method="POST" action="do_redirect.php">
```

Now create a drop-down list box containing some menu options:

```
<P>I want to go to:
<SELECT name="location" size="1">
    <OPTION value="http://www.prima-tech.com/">Prima-Tech</OPTION>
    <OPTION value="http://www.php.net/">PHP.net</OPTION>
    <OPTION value="http://www.slashdot.org/">Slashdot</OPTION>
    <OPTION value="http://www.linuxchix.org/">Linuxchix</OPTION>
</SELECT>
```

Finally, add a submit button:

```
<INPUT type="submit" value="Go!">
```

Don't forget the closing `</FORM>` tag!

Your HTML source code should look something like this:

```
<!DOCTYPE HTML PUBLIC "-//W3C//DTD HTML 3.2//EN">
<HTML>
<HEAD>
<TITLE>Redirection Menu</TITLE>
</HEAD>
<BODY>
    <FORM method="POST" action="do_redirect.php">
    <P>I want to go to:
    <SELECT name="location" size="1">
    <OPTION value="http://www.prima-tech.com/">Prima-Tech</OPTION>
    <OPTION value="http://www.php.net/">PHP.net</OPTION>
    <OPTION value="http://www.slashdot.org/">Slashdot</OPTION>
    <OPTION value="http://www.linuxchix.org/">Linuxchix</OPTION>
    </SELECT>
        <INPUT type="submit" value="Go!">
    </FORM>
</BODY>
</HTML>
```

Place this file on your Web server, and access it with your browser at its URL, http://www.yourserver.com/show_menu.html. In your browser window, you should see what is shown in Figure 2.3.

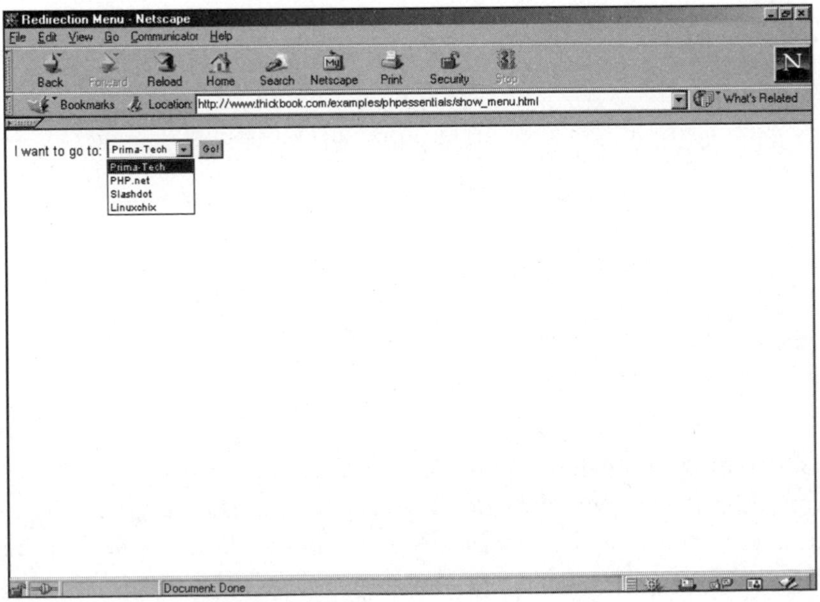

Figure 2.3 *Redirection menu*

Now, create the `do_redirect.php` script, which simply captures the value in `$location` and sends the redirection header:

```php
<?php
header("Location: $location");
exit;
?>
```

Save this file and place it on your server, and then access the menu at its URL, http://www.yourserver.com/show_menu.html.

Select a destination, click the "Go!" button, and away you (should) go!

If you want to hide the redirection URLs from your users, modify the HTML form elements so that `$location` holds just an identification string:

```html
<SELECT name="id" size="1">
<OPTION value="prima">Prima-Tech</OPTION>
<OPTION value="php">PHP.net</OPTION>
<OPTION value="slashdot">Slashdot</OPTION>
<OPTION value="linuxchix">Linuxchix</OPTION>
</SELECT>
```

Then modify your PHP script to add a series of conditional statements, ultimately assigning the proper value to `$location` based on the value of `$id`:

```php
<?php
    if ($id == "prima") {
        $location = "http://www.prima-tech.com/";
    } else if ($id == "php") {
        $location = "http://www.php.net/";
    } else if ($id == "slashdot") {
        $location = "http://www.slashdot.org/";
    } else if ($id == "linuxchix") {
        $location = "http://www.linuxchix.org/";
    }
    header("Location: $location");
    exit;
?>
```

Although coding the URLs in the script works as well as coding the URLs into the HTML form values, it adds twice the work. If you choose to code the URLs in the script, anytime you want to add a new location, you must add the option to the form, and also add the corresponding `if`... statement to the script.

Either way, you've now mastered the art of sending redirection headers via a PHP script!

Displaying Browser-Specific Code

As of this writing, the Browser War still rages on: no single Web browser is used by a vast majority of Web surfers. Various flavors of Microsoft Internet Explorer (MSIE) account for approximately 75 percent of Web browsers in use, while versions of Netscape (NS) take up about 24 percent. Throw in the die-hard Lynx, Opera, and WebTV users to reach 100 percent.

Although a 75/25 split might seem like a vast majority, if 150 million people have access to the Internet, 25 million non-Microsoft users is a huge number of users to consider when developing a good Web site. There are many nuances to browser-specific HTML development, but here are some highlights:

- MSIE 5.0 includes some XML support. NS 4.x does not.
- MSIE and NS versions 3.x and higher include support for style sheets. Other browsers do not.
- Some versions of NS on UNIX do not include support for style sheets.

And so on. HotWired maintains a browser reference at http://hotwired.lycos.com/webmonkey/reference/browser_chart/.

Using the HTTP_USER_AGENT environment variable, you can discern the specific attributes of the browser accessing your page and display code specifically designed for that browser type and platform.

However, having seen some HTTP_USER_AGENT values, you can imagine that there are hundreds of slightly different values. It's time to learn basic pattern matching!

Create a script called browser_match.php, containing the following code:

```
<?php
    $browser_type = getenv("HTTP_USER_AGENT");
?>
```

Using the preg_match() PHP function, find a specific block of text within the value of $HTTP_USER_AGENT. The syntax of preg_match() is

```
preg_match("/[what you want to find]/", "[where you're looking]");
```

To find "MSIE" somewhere in the HTTP_USER_AGENT value, which you have already assigned to the variable $browser_type, use

```
preg_match("/MSIE/i", "$browser_type");
```

The "i" following /MSIE/ tells the script to match any instances, in uppercase or lowercase.

To find "Mozilla" in the HTTP_USER_AGENT value, use

```
(preg_match("/Mozilla/i", "$browser_type");
```

Put all the pieces together within an if...else statement so that if the browser is MSIE, "Using MSIE" will be printed on the screen. Or, if the browser is Netscape, "Using Netscape" will be printed on the screen. Or, if the browser is neither of those types, the HTTP_USER_AGENT value for that browser will be printed. Your code should look something like this:

```php
<?php
    $browser_type = getenv("HTTP_USER_AGENT");
    if (preg_match("/MSIE/i", "$browser_type")) {
        echo "Using MSIE.";
    } else if (preg_match("/Mozilla/i", "$browser_type")) {
        echo "Using Netscape.";
    } else {
        echo "$browser_type";
    }
?>
```

Save this file and place it on your server, and then access it with your browser at its URL, http://www.yourserver.com/browser_match.php.

In your browser window, you should see "Using MSIE," "Using Netscape," or the HTTP_USER_AGENT value for the browser you are using (see Figure 2.4).

If you are developing a Web site using style sheets, and you have one set of styles for MSIE and another set of styles for Netscape, you can use this same construct to print the style sheet link within the context of your code.

For example, a link to the style sheet:

```
<LINK REV="stylesheet" HREF="msie_style.css">
```

would appear in the area indicated by

```
<!-- stylesheet code goes here -->
```

in the following HTML example:

```
<!DOCTYPE HTML PUBLIC "-//W3C//DTD HTML 3.2//EN">
<HTML>
<HEAD>
```

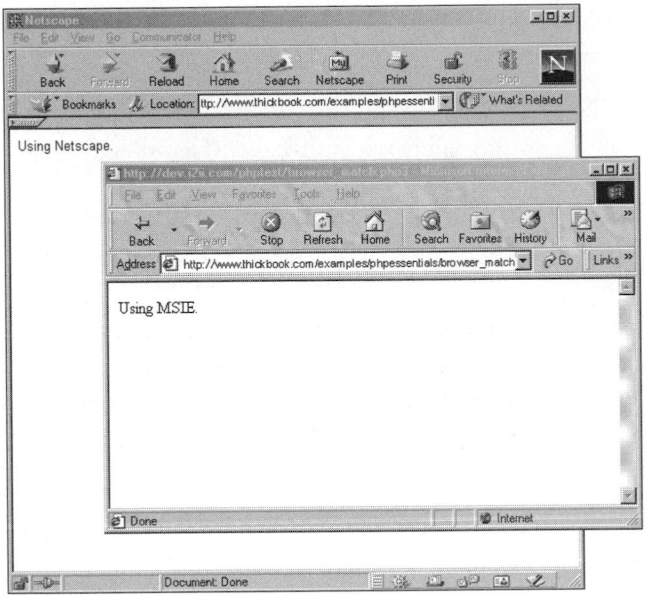

Figure 2.4   *Displaying a custom message based on browser type*

```
<TITLE>Your Page</TITLE>
<!-- stylesheet code goes here -->
</HEAD>
<BODY>
</BODY>
</HTML>
```

If you have two style sheets, `msie_style.css` for MSIE-specific styles and `ns_style.css` for Netscape-specific styles, replace the style sheet comment with this block of PHP:

```php
<?php
    $browser_type = getenv("HTTP_USER_AGENT");
    if (preg_match("/MSIE/i", "$browser_type")) {
        echo "<LINK REV=\"stylesheet\" HREF=\"msie_style.css\">.";
    } else if (preg_match("/Mozilla/i", "$browser_type")) {
        echo "<LINK REV=\"stylesheet\" HREF=\"ns_style.css\">.";
    }
?>
```

Note the use of escaped quotation marks (\"\") in the echo statement. When you use quotation marks inside other quotation marks, the inner pairs must delineated from the outside pair using the escape (\) character (also known as a backslash). Otherwise, nasty parse errors will occur.

This section of PHP code will seamlessly print the correct style sheet link in your HTML document, thus allowing you to safely use all the browser-specific styles you can think up.

Sending E-Mail

I can't think of any successful Web site that doesn't have some sort of feedback form or other mechanism for contact. When you see how incredibly easy it is to send e-mail with PHP, you might scratch your head in amazement and wonder why the rest of the world doesn't do this. That's a perfectly normal reaction (I still feel that way).

The `mail()` function takes four arguments: the recipient, the subject, the message, and the mail headers. So, if you want to send an e-mail to joe@yourcompany.com, with a subject of "Check this out!" and a message of "PHP is the best!", your entire PHP mail script could look like this:

```
<?php
    mail("joe@yourcompany.com", "Check this out!", "PHP is the best!", "From:
\"You\" <\"you@yourcompany.com\">\n");
?>
```

The e-mail will arrive in your mailbox like any other mail message:

Subject:	Check this out!
Date:	[date sent]
From:	You <you@yourcompany.com>
To:	joe@yourcompany.com

PHP is the best!

Now that you know how to send a simple e-mail, you can create a feedback form in HTML. A basic feedback form can contain text fields for the sender's name and e-mail address, a set of radio buttons asking if the user liked the site, and a text area for any additional message.

To begin, open your favorite text editor, create a file called `show_feedback.html`, and set up an HTML "shell":

```
<!DOCTYPE HTML PUBLIC "-//W3C//DTD HTML 3.2//EN">
<HTML>
<HEAD>
```

```
<TITLE>Feedback Form</TITLE>
</HEAD>
<BODY>
    <!-- your HTML form will go here -->
</BODY>
</HTML>
```

To create the form code, assume that your PHP script will be called `do_sendfeedback.php` and your form will use the POST method:

```
<FORM method="POST" action="do_sendfeedback.php">
```

Next, create two text fields to capture the values for `$sender_name` and `$sender_email`:

```
<P>Your Name: <br><INPUT type="text" name="sender_name" size=30></P>
<P>Your E-Mail Address: <br><INPUT type="text" name="sender_email" size=30></P>
```

Add the radio button group to gather the value of `$like_site`:

```
<P>Did you like this site?
<INPUT type="radio" name="like_site" value="Yes" checked> yes
<INPUT type="radio" name="like_site" value="No"> no
</p>
```

Add a text area so that the user can enter any additional message (captured in the variable `$message`):

```
<P>Additional Message: <br>
    <textarea name="message" cols=30 rows=5></textarea>
</P>
```

Finally, add the Send This Form button:

```
<INPUT type="submit" value="Send This Form">
```

Don't forget the closing `</FORM>` tag!

Your HTML source code should look something like this:

```
<!DOCTYPE HTML PUBLIC "-//W3C//DTD HTML 3.2//EN">
<HTML>
<HEAD>
<TITLE>Feedback</TITLE>
</HEAD>
<BODY>
<FORM method="POST" action="do_sendfeedback.php">
    <P>Your Name: <INPUT type="text" name="sender_name" size=30></P>
```

```
    <P>Your E-Mail Address: <INPUT type="text" name="sender_email" size=30></P>
    <P>Did you like this site?
    <INPUT type="radio" name="like_site" value="Yes" checked> yes
    <INPUT type="radio" name="like_site" value="No"> no
    </P>
    <P>Additional Message: <br>
        <textarea name="message" cols=30 rows=5></textarea>
    </P>
    <INPUT type="submit" value="Send This Form">
</FORM>
</BODY>
</HTML>
```

Place this file on your Web server, and access it with your browser at its URL, http://www.yourserver.com/show_feedback.html. In your browser window, you should see what is shown in Figure 2.5.

Next, create the do_sendfeedback.php script. This script will capture the form values $sender_name, $sender_email, $like_site, and $message.

Begin the script with:

```
<?php_track_vars?> // ensures variables are tracked
```

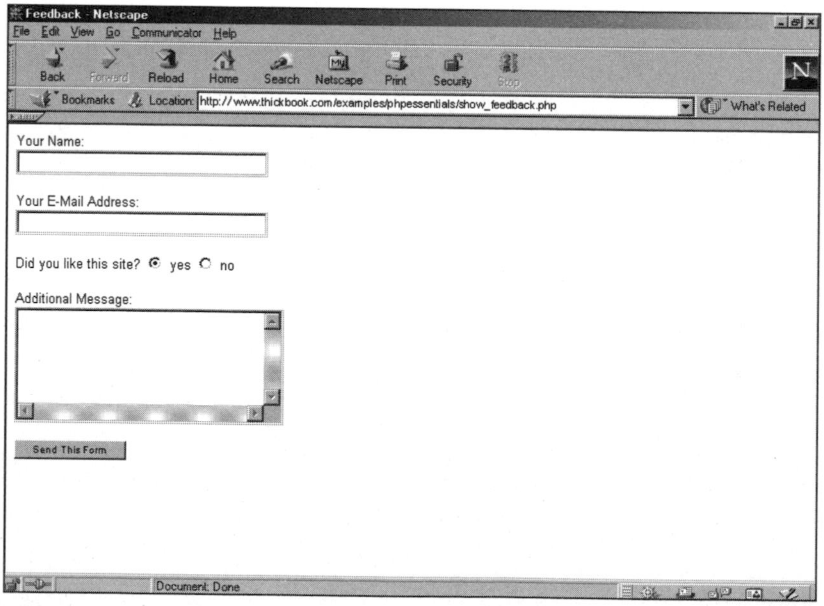

Figure 2.5 *Feedback form*

You must build the e-mail by concatenating strings to form one big message string. "Concatenating" is a fancy word for "smash strings together." Use the newline (\n) and tab (\t) characters to add spacing where appropriate. Start building the message string in a variable called $msg:

```php
<?php
    $msg = "Sender's Full Name:\t$sender_name\n";
?>
```

In this line, you want the e-mail to display a field label before the variable $sender_name so that you know what $sender_name is. For all you know, $sender_name could be "Dog's Name."

Repeat the process, setting up field labels and results for $sender_email, $like_site, and $message. In these lines, however, use the concatenation operator (.=) instead of the assignment operator (=).

```php
$msg .= "Sender's E-Mail:\t$sender_email\n";
$msg .= "Did You Like the Site?\t$like_site\n";
$msg .= "Additional Message:\t$message\n\n";
// use two newline characters at the end of your content,
// or to insert additional spacing
```

Your message string ($msg) is now

```php
"Sender's Full Name:\t$sender_name\nSender's E-Mail:\t$sender_email\nDid You Like
the Site?\t$like_site\nAdditional Message:\t$message\n\n";
```

The e-mail client will format this into a nice e-mail with line breaks and tabs between elements.

Now create a variable called $mailheaders to force particular values in the From and Reply-To headers of your e-mail:

```php
$mailheaders = "From: My Web Site\n";
$mailheaders .= "Reply-To: $sender_email\n\n";
```

Create the mail function. In this case, I'll use my own e-mail address:

```php
mail("julie@thickbook.com", "Feedback Form", $msg, $mailheaders);
```

After your mail is sent, you should return some sort of text message to the browser so that the person doesn't sit there, wondering if the message was sent or not. If a user doesn't know if a message has been sent, chances are good that he or she will continue to click the Submit This Form button, thereby flooding your mailbox with the same feedback form repeatedly.

Add a few echo statements. You can even include the user's name in your response, since you have access to the variable $sender_name:

```
echo "<H1 align=center>Thank You, $sender_name</J1>";
echo "<P align=center>We appreciate your feedback.</P>";
```

Your entire PHP script should look something like this:

```
<?php_track_vars?>
<?php

    $msg = "Sender's Full Name:\t$sender_name\n";
    $msg .= "Sender's E-Mail:\t$sender_email\n";
    $msg .= "Did You Like the Site?\t$like_site\n";
    $msg .= "Additional Message:\t$message\n\n";
    // use two newline characters at the end of your content,
    // or to insert additional spacing

    $mailheaders = "From: My Web Site\n";
    $mailheaders .= "Reply-To: $sender_email\n\n";

    mail("julie@thickbook.com", "Feedback Form", $msg, $mailheaders);

    echo "<H1 align=center>Thank You, $sender_name</H1>";
    echo "<P align=center>We appreciate your feedback.</P>";

?>
```

Return to your Web browser, open the feedback form at its URL, http://www.yourserver.com/show_feedback.html, and enter your name, e-mail address, and a message. For testing purposes, I entered "Julie Meloni," "jcm@i2ii.com," selected "yes" when asked if I liked this site, and "This is a great site!" in the message box.

After I submitted the form, the resulting page properly displayed my name and provided a thank-you message, as shown in Figure 2.6.

I checked my e-mail, and I had received a properly-formatted message, including the $sender_name, $sender_email, $like_site, and $message values (see Figure 2.7).

What about form validation? While ensuring that all fields are completed is not terribly crucial in this simple mail example, it will be important down the road when you start creating order forms. A very easy way to deal with required fields using PHP is to check for the required value and simply redirect the user back to the form if one of those values doesn't exist.

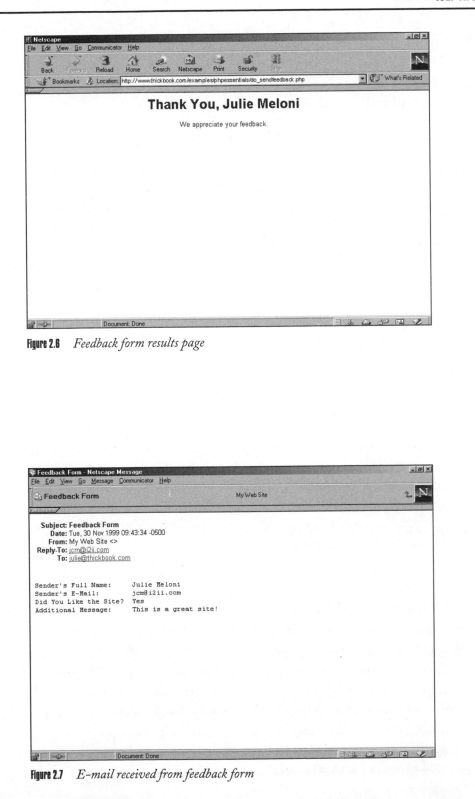

Figure 2.6   *Feedback form results page*

Figure 2.7   *E-mail received from feedback form*

In the `do_sendfeedback.php` script, add this code before building the message string to check for an e-mail address and a message:

```
if (($sender_email == "") || ($message == "")) {
   header("Location: http://www.yourserver.com/show_feedback.html");
   exit;
}
```

This code simply states "if the value of `$sender_email` is blank or if the value of `$message` is blank, redirect the user back to a blank form so they can start again." In the "Tutorials" section at http://www.thickbook.com/ you can learn how to print specific error messages after a user is redirected, so they know the mistake they made (in this case, the error was not completing the form).

In the next section, you'll learn how to read and write data files from the file system, including how to place the contents of a file into an e-mail and send it to a particular e-mail address.

Reading and Writing Data Files

In addition to sending an e-mail full of data, you can create simple PHP scripts to create, open, and write to files on your Web server using the `fopen()` function.

Writing Data Files

The `fopen()` function takes two arguments, file name and mode, and returns a file pointer. A file pointer provides information about the file and is used as a reference. The file name is the full path to the file you want to create or open, and mode can be any of the following:

- r Opens the existing file in order to read data from it. The file pointer is placed at the beginning of the file, before any data.

- r+ Opens the existing file for reading or writing. The file pointer is placed at the beginning of the file, before any data.

- w Opens a file only for writing. If a file with that name does not exist, attempts to create a new file. If the file does exist, deletes all existing contents and places the file pointer at the beginning of the file.

- w+ Opens a file for reading and writing. If a file with that name does not exist, attempts to create a new file. If the file does exist, deletes all existing contents and places the file pointer at the beginning of the file.

- a Opens a file only for writing. If a file with that name does not exist, attempts to create a new file. If the file does exist, places the file pointer at the end of the file, after all other data.

- a+ Opens a file for reading and writing. If a file with that name does not exist, attempts to create a new file. If the file does exist, places the file pointer at the end of the file, after all other data.

So, to create a new file in your Web server document root (for example, /usr/local/apache/htdocs/) called mydata.txt, to be used to read and write data, use this code:

```php
<?php
$newfile = fopen("/usr/local/apache/htdocs/mydata.txt", "a+");
?>
```

In this example, $newfile is the file pointer. You can refer to this file pointer when reading, closing, or performing other functions with the file.

> Remember to read to and write from files that are in an area accessible by your server process.

After you open a file, be sure to close it using the fclose() function:

```php
fclose($newfile);
```

But opening a file just to close it again can get boring, so use the fwrite() or fputs() function to place data in the open file:

```php
fwrite([file], [data]);
```

> For all intents and purposes, fwrite() and fputs() are exactly the same.

Create a script called write_data.php, containing the following code:

```php
<?php
$newfile = fopen("/usr/local/apache/htdocs/mydata.txt", "a+");
fwrite($newfile, "This is a new file.");
fclose($newfile);
echo "All done!";
?>
```

Be sure to modify the path to the file to match your own environment. Adding the echo statement after the file has been opened, written to, and closed will cause the message to display after the actions have occurred. If any errors arise, such as problems with file permissions, you'll see those on the screen as well.

If your Web server runs on the Windows platform, escape the backslashes in your file path, like this:

```
$newfile = fopen("c:\\Apache\\htdocs\\mydata.txt", "a+");
```

Place the PHP script on your Web server, and access it with your browser at its URL, http://www.yourserver.com/write_data.php. In your browser window, you should now see this:

All done!

To verify that the message "This is a new file." has been written to mydata.txt, you can access it via URL if it has been placed above the document root: http://www.yourserver.com/mydata.txt. If you placed the file in your home directory, such as /home/username/, navigate through your filesystem and open the file.

Reading Data Files

You can also use PHP to verify that a file has been written to by using the fread() function to gather the data into a variable. The fread() function takes two arguments:

```
fread([filename], [length]);
```

To read the complete file, length can be found using the filesize() function:

```
fread([filename], filesize([filename]));
```

To verify that the file mydata.txt, created in the preceding section, contains the string "This is a new file.", first create a script called read_data.php containing the following code:

```php
<?php
    $file_loc = "/usr/local/apache/htdocs/mydata.txt";
    // this variable contains the full path to the filename
    $whattoread = fopen($file_loc, "r");
    // opens the file for reading only
    $file_contents = fread($whattoread, filesize($file_loc));
    // puts the contents of the entire file into a variable
    fclose($whattoread);
    // close the file
    echo "The file contains:<br>$file_contents";
?>
```

Be sure to modify the path to the file to match your own environment.

Place the PHP script on your Web server, and access it with your browser at its URL, http://www.yourserver.com/read_data.php. In your browser window, you should now see this:

> The file contains:
>
> This is a new file.

As well as reading the results on the screen, you can also send the contents in an e-mail. Add the following lines before the echo statement:

```
$mailheaders = "From: My Web Site <> \n";
mail("julie@thickbook.com", "File Contents", $file_contents, $mailheaders);
```

And change the echo statement to:

```
echo "Check your mail!";
```

The complete script should now look something like this:

```php
<?php
    $file_loc = "/usr/local/apache/htdocs/mydata.txt";
    // this variable contains the full path to the filename
    $whattoread = fopen($file_loc, "r");
    // opens the file for reading only
    $file_contents = fread($whattoread, filesize($file_loc));
    // puts the contents of the entire file into a variable
    fclose($whattoread);
    // close the file
    $mailheaders = "From: My Web Site <> \n";
    mail("julie@thickbook.com", "File Contents", $file_contents, $mailheaders);
    echo "Check your mail!";
?>
```

Place the PHP script on your Web server, and access it with your browser at its URL, http://www.yourserver.com/read_data.php. In your browser window, you should now see this:

> Check your mail!

When you check your mail, a message similar to this one should be waiting for you:

> Subject: File Contents
>
> Date: [date sent]

From: My Web Site <>

To: julie@thickbook.com

This is a new file.

Later, you'll learn how to save form data on the filesystem and e-mail it to yourself on demand. You'll also learn how to launch applications with PHP to encrypt files, and then delete the unencrypted versions.

Chapter 3: Working with Databases

Basic Database Theory

Basic SQL

Establishing a Database Connection with PHP

can't think of a time when I wouldn't want to use some sort of database in a Web application, be it a simple flat-file operational database or a complex relational database. Whether saving form data, tracking inventory, or creating dynamic content, if you can grasp basic database concepts, you can begin to create simple database-driven Web applications. With the advent of open source, fully-functional relational databases, these types of applications are no longer only for those with enough money to play the game.

In this chapter, you'll learn some rudimentary database theory, basic SQL statements, and how to use PHP to connect and retrieve information stored in database tables. Although PHP supports numerous database types as well as generic ODBC connections, the in-depth examples used throughout this book are based on the MySQL database functions. If you are not using MySQL, refer to the PHP Manual online at http://www.php.net/ to find the functions for your particular database type.

Basic Database Theory

Before I lead you far down the path of database development, you should become familiar with the basic structure of a database. Here's a listing from the largest element to the smallest:

1. A database is a collection of tables.
2. A table contains a set of records.
3. All records have the same number of fields.
4. Each field categorizes a piece of data.

Starting with the smallest element, suppose you have a few uncategorized, seemingly random pieces of data: Joe Smith, 1970-10-03, and blue. These pieces of data can be placed into categories such as Full Name, Birthday, and Favorite Color. Give these fields some database-friendly names, such as:

- FULL_NAME
- BIRTH_DATE
- FAVE_COLOR

Now visualize these fields horizontally, where they become the labels for columns in a table:

```
+-------------+-------------+-------------+
| FULL_NAME   | BIRTH_DATE  | FAVE_COLOR  |
+-------------+-------------+-------------+
```

To create the first record (row) in this table, enter Joe Smith's information. Your table then looks like this:

```
+-------------+-------------+-------------+
| FULL_NAME   | BIRTH_DATE  | FAVE_COLOR  |
+-------------+-------------+-------------+
| Joe Smith   | 1970-10-03  | blue        |
+-------------+-------------+-------------+
```

Add additional records to your table by adding more friends:

```
+-------------+-------------+-------------+
| FULL_NAME   | BIRTH_DATE  | FAVE_COLOR  |
+-------------+-------------+-------------+
| Joe Smith   | 1970-10-03  | blue        |
| Mary Smith  | 1962-07-25  | red         |
| Jane Smith  | 1968-04-28  | black       |
+-------------+-------------+-------------+
```

Give your table a name, such as FRIEND_INFO, and that's all there is to it. Tables, records, and fields are the basic elements of a database.

The Importance of Unique Identifiers

The FRIEND_INFO table from the preceding section is missing something: a unique identifier. You might think that the FULL_NAME field is the unique identifier. If so, you better not have additional friends named Joe Smith, Mary Smith, or Jane Smith. If FULL_NAME is the unique identifier, no one else with those exact names can be included in your FRIEND_INFO table.

Instead, how about a simple FRIEND_ID field? If you have two friends named Joe Smith, this ensures that you'll know their favorite color when it's time to get them a birthday present.

Add the FRIEND_ID field to your FRIEND_INFO table:

```
+-------------+-------------+-------------+-------------+
| FRIEND_ID   | FULL_NAME   | BIRTH_DATE  | FAVE_COLOR  |
+-------------+-------------+-------------+-------------+
| 1           | Joe Smith   | 1970-10-03  | blue        |
| 2           | Mary Smith  | 1962-07-25  | red         |
| 3           | Jane Smith  | 1968-04-28  | black       |
+-------------+-------------+-------------+-------------+
```

You can now add your other friend named Joe Smith. The FRIEND_INFO table will now look like this:

```
+-------------+-------------+-------------+-------------+
| FRIEND_ID   | FULL_NAME   | BIRTH_DATE  | FAVE_COLOR  |
+-------------+-------------+-------------+-------------+
| 1           | Joe Smith   | 1970-10-03  | blue        |
| 2           | Mary Smith  | 1962-07-25  | red         |
| 3           | Jane Smith  | 1968-04-28  | black       |
| 4           | Joe Smith   | 1975-11-07  | green       |
+-------------+-------------+-------------+-------------+
```

I hope this simple example conveys the importance of having a unique identifier for each record in your table.

What About Relationships?

Relational databases get their name from the relationships that exist between the multiple tables contained in them. You could have a series of disconnected tables in a relational database, but where's the fun in that?

Relationships between tables occur because they have fields in common. Usually these common fields are the unique fields, or *keys,* which you learned about a moment ago.

The simplest example of a relational database is a product catalog and ordering mechanism. One table has product information. Another contains customer information. A third table has order information. Instead of creating one large table for orders, containing all product and customer information, simply use unique identifiers in the orders table to reference products in the product table and customers in the customer table.

For example, records in the MY_PRODUCTS table will have a unique PRODUCT_ID, a TITLE, a DESCRIPTION, and a PRICE:

```
+--------------+-----------+--------------------+-------------+
| PRODUCT_ID   | TITLE     | DESCRIPTION        | PRICE       |
+--------------+-----------+--------------------+-------------+
| 12557        | Hat       | Warm and fuzzy.    | 7.50        |
| 12558        | Jacket    | Waterproof.        | 32.50       |
| 12559        | Shirt     | Shiny and stylish. | 48.00       |
| 12560        | Pants     | Pleated chinos.    | 52.00       |
+--------------+-----------+--------------------+-------------+
```

Next, records in the MY_CUSTOMERS table will have a unique CUSTOMER_ID, a NAME, and an ADDRESS:

```
+--------------+-------------+-----------------------------------+
| CUSTOMER_ID  | NAME        | ADDRESS                           |
+--------------+-------------+-----------------------------------+
| 125          | Mike Jones  | 112 Main St, Anywhere CA 95228    |
| 268          | Jim Smith   | 458 Bee Ave, Blankville IN 55248  |
| 275          | Nancy Jones | 751 14th St NW, Notown MI 44322   |
+--------------+-------------+-----------------------------------+
```

Records in the MY_ORDERS table will have a unique ORDER_ID. You can use the CUSTOMER_ID and PRODUCT_ID identifiers to fill in the CUSTOMER and PRODUCT_ORDERED fields. Finally, if you're ordering something, you have to have a QUANTITY.

```
+-----------+-------------+-------------------+-----------+
| ORDER_ID  | CUSTOMER    | PRODUCT_ORDERED   | QUANTITY  |
+-----------+-------------+-------------------+-----------+
| 1         | 125         | 12558             | 1         |
| 2         | 268         | 12560             | 1         |
| 3         | 275         | 12557             | 1         |
+-----------+-------------+-------------------+-----------+
```

To create an invoice for these orders, you would use the values in the CUSTOMER and PRODUCT_ORDERED fields to find the extended information about these people and items in their respective tables: MY_CUSTOMERS and MY_PRODUCTS.

Using the relationships between your tables, you could create an invoice like this:

```
ORDER NUMBER:    001
SHIP TO:         Mike Jones, 112 Main St, Anywhere CA 95228
ITEMS ORDERED:   1 Hat (Warm and Fuzzy)
TOTAL COST:      $ 7.50
```

With this basic understanding of unique fields and the relationships between tables in a database, it's time to learn some of the language of relational databases: SQL, or Structured Query Language.

Basic SQL

Although the Structured Query Language (SQL) was developed by IBM, SQL is currently under the watchful eye of the American National Standards Institute (ANSI). As with all "standards," there are variations of SQL—"proprietary enhancements," if you will—for use with Microsoft SQL Server, Oracle databases, and others. However, learning the standard set of SQL commands will provide you with a fundamental knowledge of SQL that you can use with multiple database systems. Here are the standard commands:

- CREATE. Creates a new table.
- ALTER. Modifies the definition (structure, data types, and so on) of an existing table.
- DROP. Permanently removes elements such as tables and fields.
- INSERT. Adds a record to a table.
- UPDATE. Modifies data in an existing record.
- SELECT. Performs a query on a table, including mathematical functions, field comparison, pattern matching, and so on.
- DELETE. Permanently removes elements from a table.

The next several sections contain further descriptions and examples of these basic SQL commands. Be sure to read your database documentation thoroughly for the exact usage of these commands in your own environment, because they might differ slightly from these examples, which are geared toward the MySQL user. Additionally, you may enter SQL commands directly through a graphical user interface (GUI) or via the command line, depending on your database type. The next sections provide only examples of the SQL commands themselves; at the end of this chapter, you'll learn to send SQL commands to your database via PHP scripts.

CREATE

The CREATE command creates a table in the selected database. The basic syntax is as follows:

```
CREATE TABLE [table name] [(field_name field_data_type,…)] [options]
```

> Some common data types are int, double, char, varchar, date, time, datetime, text, and blob. Refer to your database documentation for a list of supported data types and any size and data restrictions.

To create the `FRIEND_INFO` table used at the beginning of this chapter, the SQL statement would be something like this:

```
CREATE TABLE FRIEND_INFO (
FRIEND_ID char(5) not null,
FULL_NAME varchar (100),
BIRTH_DATE date,
FAVE_COLOR varchar (25),
UNIQUE FRIEND_ID (FRIEND_ID)
);
```

This sample code uses a lot of white space. White space is irrelevant in SQL statements, but it certainly makes your code easier to read (and easier to edit later!). The preceding statement could just as easily have been written like this:

```
CREATE TABLE FRIEND_INFO (FRIEND_ID char(5) not null, FULL_NAME varchar (100),
BIRTH_DATE date, FAVE_COLOR varchar (25), UNIQUE FRIEND_ID (FRIEND_ID));
```

The `CREATE` command defines the attributes of the fields in your table; it gives each a type and a length. In this example, the `FRIEND_ID` field is defined as "not null," meaning that when a record is added, if the field is empty, it is simply empty, or has a default value such as "0" for numeric fields. A value of NULL means something entirely different from "empty," and is an important distinction to remember. `FRIEND_ID` is also identified as *unique*, by adding `UNIQUE FRIEND_ID (FRIEND_ID)` to the SQL statement, meaning that `FRIEND_ID` always holds unique data: Although there may be multiple entries for Joe Smith, there will be only one `FRIEND_ID` of 1, 2, and so on.

ALTER

The `ALTER` command gives you the opportunity to modify elements of a particular table. For example, you can use `ALTER` to add fields or change field types. For instance, if you want to change the size of the `FULL_NAME` field of the `FRIEND_INFO` table from 100 to 150, you could issue this statement:

```
ALTER TABLE FRIEND_INFO
CHANGE FULL_NAME
FULL_NAME VARCHAR (150);
```

To add a column to the table, you could use the following statement, which adds a field called HAT_SIZE:

```
ALTER TABLE FRIEND_INFO
ADD HAT_SIZE char(5);
```

Using the ALTER command alleviates the need to delete an entire table and recreate it just because you spelled a field name incorrectly or made other minor mistakes.

DROP

The DROP command is quite dangerous if you're not paying attention to what you're doing, because it will delete your entire table in the blink of an eye. The syntax is very simple:

```
DROP TABLE [table name];
```

If you wanted to delete the FRIEND_INFO table and rely on your brain to remember your friends' birthdays, the command would be

```
DROP TABLE FRIEND_INFO;
```

You can use the DROP command in conjunction with the ALTER command to delete specific fields (and all the data contained in them). To delete the HAT_SIZE field from the FRIEND_INFO table, issue this statement:

```
ALTER TABLE FRIEND_INFO
DROP HAT_SIZE;
```

The HAT_SIZE field will no longer exist, but all other fields in your table will still be intact.

INSERT

You use the INSERT command to populate your tables one record at a time. The basic syntax of the INSERT command is

```
INSERT INTO [table name] ([name of field1] , [name of field2], …)
VALUES ('[value of field 1]', '[value of field 2]'…);
```

To add a record to the FRIEND_INFO table, where the fields are FRIEND_ID, FULL_NAME, BIRTH_DATE, and FAVE_COLOR, the command would be:

```
INSERT INTO FRIEND_INFO (FRIEND_ID, FULL_NAME, BIRTH_DATE, FAVE_COLOR)
VALUES ('1', 'Joe Smith', '1970-10-03', 'blue');
```

To add the rest of your friends, issue additional INSERT statements:

```
INSERT INTO FRIEND_INFO (FRIEND_ID, FULL_NAME, BIRTH_DATE, FAVE_COLOR)
VALUES ('2', 'Mary Smith', '1962-07-25', 'red');

INSERT INTO FRIEND_INFO (FRIEND_ID, FULL_NAME, BIRTH_DATE, FAVE_COLOR)
VALUES ('3', 'Jane Smith', '1968-04-28', 'black');

INSERT INTO FRIEND_INFO (FRIEND_ID, FULL_NAME, BIRTH_DATE, FAVE_COLOR)
VALUES ('4', 'Joe Smith', '1975-11-07', 'green');
```

When inserting records, be sure to separate your strings with single quotes or double quotes. If you use single quotes around your strings, and the data you are adding contains apostrophes, avoid errors by escaping the apostrophe (\') within the INSERT statement. Similarly, if you use double quotes around your strings and you want to include double quotes as part of the data, escape them (\") within your INSERT statement.

For example, if you use single quotes around your strings and you want to insert a record for a friend named Mark O'Hara, you can use this statement:

```
INSERT INTO FRIEND_INFO (FRIEND_ID, FULL_NAME, BIRTH_DATE, FAVE_COLOR)
VALUES ('5', 'Mark O\'Hara', '1968-12-12', 'orange');
```

Or, you can surround your strings with double quotes:

```
INSERT INTO FRIEND_INFO (FRIEND_ID, FULL_NAME, BIRTH_DATE, FAVE_COLOR)
VALUES ("5", "Mark O'Hara", "1968-12-12", "orange");
```

UPDATE

The UPDATE command modifies parts of a record without replacing the entire record. Here is the basic syntax of the UPDATE command:

```
UPDATE [table name]
SET [field name] = '[new value]'
WHERE [some expression];
```

For instance, suppose you have an incorrect birth date in the FRIEND_INFO table: Joe Smith, with a FRIEND_ID of 1, was born on November 3 instead of October 3. Instead of deleting the record and inserting a new one, just use the UPDATE command to change the data in the BIRTH_DATE field:

```
UPDATE FRIEND_INFO
SET BIRTH_DATE = '1970-11-03'
WHERE FRIEND_ID = '1';
```

If you issue an UPDATE statement without specifying a WHERE expression, you will update all the records. For example, to change everyone's favorite color to red, use this UPDATE statement:

```
UPDATE FRIEND_INFO
    SET FAVE_COLOR = 'red';
```

UPDATE can be a very powerful SQL command. For example, you can perform string functions and mathematical functions on existing records and use the UPDATE command to modify their values.

SELECT

When you're creating database-driven Web sites, the SELECT command will likely be the most often-used command in your arsenal. The SELECT command causes certain records in your table to be chosen, based on criteria that you define. Here is the basic syntax of the SELECT command:

```
SELECT [field names]
FROM [table names]
WHERE [some expression]
ORDER BY [field names];
```

To select all the records in a table, such as the FRIEND_INFO table, use this statement:

```
SELECT *
FROM FRIEND_INFO;
```

To select just the entries in the FULL_NAME field of the FRIEND_INFO table, use this:

```
SELECT FULL_NAME
FROM FRIEND_INFO;
```

To select all the records in a table and have them returned in a particular order, use an expression for ORDER BY. For example, to view the FRIEND_ID, FULL_NAME, and BIRTH_DATE in each record in the FRIEND_INFO table, ordered by youngest friend to oldest friend, use the following:

```
SELECT FRIEND_ID, FULL_NAME, BIRTH_DATE
    FROM FRIEND_INFO
    ORDER BY BIRTH_DATE DESC;
```

DESC stands for "descending." To view from oldest to youngest, use ASC for "ascending":

```
SELECT FRIEND_ID, FULL_NAME, BIRTH_DATE
    FROM FRIEND_INFO
    ORDER BY BIRTH_DATE ASC;
```

This statement produces results like this:

```
+-------------+-------------+--------------+
|  FRIEND_ID  |  FULL_NAME  |  BIRTH_DATE  |
+-------------+-------------+--------------+
|  2          |  Mary Smith |  1962-07-25  |
|  3          |  Jane Smith |  1968-04-28  |
|  1          |  Joe Smith  |  1970-11-03  |
|  4          |  Joe Smith  |  1975-11-07  |
+-------------+-------------+--------------+
```

When preparing ORDER BY clauses, the default order is ASC (ascending).

You can also perform mathematical and string functions within SQL statements, thereby using SELECT to do more than just echo existing data. For example, to quickly find the number of friends in your FRIEND_INFO table, use

```
SELECT COUNT(FRIEND_ID) FROM FRIEND_INFO;
```

The result of this statement is 4. You could also use the COUNT() function on any other field to count the number of those entries in the table.

I could write volumes on the many variations of SELECT commands, but luckily, others already have. Additionally, if you are using the MySQL database, the MySQL manual contains a wonderful SQL reference. Later in this chapter, as well as in Chapters 7 and 8, "Advanced PHP Techniques: Web-Based Database Administration" and "Advanced PHP Techniques: e-Commerce," you'll learn more uses of the SELECT command.

DELETE

The DELETE command is not nearly as fun as SELECT, but it's useful nonetheless. Like the DROP command, using DELETE without paying attention to what you're doing can have horrible consequences in a production environment. Once you DROP a table or DELETE a record, it's gone forever. The basic syntax of the DELETE command is as follows:

```
DELETE FROM [table name]
    WHERE [some expression];
```

For example, to delete entries for Joe Smith from your FRIEND_INFO table, you could use:

```
DELETE FROM FRIEND_INFO
    WHERE FULL_NAME = 'Joe Smith';
```

But wait a minute! If you execute this statement, you'll delete *both* Joe Smith entries. So, use another identifier in addition to the name:

```
DELETE FROM FRIEND_INFO
    WHERE FULL_NAME = 'Joe Smith' AND BIRTH_DATE = '1970-11-03';
```

Or, since you now know the importance of unique identifiers, you could use this:

```
DELETE FROM FRIEND_INFO
    WHERE FRIEND_ID = '1';
```

If you issue a DELETE command without specifying a WHERE expression, you will delete all the records. For example, this bit of SQL deletes all the records in the FRIEND_INFO table:

```
DELETE FROM FRIEND_INFO
```

Also remember, if you don't want to delete an entire record, just a certain field from a table, you can use this:

```
ALTER TABLE [table name]
    DROP [field name];
```

Always back up your data if you're going to be using the DELETE and DROP commands, just in case something goes wrong.

Establishing a Database Connection with PHP

Using the built-in database connectivity functions in PHP, you can connect to virtually any database type and access its data (if you have the proper permissions, of course!). If PHP does not contain specific functions for your particular database type, you can make generic ODBC connections using PHP's ODBC functions. Before trying to use any of the database connectivity functions, be sure that you have a database installed and the proper extensions are loaded and indicated in your php3.ini or php.ini file.

In the next several pages, you'll find function definitions and code samples for numerous database types. The PHP Manual at http://www.php.net/manual/ is the first place you should look to find a complete list of all the functions for supported databases. After searching the manual and the FAQ, search the PHP Mailing List Archives. Chances are good that if you have a database connectivity question, someone else has asked it and a developer has answered it. If not, asking a well-phrased question will undoubtedly elicit numerous responses.

The following sections are by no means all there is to know about connecting to databases with PHP. Instead, these sections detail the basic elements of database connectivity:

1. Connect to a server
2. Select a database
3. Query
4. View results

The code samples provided in the next sections are not the only ways to make a simple connection and print results. Some of the examples are more verbose than they really need to be, but they give you a solid foundation for understanding the steps that follow. When you become an expert with your database type, you can find your own ways to optimize your code, eliminating extra steps and some processing time and resource overhead.

Connecting to Informix Databases

There are more than 35 different PHP functions for Informix connectivity, documented in detail in the PHP Manual. However, you need only a few of these functions in order to make a simple connection and select some data:

- `ifx_connect()` Opens a connection to the Informix server. Requires a database name, username, and password.
- `ifx_query()` Issues the SQL statement.
- `ifx_htmltbl_result()` Places the results of your SQL statement into a nicely-formatted HTML table.
- `ifx_free_result()` Frees the resources in use by the current connection.
- `ifx_close()` Closes the current connection.

First, you must know the name of your database and the name of the server on which it resides. You must also have a valid username and password for that database. In this example, the database name is `secretDB` on `localhost`, your username is `sandman`, and your password is `34Nhjp`. Start your PHP code by creating a connection variable:

```
$connection = ifx_connect("secretDB@localhost", "sandman", "34Nhjp")
or die ("Couldn't connect to the database.");
```

The `die()` function is used to print an error message and exit a script when the function cannot perform as required. In this case, `die()` would execute if the connection failed. The error message would be printed so you know where the error occurred ("Couldn't connect to the database."), and no further actions would take place. Using `die()` properly will alleviate many headaches as you attempt to debug your code.

If you make it through the connection, the next step is to create the SQL statement. Suppose that the FRIEND_INFO table, used in previous examples, exists in your Informix database. You want to view your friends' names, birthdays, and favorite colors, ordered from oldest to youngest friend. Create a variable that holds your SQL statement:

```
$sql = "SELECT FULL_NAME, BIRTH_DATE, FAVE_COLOR FROM FRIEND_INFO
  ORDER BY BIRTH_DATE ASC";
```

Next, create a variable to hold the result ID of the query, carried out by the ifx_query() function. The ifx_query() function takes two arguments: the connection and the SQL statement variables you just created.

```
$sql_result = ifx_query($sql,$connection) or die ("Couldn't execute query.");
```

To format the results currently held in $sql_result, use the very handy ifx_htmltbl_result() function. This function uses the result ID variable and HTML table options such as "border=1".

```
ifx_htmltbl_result($sql_result,"border=1");
```

Finally, you'll want to free up the resources used to perform the query, and close the database connection. Failing to do so could cause memory leaks and other nasty resource-hogging things to occur.

```
ifx_free_result($sql_result);
ifx_close($connection);
```

The full script to perform a simple connection and data selection from an Informix database could look something like this:

```
<?php
// create connection
$connection = ifx_connect("secretDB@localhost", "sandman", "34Nhjp")
or die ("Couldn't connect to the database.");

// create SQL statement
$sql = "SELECT FULL_NAME, BIRTH_DATE, FAVE_COLOR FROM FRIEND_INFO
  ORDER BY BIRTH_DATE ASC";

// execute SQL query and get result
$sql_result = ifx_query($sql,$connection) or die ("Couldn't execute query.");
```

```
// format result in HTML table, then free resources
ifx_htmltbl_result($sql_result,"border=1");
ifx_free_result($sql_result);
ifx_close($connection);
?>
```

See the PHP Manual for additional Informix database functions, and try using your own tables and SQL statements instead of the examples just shown. Remember, don't use the DELETE or DROP commands unless you're really ready and you've backed up your data!

Connecting to Microsoft SQL Server

There are numerous PHP functions for Microsoft SQL Server connectivity, documented in detail in the PHP Manual. However, you need only a few of these functions in order to make a simple connection and select some data:

- mssql_connect() Opens a connection to Microsoft SQL Server. Requires a server name, username, and password.
- mssql_select_db() Selects a database on the Microsoft SQL Server.
- mssql_query() Issues the SQL statement.
- mssql_fetch_array() Puts an SQL statement result row in an array.
- mssql_free_result() Frees the resources in use by the current connection.
- mssql_close() Closes the current connection.

First, you must know the name of the server on which the database resides, as well as a valid username and password for that database. In this example, the database name is secretDB on localhost, your username is sandman, and your password is 34Nhjp. Start your PHP code by creating a connection variable:

```
$connection = mssql_connect("localhost","sandman","34Nhjp")
or die ("Couldn't connect to the server.");
```

The die() function is used to print an error message and exit a script when the function cannot perform as required. In this case, die() would execute if the connection failed. The error message would be printed so you know where the error occurred ("Couldn't connect to the server."), and no further actions would take place. Using die() properly will alleviate many headaches as you attempt to debug your code.

> If you have problems making a connection, try using an empty string for the password (" ").

If you make it through the connection test, the next step is to select the database and create the SQL statement. Suppose that the FRIEND_INFO table, used in previous examples, exists in a database called secretDB. Create a database variable such as this:

```
$db = mssql_select_db("secretDB", $connection) or die ("Couldn't select
database.");
```

Up to this point, you've told PHP to connect to a server and select a database. If you've made it this far, you can issue an SQL statement and hopefully see some results!

Using the FRIEND_INFO table, suppose you want to view your friends' names, birthdays, and favorite colors, ordered from oldest to youngest friend. Create a variable that holds your SQL statement:

```
$sql = "SELECT FULL_NAME, BIRTH_DATE, FAVE_COLOR FROM FRIEND_INFO
  ORDER BY BIRTH_DATE ASC";
```

Next, create a variable to hold the result of the query, carried out by the mssql_query() function. The mssql_query() function takes two arguments: the connection and the SQL statement variables you just created.

```
$sql_result = mssql_query($sql,$connection) or die ("Couldn't execute query.");
```

To format the results currently held in $sql_result, first separate the results by row, using the mssql_fetch_array() function:

```
while ($row = mssql_fetch_array($sql_result)) {
    // more code here…
}
```

The while loop creates an array called $row for each record in the result set. To get the individual elements of the record (FULL_NAME, BIRTH_DATE, FAVE_COLOR), create specific variables:

```
$full_name = $row["FULL_NAME"];
$birth_date = $row["BIRTH_DATE"];
$fave_color = $row["FAVE_COLOR"];
```

You'll probably want to print the results in a simple HTML table. Step back and place this statement before the while loop begins, to open the table tag and create the row headings:

```
echo "<TABLE BORDER=1>";
echo "<TR><TH>Full Name</TH><TH>Birthday</TH><TH>Favorite Color</TH></TR>";
```

After defining the variables within the while loop, print them in table format:

```
echo "<TR><TD>$full_name</TD><TD>$birth_date</TD><TD>$fave_color</TD></TR>";
```

The new while loop looks like this:

```
while ($row = mssql_fetch_array($sql_result)) {
$full_name = $row["FULL_NAME"];
$birth_date = $row["BIRTH_DATE"];
$fave_color = $row["FAVE_COLOR"];
echo "<TR><TD>$full_name</TD><TD>$birth_date</TD><TD>$fave_color</TD></TR>";
}
```

After the while loop, close the HTML table:

```
echo "</TABLE>";
```

Finally, you'll want to free up the resources used to perform the query and close the database connection. Failing to do so could cause memory leaks and other nasty resource-hogging things to occur.

```
mssql_free_result($sql_result);
mssql_close($connection);
```

The full script to perform a simple connection and data selection from a database on Microsoft SQL Server could look something like this:

```
<?php
// create connection
$connection = mssql_connect("localhost","sandman","34Nhjp")
or die ("Couldn't connect to the server.");

// select database
// substitute your own database name
$db = mssql_select_db("secretDB", $connection) or die ("Couldn't select
database.");

// create SQL statement
$sql = "SELECT FULL_NAME, BIRTH_DATE, FAVE_COLOR FROM FRIEND_INFO
        ORDER BY BIRTH_DATE ASC";
```

```
// execute SQL query and get result
$sql_result = mssql_query($sql,$connection) or die ("Couldn't execute query.");

// start results formatting
echo "<TABLE BORDER=1>";
echo "<TR><TH>Full Name</TH><TH>Birthday</TH><TH>Favorite Color</TH></TR>";

// format results by row
while ($row = mssql_fetch_array($sql_result)) {
$full_name = $row["FULL_NAME"];
$birth_date = $row["BIRTH_DATE"];
$fave_color = $row["FAVE_COLOR"];
echo "<TR><TD>$full_name</TD><TD>$birth_date</TD><TD>$fave_color</TD></TR>";
}
echo "</TABLE>";

// free resources and close connection
mssql_free_result($sql_result);
mssql_close($connection);
?>
```

See the PHP Manual for additional Microsoft SQL Server functions, and try using your own tables and SQL statements instead of the examples just shown. Remember, don't use the DELETE or DROP commands unless you're really ready and you've backed up your data!

Connecting to an mSQL Database

There are numerous PHP functions you can use in conjunction with your mSQL databases, all documented in detail in the PHP Manual. However, you need only a few of these functions in order to make a simple connection and select some data:

- msql_connect() Opens a connection to the mSQL server. Requires a hostname.
- msql_select_db() Selects a database on the mSQL server.
- msql_query() Issues the SQL statement.
- msql_fetch_array() Puts an SQL statement result row in an array.
- msql_free_result() Frees the resources in use by the current connection.
- msql_close() Closes the current connection.

First, you must know the name of the server on which the database resides. In this example, the database name is `secretDB` on `localhost`. Start your PHP code by creating a connection variable:

```
$connection = msql_connect("localhost")
or die ("Couldn't connect to the server.");
```

The `die()` function is used to print an error message and exit a script when the function cannot perform as required. In this case, `die()` would execute if the connection failed. The error message would be printed so you know where the error occurred ("Couldn't connect to the server."), and no further actions would take place. Using `die()` properly will alleviate many headaches as you attempt to debug your code.

If you make it through the connection test, the next step is to select the database and create the SQL statement. Suppose that the `FRIEND_INFO` table, used in previous examples, exists in an mSQL database called `secretDB`. Create a database variable such as this:

```
$db = msql_select_db("secretDB", $connection) or die ("Couldn't select database.");
```

Up to this point, you've told PHP to connect to a server and select a database. If you've made it this far, you can issue an SQL statement and hopefully see some results!

Using the `FRIEND_INFO` table, suppose you want to view your friends' names, birthdays, and favorite colors, ordered from oldest to youngest friend. Create a variable that holds your SQL statement:

```
$sql = "SELECT FULL_NAME, BIRTH_DATE, FAVE_COLOR FROM FRIEND_INFO
   ORDER BY BIRTH_DATE ASC";
```

Next, create a variable to hold the result of the query, carried out by the `msql_query()` function. The `msql_query()` function takes two arguments: the connection and the SQL statement variables you just created.

```
$sql_result = msql_query($sql,$connection) or die ("Couldn't execute query.");
```

To format the results currently held in `$sql_result`, first separate the results by row, using the `msql_fetch_array()` function:

```
while ($row = msql_fetch_array($sql_result)) {
   // more code here...
}
```

The `while` loop creates an array called `$row` for each record in the result set. To get the individual elements of the record (`FULL_NAME`, `BIRTH_DATE`, `FAVE_COLOR`), create specific variables:

```
$full_name = $row["FULL_NAME"];
$birth_date = $row["BIRTH_DATE"];
$fave_color = $row["FAVE_COLOR"];
```

You'll probably want to print the results in a simple HTML table. Step back and place this statement before the `while` loop begins, to open the table tag and create the row headings:

```
echo "<TABLE BORDER=1>";
echo "<TR><TH>Full Name</TH><TH>Birthday</TH><TH>Favorite Color</TH></TR>";
```

After defining the variables within the `while` loop, print them in table format:

```
echo "<TR><TD>$full_name</TD><TD>$birth_date</TD><TD>$fave_color</TD></TR>";
```

The new `while` loop looks like this:

```
while ($row = msql_fetch_array($sql_result)) {
$full_name = $row["FULL_NAME"];
$birth_date = $row["BIRTH_DATE"];
$fave_color = $row["FAVE_COLOR"];
echo "<TR><TD>$full_name</TD><TD>$birth_date</TD><TD>$fave_color</TD></TR>";
}
```

After the `while` loop, close the HTML table:

```
echo "</TABLE>";
```

Finally, you'll want to free up the resources used to perform the query and close the database connection. Failing to do so could cause memory leaks and other nasty resource-hogging things to occur.

```
msql_free_result($sql_result);
msql_close($connection);
```

The full script to perform a simple connection and data selection from an mSQL database could look something like this:

```
<?php
// create connection
$connection = msql_connect("localhost","sandman","34Nhjp") or die ("Couldn't connect to server.");

// select database
```

```
// substitute your own database name
$db = msql_select_db("secretDB", $connection) or die ("Couldn't select database");

// create SQL statement
$sql = "SELECT FULL_NAME, BIRTH_DATE, FAVE_COLOR FROM FRIEND_INFO
        ORDER BY BIRTH_DATE ASC";

// execute SQL query and get result
$sql_result = msql_query($sql,$connection) or die ("Couldn't execute query.");

// start results formatting
echo "<TABLE BORDER=1>";
echo "<TR><TH>Full Name</TH><TH>Birthday</TH><TH>Favorite Color</TH></TR>";

// format results by row
while ($row = msql_fetch_array($sql_result)) {
$full_name = $row["FULL_NAME"];
$birth_date = $row["BIRTH_DATE"];
$fave_color = $row["FAVE_COLOR"];
echo "<TR><TD>$full_name</TD><TD>$birth_date</TD><TD>$fave_color</TD></TR>";
}
echo "</TABLE>";

// free resources and close connection
msql_free_result($sql_result);
msql_close($connection);
?>
```

See the PHP Manual for additional mSQL functions, and try using your own tables and SQL statements instead of the examples just shown. Remember, don't use the DELETE or DROP commands unless you're really ready and you've backed up your data!

Connecting to a MySQL Database

The MySQL database is one of the most popular among PHP developers. It's my database of choice, as well as the database used in the examples found in this book. Understandably, there are numerous well-documented PHP functions you can use in conjunction with your MySQL databases; see the PHP Manual for a complete list. However, you need only a few of these functions in order to make a simple connection and select some data:

- `mysql_connect()` Opens a connection to the MySQL server. Requires a hostname, username, and password.
- `mysql_select_db()` Selects a database on the MySQL server.
- `mysql_query()` Issues the SQL statement.
- `mysql_fetch_array()` Puts an SQL statement result row in an array.
- `mysql_free_result()` Frees the resources in use by the current connection.
- `mysql_close()` Closes the current connection.

First, you must know the name of the server on which the database resides, as well as a valid username and password for that server. In this example, the database name is `secretDB` on `localhost`, your username is `sandman`, and your password is `34Nhjp`. Start your PHP code by creating a connection variable:

```
$connection = mysql_connect("localhost","sandman","34Nhjp")
or die ("Couldn't connect to the server.");
```

The `die()` function is used to print an error message and exit a script when the function cannot perform as required. In this case, `die()` would execute if the connection failed. The error message would be printed so you know where the error occurred ("Couldn't connect to the server."), and no further actions would take place. Using `die()` properly will alleviate many headaches as you attempt to ·debug your code.

If you make it through the connection test, the next step is to select the database and create the SQL statement. Suppose that the `FRIEND_INFO` table, used in previous examples, exists in a MySQL database called `secretDB`. Create a database variable such as this:

```
$db = mysql_select_db("secretDB", $connection) or die ("Couldn't select database.");
```

Up to this point, you've told PHP to connect to a server and select a database. If you've made it this far, you can issue an SQL statement and hopefully see some results!

Using the `FRIEND_INFO` table, suppose you want to view your friends' names, birthdays, and favorite colors, ordered from oldest to youngest friend. Create a variable that holds your SQL statement:

```
$sql = "SELECT FULL_NAME, BIRTH_DATE, FAVE_COLOR FROM FRIEND_INFO
   ORDER BY BIRTH_DATE ASC";
```

Next, create a variable to hold the result of the query, carried out by the `mysql_query()`

function. The mysql_query() function takes two arguments: the connection and the SQL statement variables you just created.

```
$sql_result = mysql_query($sql,$connection) or die ("Couldn't execute query.");
```

To format the results currently held in $sql_result, first separate the results by row, using the mysql_fetch_array() function:

```
while ($row = mysql_fetch_array($sql_result)) {
    // more code here…
}
```

The while loop creates an array called $row for each record in the result set. To get the individual elements of the record (FULL_NAME, BIRTH_DATE, FAVE_COLOR), create specific variables:

```
$full_name = $row["FULL_NAME"];
$birth_date = $row["BIRTH_DATE"];
$fave_color = $row["FAVE_COLOR"];
```

You'll probably want to print the results in a simple HTML table. Step back and place this statement before the while loop begins, to open the table tag and create the row headings:

```
echo "<TABLE BORDER=1>";
echo "<TR><TH>Full Name</TH><TH>Birthday</TH><TH>Favorite Color</TH></TR>";
```

After defining the variables within the while loop, print them in table format:

```
echo "<TR><TD>$full_name</TD><TD>$birth_date</TD><TD>$fave_color</TD></TR>";
```

The new while loop looks like this:

```
while ($row = mysql_fetch_array($sql_result)) {
$full_name = $row["FULL_NAME"];
$birth_date = $row["BIRTH_DATE"];
$fave_color = $row["FAVE_COLOR"];
echo "<TR><TD>$full_name</TD><TD>$birth_date</TD><TD>$fave_color</TD></TR>";
}
```

After the while loop, close the HTML table:

```
echo "</TABLE>";
```

Finally, you'll want to free up the resources used to perform the query and close the database connection. Failing to do so could cause memory leaks and other nasty resource-hogging things to occur.

```
mysql_free_result($sql_result);
mysql_close($connection);
```

The full script to perform a simple connection and data selection from a MySQL database could look something like this:

```php
<?php
// create connection
$connection = mysql_connect("localhost","sandman","34Nhjp") or die ("Couldn't
connect to server.");

// select database
$db = mysql_select_db("secretDB", $connection) or die ("Couldn't select
database.");

// create SQL statement
$sql = "SELECT FULL_NAME, BIRTH_DATE, FAVE_COLOR FROM FRIEND_INFO
        ORDER BY BIRTH_DATE ASC";

// execute SQL query and get result
$sql_result = mysql_query($sql,$connection) or die ("Couldn't execute query.");

// start results formatting
echo "<TABLE BORDER=1>";
echo "<TR><TH>Full Name</TH><TH>Birthday</TH><TH>Favorite Color</TH></TR>";

// format results by row
while ($row = mysql_fetch_array($sql_result)) {
$full_name = $row["FULL_NAME"];
$birth_date = $row["BIRTH_DATE"];
$fave_color = $row["FAVE_COLOR"];
echo "<TR><TD>$full_name</TD><TD>$birth_date</TD><TD>$fave_color</TD></TR>";
}
   echo "</TABLE>";

// free resources and close connection
mysql_free_result($sql_result);
mysql_close($connection);
?>
```

See the PHP Manual for additional MySQL functions, and try using your own tables and SQL statements instead of the examples just shown. Remember, don't use the DELETE or DROP commands unless you're really ready and you've backed up your data!

Connecting to an Oracle Database

PHP has numerous functions for connecting to Oracle databases. This is good because if you've spent the money to purchase an Oracle database, you'll want to be able to connect to it using this newfangled programming language that's all the rage. The PHP Manual has the definitive list of PHP-to-Oracle connectivity functions; however, you need only a few in order to make a simple connection and select some data:

- OCILogon() Opens a connection to Oracle. Requires that the environment variable ORACLE_SID has been set and that you have a valid username and password.
- OCIParse() Parses an SQL statement.
- OCIExecute() Executes the SQL statement.
- OCINumCols() Gets the number of columns used in the SQL statement.
- OCIFetch() Gets the next row in the result of a SQL statement and places it in a results buffer.
- OCIResult() Gets the value of the named column in the current result row.
- OCIFreeStatement() Frees the resources in use by the current statement.
- OCILogoff() Closes the connection to Oracle.

First, you must have a valid username and password for the database defined by ORACLE_SID. In this example, the username is sandman, and your password is 34Nhjp. Start your PHP code by creating a connection variable:

```
$connection = OCILogon("sandman","34Nhjp") or die ("Couldn't logon.");
```

The die() function is used to print an error message and exit a script when the function cannot perform as required. In this case, die() would execute if the connection failed. The error message would be printed so you know where the error occurred ("Couldn't logon."), and no further actions would take place. Using die() properly will alleviate many headaches as you attempt to debug your code.

If you make it through the connection test, the next step is to create the SQL statement. Suppose that the FRIEND_INFO table, used in previous examples, exists in your Oracle database.

Using the FRIEND_INFO table, suppose you want to view your friends' names, birthdays, and favorite colors, ordered from oldest to youngest friend. Create a variable that holds your SQL statement:

```
$sql = "SELECT FULL_NAME, BIRTH_DATE, FAVE_COLOR FROM FRIEND_INFO
       ORDER BY BIRTH_DATE ASC";
```

Next, use the `OCIParse()` function to parse the statement in the context of your database connection:

```
$sql_statement = OCIParse($connection,$sql) or die ("Couldn't parse statement.");
```

The next step is to execute the statement:

```
OCIExecute($sql_statement) or die ("Couldn't execute query.");
```

Now it's time to get the results. Use the `OCIFetch()` function within a `while` statement to get each row in your results:

```
while (OCIFetch($sql_statement));
    // more code here…
}
```

The code within the `while` loop will continue to execute as long as there are rows in the result set. So let's put some code inside the loop!

For each row in your result set, you will have a number of columns. The number of columns is important to know, because you'll use this number to step incrementally through the data. Before your `while` loop, add this variable to get the number of columns used in your SQL statement:

```
$num_columns = OCINumCols($sql_statement);
```

Return to your `while` loop, and place the following `for` expression within it to step through your result row:

```
for ($i = 0; $i < $num_columns; $i++) {
    $column_value = OCIResult($sql_statement,$i);
    }
```

For as long as `$i` is less than the number of columns in the result row, the loop will execute. This loop will be repeated for every row in the result set.

You'll probably want to print the results in a simple HTML table. Step back and place this statement before the `while` loop begins, to open the table tag and create the row headings:

```
echo "<TABLE BORDER=1>";
echo "<TR><TH>Full Name</TH><TH>Birthday</TH><TH>Favorite Color</TH></TR>";
```

Now, add some code within the `while` loop to start the table row that will hold the data from the result row:

```
echo "<TR>";
```

Next, add a line within your `for` statement to enclose each individual piece of data inside a table cell:

```
echo "<TD>$column_value</TD>";
```

Before closing the `while` loop, close the table row:

```
echo "</TR>";
```

The new `while` loop should look something like this:

```
while (OCIFetch($sql_statement)) ;
echo "<TR>";
for ($i = 0; $i < $num_columns; $i++) {
        $column_value = OCIResult($sql_statement,$i);
echo "<TD>$column_value</TD>";
    }
    echo "</TR>";
}
```

After the `while` loop, close the HTML table:

```
echo "</TABLE>";
```

Finally, you'll want to free up the resources used to perform the query and close the database connection. Failing to do so could cause memory leaks and other nasty resource-hogging things to occur.

```
OCIFreeStatement($sql_result);
OCILogoff($connection);
```

The full script to perform a simple connection and data selection from an Oracle database could look something like this:

```
<?php
// create a connection
$connection = OCILogon("sandman","34Nhjp") or die ("Couldn't logon.");

// create SQL statement
$sql = "SELECT FULL_NAME, BIRTH_DATE, FAVE_COLOR FROM FRIEND_INFO
        ORDER BY BIRTH_DATE ASC";
```

```
// parse SQL statement
$sql_statement = OCIParse($connection,$sql) or die ("Couldn't parse statement.");

// execute SQL query
OCIExecute($sql_statement) or die ("Couldn't execute query.");

// start results formatting
echo "<TABLE BORDER=1>";
echo "<TR><TH>Full Name</TH><TH>Birthday</TH><TH>Favorite Color</TH></TR>";

// format results by row
while (OCIFetch($sql_statement);
echo "<TR>";
for ($i = 0; $i < $num_columns; $i++) {
            $column_value = OCIResult($sql_statement,$i);
echo "<TD>$column_value</TD>";
        }
    echo "</TR>";
}
echo "</TABLE>";

// free resources and close connection
OCIFreeStatement($sql_result);
OCILogoff($connection);
?>
```

See the PHP Manual for additional Oracle functions, and try using your own tables and SQL statements instead of the examples just shown. Remember, don't use the DELETE or DROP commands unless you're really ready and you've backed up your data!

Connecting to a PostgreSQL Database

Like MySQL, the PostgreSQL database is quite popular among PHP developers. Understandably, there are numerous well-documented PHP functions you can use in conjunction with PostgreSQL. However, you need only a few of these functions in order to make a simple connection and select some data:

- pg_connect() Opens a connection to PostgreSQL. Requires a hostname, database name, username, and password.

- `pg_exec()` Executes the SQL statement.
- `pg_numrows()` Returns the number of rows in a result set.
- `pg_fetch_array()` Puts an SQL statement result row in an array.
- `pg_freeresult()` Frees the resources in use by the current connection.
- `pg_close()` Closes the current connection.

First, you must know the name of the server on which the database resides, as well as a valid username and password for that server. In this example, the database name is `secretDB` on `localhost`, your username is `sandman`, and your password is `34Nhjp`. Start your PHP code by creating a connection variable:

```
$connection = pg_connect("host=localhost dbname=secretDB user=sandman
password=34Nhjp") or die ("Couldn't make a connection.");
```

The `die()` function is used to print an error message and exit a script when the function cannot perform as required. In this case, `die()` would execute if the connection failed. The error message would be printed so you know where the error occurred ("Couldn't make a connection."), and no further actions would take place. Using `die()` properly will alleviate many headaches as you attempt to debug your code.

If you make it through the connection test, the next step is to create the SQL statement. Using the `FRIEND_INFO` table, suppose you want to view your friends' names, birthdays, and favorite colors, ordered from oldest to youngest friend. Create a variable that holds your SQL statement:

```
$sql = "SELECT FULL_NAME, BIRTH_DATE, FAVE_COLOR FROM FRIEND_INFO
        ORDER BY BIRTH_DATE ASC";
```

Next, create a variable to hold the result of the query, carried out by the `pg_exec()` function. The `pg_exec()` function takes two arguments: the connection and the SQL statement variables you just created.

```
$sql_result = pg_exec($connection,$sql) or die ("Couldn't execute query.");

   //get number of rows in result set

   $num = pg_numrows($sql_result);
```

To format the results currently held in `$sql_result`, first separate the results by row, using the `pg_fetch_array()` function. But, put this within another while loop to go row-by-row throught the results.

```
$i=0
while ($i<$num) {
```

```
    $row = pg_fetch_array($sql_result,$i);
   // more code here...
     $i++;
}
```

The `while` loop creates an array called `$row` for each record in the result set. To get the individual elements of the record (`FULL_NAME`, `BIRTH_DATE`, `FAVE_COLOR`), create specific variables:

```
$full_name = $row["FULL_NAME"];
$birth_date = $row["BIRTH_DATE"];
$fave_color = $row["FAVE_COLOR"];
```

You'll probably want to print the results in a simple HTML table. Step back and place this statement before the `while` loop begins, to open the table tag and create the row headings:

```
echo "<TABLE BORDER=1>";
echo "<TR><TH>Full Name</TH><TH>Birthday</TH><TH>Favorite Color</TH></TR>";
```

After defining the variables within the `while` loop, print them in table format:

```
echo "<TR><TD>$full_name</TD><TD>$birth_date</TD><TD>$fave_color</TD></TR>";
```

The new `while` loop looks like this:

```
while ($row = pg_fetch_array($sql_result)) {
$full_name = $row["FULL_NAME"];
$birth_date = $row["BIRTH_DATE"];
$fave_color = $row["FAVE_COLOR"];
echo "<TR><TD>$full_name</TD><TD>$birth_date</TD><TD>$fave_color</TD></TR>";
}
```

After the `while` loop, close the HTML table:

```
echo "</TABLE>";
```

Finally, you'll want to free up the resources used to perform the query, and close the database connection:

```
pg_freeresult($sql_result);
pg_close($connection);
```

The full script to perform a simple connection and data selection from a PostgreSQL database could look something like this:

```
<?php
// create connection
```

```php
$connection = pg_connect("host=localhost dbname=secretDB user=sandman
password=34Nhjp") or die ("Couldn't make a connection.");

// create SQL statement
$sql = "SELECT FULL_NAME, BIRTH_DATE, FAVE_COLOR FROM FRIEND_INFO
        ORDER BY BIRTH_DATE ASC";

// execute SQL query and get result
$sql_result = pg_exec($connection,$sql) or die ("Couldn't execute query.");

//get number of rows in result set
$num = pg_numrows($sql_result);

// start results formatting
echo "<TABLE BORDER=1>";
echo "<TR><TH>Full Name</TH><TH>Birthday</TH><TH>Favorite Color</TH></TR>";

// format results by row
$i=0;
while ($i<$num) {
   $row = pg_fetch_array($sql_result,$i);
   $full_name = $row["FULL_NAME"];
   $birth_date = $row["BIRTH_DATE"];
   $fave_color = $row["FAVE_COLOR"];
   echo "<TR>
        <TD>$full_name</TD>
        <TD>$birth_date</TD>
        <TD>$fave_color</TD>
        </TR>";
   $i++;
}
echo "</TABLE>

// free resources and close connection
pg_freeresult($sql_result);
pg_close($connection);
?>
```

See the PHP Manual for additional PostgreSQL functions, and try using your own tables and SQL statements instead of the examples just shown. Remember, don't use the DELETE or DROP commands unless you're really ready and you've backed up your data!

Connecting to a Sybase Database

There are numerous PHP functions you can use in conjunction with your Sybase databases, all documented in detail in the PHP Manual. However, you need only a few of these functions in order to make a simple connection and select some data:

- sybase_connect() Opens a connection to Sybase. Requires a server name, username, and password.
- sybase_select_db() Selects a database on the server.
- sybase_query() Issues the SQL statement.
- sybase_fetch_array() Puts an SQL statement result row in an array.
- sybase_free_result() Frees the resources in use by the current connection.
- sybase_close() Closes the current connection.

First, you must know the name of the server on which the database resides, as well as a valid username and password for that server. In this example, the database name is secretDB on localhost, your username is sandman, and your password is 34Nhjp. Start your PHP code by creating a connection variable:

```
$connection = sybase_connect("localhost","sandman","34Nhjp")
or die ("Couldn't connect to the server.");
```

The die() function is used to print an error message and exit a script when the function cannot perform as required. In this case, die() would execute if the connection failed. The error message would be printed so you know where the error occurred ("Couldn't connect to the server."), and no further actions would take place. Using die() properly will alleviate many headaches as you attempt to debug your code.

If you make it through the connection test, the next step is to select the database and create the SQL statement. Suppose that the FRIEND_INFO table, used in previous examples, exists in a Sybase database called secretDB. First, create a database variable such as this:

```
$db = sybase_select_db("secretDB", $connection) or die ("Couldn't select database.");
```

Up to this point, you've told PHP to connect to a server and select a database. If you've made it this far, you can issue an SQL statement and hopefully see some results!

Using the `FRIEND_INFO` table, suppose you want to view your friends' names, birth-days, and favorite colors, ordered from oldest to youngest friend. Create a variable that holds your SQL statement:

```
$sql = "SELECT FULL_NAME, BIRTH_DATE, FAVE_COLOR FROM FRIEND_INFO
        ORDER BY BIRTH_DATE ASC";
```

Next, create a variable to hold the result of the query, carried out by the `sybase_query()` function. The `sybase_query()` function takes two arguments: the connection and the SQL statement variables you just created.

```
$sql_result = sybase_query($sql,$connection) or die ("Couldn't execute query.");
```

To format the results currently held in `$sql_result`, first separate the results by row, using the `sybase_fetch_array()` function:

```
while ($row = sybase_fetch_array($sql_result)) {
    // more code here…
}
```

The `while` loop creates an array called `$row` for each record in the result set. To get the individual elements of the record (`FULL_NAME`, `BIRTH_DATE`, `FAVE_COLOR`), create specific variables:

```
$full_name = $row["FULL_NAME"];
$birth_date = $row["BIRTH_DATE"];
$fave_color = $row["FAVE_COLOR"];
```

You'll probably want to print the results in a simple HTML table. Step back and place this statement before the `while` loop begins, to open the table tag and create the row headings:

```
echo "<TABLE BORDER=1>";
echo "<TR><TH>Full Name</TH><TH>Birthday</TH><TH>Favorite Color</TH></TR>";
```

After defining the variables within the `while` loop, print them in table format:

```
echo "<TR><TD>$full_name</TD><TD>$birth_date</TD><TD>$fave_color</TD></TR>";
```

The new `while` loop looks like this:

```
while ($row = sybase_fetch_array($sql_result)) {
$full_name = $row["FULL_NAME"];
$birth_date = $row["BIRTH_DATE"];
$fave_color = $row["FAVE_COLOR"];
echo "<TR><TD>$full_name</TD><TD>$birth_date</TD><TD>$fave_color</TD></TR>";
}
```

After the `while` loop, close the HTML table:

```
echo "</TABLE>";
```

Finally, you'll want to free up the resources used to perform the query and close the database connection. Failing to do so could cause memory leaks and other nasty resource-hogging things to occur.

```
sybase_free_result($sql_result);
sybase_close($connection);
```

The full script to perform a simple connection and data selection from a Sybase database could look something like this:

```php
<?php
// create connection
$connection = sybase_connect("localhost","sandman","34Nhjp") or die ("Couldn't
connect to the server.");

// select database
$db = sybase_select_db("secretDB", $connection) or die ("Couldn't select
database.");

// create SQL statement
$sql = "SELECT FULL_NAME, BIRTH_DATE, FAVE_COLOR FROM FRIEND_INFO
        ORDER BY BIRTH_DATE ASC";

// execute SQL query and get result
$sql_result = sybase_query($sql,$connection) or die ("Couldn't execute query.");

// start results formatting
echo "<TABLE BORDER=1>";
echo "<TR><TH>Full Name</TH><TH>Birthday</TH><TH>Favorite Color</TH></TR>";

// format results by row
while ($row = sybase_fetch_array($sql_result)) {
$full_name = $row["FULL_NAME"];
$birth_date = $row["BIRTH_DATE"];
$fave_color = $row["FAVE_COLOR"];
echo "<TR><TD>$full_name</TD><TD>$birth_date</TD><TD>$fave_color</TD></TR>";
}
echo "</TABLE>";
```

```
// free resources and close connection
sybase_free_result($sql_result);
sybase_close($connection);
?>
```

See the PHP Manual for additional Sybase functions, and try using your own tables and SQL statements instead of the examples just shown. Remember, don't use the DELETE or DROP commands unless you're really ready and you've backed up your data!

Making ODBC Connections

If your development environment does not include one of the specific databases mentioned in this chapter, have no fear! PHP includes functions for Open Database Connectivity (ODBC), which is useful if, for example, you want to connect to a Microsoft Access datasource on Windows NT.

An increasing number of PHP developers are using the ODBC functions to connect to databases; to that end, the ODBC functions are numerous and well-documented in the PHP Manual. However, you need only a few of these functions in order to make a simple connection and select some data:

- odbc_connect() Opens a connection to an ODBC datasource. Requires the datasource name, username, and password.
- odbc_prepare() Readies the SQL statement for execution.
- odbc_execute() Executes the SQL statement.
- odbc_result_all() Places the results of your SQL statement into a nicely-formatted HTML table.
- odbc_free_result() Frees the resources in use by the current connection.
- odbc_close() Closes the current connection.

First, you must know the name of the datasource to which you want to connect, as well as a valid username and password. In this example, the database name is secretDB on localhost, your username is sandman, and your password is 34Nhjp. Start your PHP code by creating a connection variable:

```
$connection = odbc_connect("secretDB","sandman","34Nhjp") or die ("Couldn't connect to the datasource.");
```

The die() function is used to print an error message and exit a script when the function cannot perform as required. In this case, `die()` would execute if the connection failed. The error message would be printed so you know where the error occurred ("Couldn't connect to the datasource."), and no further actions would take place. Using `die()` properly will alleviate many headaches as you attempt to debug your code.

Using the `FRIEND_INFO` table, used in previous examples, suppose you want to view your friends' names, birthdays, and favorite colors, ordered from oldest to youngest friend. Create a variable that holds your SQL statement:

```
$sql = "SELECT FULL_NAME, BIRTH_DATE, FAVE_COLOR FROM FRIEND_INFO
        ORDER BY BIRTH_DATE ASC";
```

Next, create a variable to hold the prepared query, within the context of the connection:

```
$sql_result = odbc_prepare($connection,$sql) or die ("Couldn't prepare statement.");
```

Now create a variable to hold the result of the query, executed by the `odbc_execute()` function:

```
odbc_execute($sql_result) or die ("Couldn't execute query.");
```

To format the results currently held in `$sql_result`, use the very handy `odbc_result_all()` function. This function uses the result variable and HTML table options such as "border=1".

```
odbc_result_all($sql_result,"border=1");
```

Finally, you'll want to free up the resources used to perform the query and close the database connection. Failing to do so could cause memory leaks and other nasty resource-hogging things to occur.

```
odbc_free_result($sql_result);
odbc_close($connection);
```

The full script to perform a simple connection and data selection from an ODBC datasource could look something like this:

```
<?php
// create connection
$connection = odbc_connect("secretDB","sandman","34Nhjp") or die ("Couldn't connect to the
datasource.");
```

```
// create SQL statement
$sql = "SELECT FULL_NAME, BIRTH_DATE, FAVE_COLOR FROM FRIEND_INFO
     ORDER BY BIRTH_DATE ASC";

// prepare SQL statement
$sql_result = odbc_prepare($connection,$sql) or die ("Couldn't prepare
statement.");

// execute SQL statement and get results
odbc_execute($sql_result) or die ("Couldn't execute query.");

// format result in HTML table, then free results
odbc_result_all($sql_result,"border=1");

odbc_free_result($sql_result);
odbc_close($connection);
?>
```

See the PHP Manual for additional ODBC functions, and try using your own tables and SQL statements instead of the examples just shown. Remember, don't use the DELETE or DROP commands unless you're really ready and you've backed up your data!

Okay, those are the basics of database connectivity; now forge ahead to Chapter 4, where you'll learn how to use PHP and HTML forms to create database tables and populate them with your data.

Chapter 4: Creating and Populating Database Tables

Create a Database Table

Inserting Data

Select and Display Data

H opefully, the previous chapter has given you a basic understanding of database connectivity with PHP. Now we'll move past the basic connection and use PHP and HTML forms to create database tables and populate these tables with data.

The following code examples use the MySQL database; however, each of the actions can be carried out on any supported database type. Check the PHP Manual at http://www.php.net/manual/ for the exact function name for your particular database—it won't be vastly different.

Create a Database Table

Essentially, to create a simple database table, you only need to give it a name. But that would make for a boring table, since it wouldn't contain any columns (fields) and couldn't hold any data. So, besides the name, you should know the number of fields and the types of fields you'd like to have in your table.

Suppose that you own a store, and you want to create a table to hold all your products. Think of the types of fields you might need: a product identification number, a title, a description, and the price of the item. Now, think of a name for the table, such as MY_PRODUCTS.

Next, you'll create a sequence of forms that will take your table information and send it to your MySQL database. In this first step, you'll submit the name of the table and the number of fields you want to include. The second step will display additional form fields so that you can define the properties of your table columns. Finally, the third step will send the request to MySQL, verify that the table was created, and display a "success!" message.

Step 1: Basic Table Definition

To begin, open your favorite text editor, create a file called show_createtable1.html, and set up an HTML "shell":

```
<!DOCTYPE HTML PUBLIC "-//W3C//DTD HTML 3.2//EN">
<HTML>
<HEAD>
<TITLE>Create a Database Table: Step 1</TITLE>
```

```
</HEAD>
<BODY>
    <!-- your HTML form will go here -->
</BODY>
</HTML>
```

To create the form code, assume that Step 2 in the sequence will be a PHP script called `do_showfielddef.php` and that your form will use the `POST` method:

```
<FORM method="POST" action="do_showfielddef.php">
```

Next, create two text fields to capture the values for `$table_name` and `$num_fields`—the name of the new table and the number of fields it contains:

```
<P>Table Name:<br><INPUT type="text" name="table_name" size=30></P>
<P>Number of Fields:<br><INPUT type="text" name="num_fields" size=5></P>
```

Finally, add the "Go to Step 2" button:

```
<INPUT type="submit" value="Go to Step 2">
```

Don't forget the closing </FORM> tag!

Your HTML source code should look something like this:

```
<!DOCTYPE HTML PUBLIC "-//W3C//DTD HTML 3.2//EN">
<HTML>
<HEAD>
<TITLE>Create a Database Table: Step 1</TITLE>
</HEAD>
<BODY>
    <FORM method="POST" action="do_showfielddef.php">
    <P>Table Name:<br><INPUT type="text" name="table_name" size=30></p>
    <P>Number of Fields:<br><INPUT type="text" name="num_fields" size=5></p>
    <INPUT type="submit" value="Go to Step 2">
    </FORM>
</BODY>
</HTML>
```

Place this file on your Web server and access it with your browser at its URL, http://www.yourserver.com/show_createtable1.html. In your browser window, you should now see what is shown in Figure 4.1.

In the next step, you'll dynamically create parts of the form in Step 2, based on the values sent through the form in Step 1.

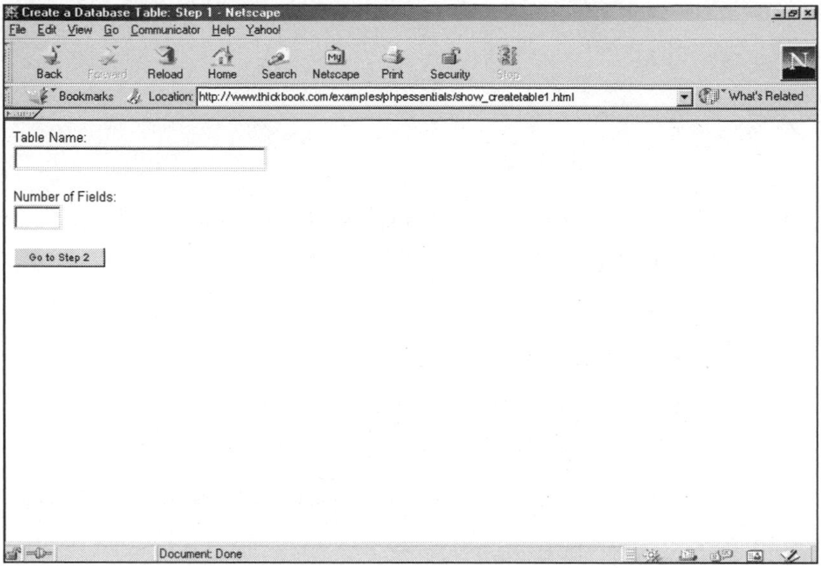

Figure 4.1   *Step 1: Name that table*

Step 2: Field Definitions

In Step 1, you created variables to hold the name of the table (`$table_name`) and the number of fields you want to place in the table (`$num_fields`). In this step, you'll create a PHP script to display additional form elements needed for further definition of the fields. To begin, open your favorite text editor and create a file called `do_showfielddef.php`.

Before your script does anything else, you'll want to check that values were actually entered in the form in Step 1. Set up a statement that looks for these values and, if they don't exist, redirects the user to the form in Step 1:

```php
<?php
    if ((!$table_name) || (!$num_fields)) {
        header("Location: http://www.yourserver.com/show_createtable1.html");
        exit;
    }
?>
```

Next, add the HTML "shell" after the `if` statement:

```html
<!DOCTYPE HTML PUBLIC "-//W3C//DTD HTML 3.2//EN">
<HTML>
```

```
<HEAD>
<TITLE>Create a Database Table: Step 2</TITLE>
</HEAD>
<BODY>
    <!-- your HTML form will go here -->
</BODY>
</HTML>
```

Now you're ready to build the form. First, though, give the page a heading so that you know what you're doing:

```
<h1>Define fields for <?php echo "$table_name"; ?></h1>
```

The inline PHP code means "Print the table name here."

To create the form code, assume that Step 3 in the sequence will be a PHP script called do_createtable.php and that your form will use the POST method:

```
<FORM method="POST" action="do_createtable.php">
```

Next, add a hidden field to your form to ensure that the value of the $table_name variable is passed along to Step 3:

```
<INPUT type="hidden" name="table_name" value="<?php echo "$table_name"; ?>">
```

The three basic field definitions are field name, field type, and field length. To create the table, you'll need to know these three elements for each field you want to create. For example, to create the MY_PRODUCTS table with four fields (product identification number, product title, product description, and product price), you'll need to provide a field name, field type, and field length for each of those four fields.

Create the beginning of an HTML table to display the three form fields:

```
<table cellspacing=5 cellpadding=5>
<tr>
<th>FIELD NAME</th><th>FIELD TYPE</th><th>FIELD LENGTH</th></tr>
```

Now you'll learn a tricky bit of PHP, which will create enough form fields to cover the number of fields you need to define in your database table.

Remember the $num_fields variable from the first step? Create a for statement that will loop until that number is reached:

```
for ($i = 0 ; $i <$num_fields; $i++) {
    // more code here
}
```

The goal is to display three form fields for each field you want to create in your database table. First, open the echo statement:

```
echo "
```

Next, start the table row and print the first input field, remembering to escape your double quotes with a backslash:

```
<tr>
<td align=center>
<input type=\"text\" name=\"field_name[]\" size=\"30\">
</td>
```

Note the use of [] after `field_name`. The [] indicates the presence of an array; for each field in your database table, you'll be adding a value to the $field_name array. An array holds many scalar variables in numbered slots, beginning with 0. Slots are added automatically as the array needs to grow.

For example, if you are creating a database table with six fields, the $field_name array will be made up of six field name variables:

```
$field_name[0] // first field name
$field_name[1] // second field name

...

$field_name[5] // sixth field name
```

After creating the first input field, create a drop-down list containing a few field types. The field types used in this example (float, int, text, varchar) are very common field types and are all that's needed for this example. A complete list of valid field types can be found in your database documentation.

```
<td align=center>
    <select name=\"field_type[]\">
    <option value=\"float\">float</option>
    <option value=\"int\">int</option>
    <option value=\"text\">text</option>
    <option value=\"varchar\">varchar</option>
    </select>
</td>
```

The last field definition is field length. Create a text field for this value, and close your table row as well as the `for` statement:

```
<td align=center>
    <input type=\"text\" name=\"field_length[]\" size=\"5\">
</td>
</tr>";
}
```

Putting it all together, your `for` statement should look something like this:

```
for ($i = 0 ; $i < $num_fields; $i++) {
    echo "
    <tr>
    <td align=center>
        <input type=\"text\" name=\"field_name[]\" size=\"30\">
    </td>

    <td align=center>
        <select name=\"field_type[]\">
        <option value=\"float\">float</option>
        <option value=\"int\">int</option>
        <option value=\"text\">text</option>
        <option value=\"varchar\">varchar</option>
        </select>
    </td>

    <td align=center>
        <input type=\"text\" name=\"field_length[]\" size=\"5\">
    </td>
    </tr>";
}
```

To finish this step, create the submit button and close the form and the HTML table:

```
<tr>
<td align=center colspan=3>
<INPUT type="submit" value="Create Table"></td>
</tr>
</table>
</FORM>
</BODY>
</HTML>
```

All in all, the `do_showfielddef.php` file should look something like this:

```php
<?php
  if ((!$table_name) || (!$num_fields)) {
      header("Location: http://www.yourserver.com/show_createtable1.html");
      exit;
  }
?>


<!DOCTYPE HTML PUBLIC "-//W3C//DTD HTML 3.2//EN">
<HTML>
<HEAD>
<TITLE>Create a Database Table: Step 2</TITLE>
</HEAD>
<BODY>
<h1>Define fields for <?php echo "$table_name"; ?></h1>
<FORM method="POST" action="do_createtable.php">
    <INPUT type="hidden" name="table_name" value="<?php echo "$table_name"; ?>">
    <table cellspacing=5 cellpadding=5>
    <tr>
    <th>FIELD NAME</th><th>FIELD TYPE</th><th>FIELD LENGTH</th></tr>
    <?php
    for ($i = 0 ; $i <$num_fields; $i++) {
        echo "
        <tr>
        <td align=center>
        <input type=\"text\" name=\"field_name[]\" size=\"30\">
        </td>

        <td align=center>
        <select name=\"field_type[]\">
        <option value=\"float\">float</option>
        <option value=\"int\">int</option>
        <option value=\"text\">text</option>
        <option value=\"varchar\">varchar</option>
        </select>
        </td>

        <td align=center>
```

```
                    <input type=\"text\" name=\"field_length[]\" size=\"5\">
                    </td>

                    </tr>";
        }
?>
<tr>
<td align=center colspan=3>
<INPUT type="submit" value="Create Table">
</td>
</tr>
</table>
</FORM>
</BODY>
</HTML>
```

Place this file on your Web server, and go back and access the form in Step 1 at its URL, http://www.yourserver.com/show_createtable1.html. Enter MY_PRODUCTS for a table name and 4 for the number of fields. In your browser window, you should now see what is shown in Figure 4.2.

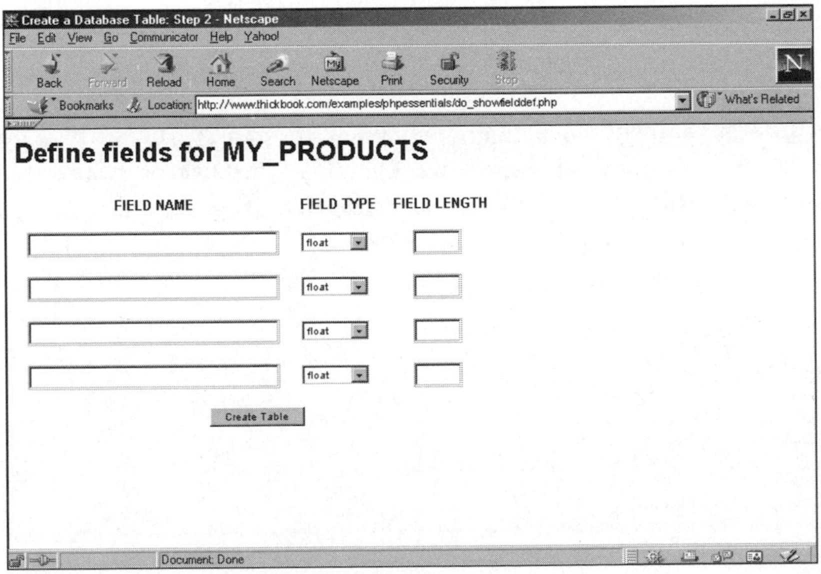

Figure 4.2   *Step 2: Form Field Definition Table*

Step 3: Connect to MySQL and Create the Table

Before you fill out the form created in Step 2, let's create the PHP script that will make it "go." Since the action of the form in Step 2 is `do_createtable.php`, open your favorite text editor and create a file called `do_createtable.php`, then add the HTML "shell":

```
<!DOCTYPE HTML PUBLIC "-//W3C//DTD HTML 3.2//EN">
<HTML>
<HEAD>
<TITLE>Create a Database Table: Step 3</TITLE>
</HEAD>
<BODY>
    <!-- your HTML form will go here -->
</BODY>
</HTML>
```

Give the page a heading so that you know what you're doing:

```
<h1>Adding table <?php echo "$table_name"; ?></h1>
```

The next section of PHP code will build the SQL statement that will be sent to MySQL. Remember, the `CREATE` syntax is

```
CREATE TABLE [table name] [(field_name field_data_type,…)] [options]
```

Hold the SQL statement in a variable called `$sql`, and initially populate this variable with the first part of the `CREATE` statement plus the value of `$table_name`:

```
$sql = "CREATE TABLE $table_name (";
```

Now create the loop that will populate the remainder of the SQL statement. The loop should repeat for as many fields as you want to add to the table, or the number of fields that you defined in Step 2. Since each field definition was placed in an array, you can count the number of elements in the `$field_name` array to get the number of times to run the loop:

```
for ($i = 0; $i < count($field_name); $i++) {
// more code here
}
```

For each new field, you'll need to add the field name, type, and length to the SQL statement using this syntax:

```
field_name field_type (field_length)
```

A comma must separate multiple field definitions.

Immediately inside the loop, add this statement to begin adding to the value of the $sql variable:

```
$sql .= "$field_name[$i] $field_type[$i]";
```

Before adding the field length, check to see that a length has been specified, add to the $sql variable accordingly, and then close the loop:

```
if ($field_length[$i] != "") {
        $sql .= " ($field_length[$i]),";
} else {
        $sql .= ",";
}
}
```

This if…else statement looks for a value for $field_length and prints it inside a set of parentheses if found. Then it adds a comma to separate the value from the next field waiting to be added. If no value is found, just the comma is added to the SQL statement.

The entire loop should look something like this:

```
for ($i = 0; $i < count($field_name); $i++) {
    $sql .= "$field_name[$i] $field_type[$i]";
    if ($field_length[$i] != "") {
        $sql .= " ($field_length[$i]),";
    } else {
        $sql .= ",";
    }
}
```

However, there's still a bit of work to do on the SQL statement: it has an extraneous comma at the end, and the parentheses have yet to be closed. To get rid of the extra comma at the end, use the substr() function to return only part of the string. In this case, you'll be returning the entire string, with the exception of the last character:

```
$sql = substr($sql, 0, -1);
```

The 0 in the argument list tells the function to begin at the first character, and the −1 tells the function to stop at the next-to-last character.

The final step in the creation of the SQL statement is to close the parentheses:

```
$sql .= ")";
```

Now use the basic connection code described earlier in this chapter to connect to and query the MySQL database using your table-creation SQL statement:

```
// create connection
// substitute your own hostname, username and password
$connection = mysql_connect("localhost","sandman","34Nhjp") or die ("Couldn't
connect to server.";

// select database
// substitute your own database name
$db = mysql_select_db("secretDB", $connection) or die ("Couldn't select
database.");

// execute SQL query and get result
$sql_result = mysql_query($sql,$connection) or die ("Couldn't execute query.");
```

Add an `if…else` statement to print a verification message, showing that the query
was successfully executed:

```
if (!$sql_result) {
    echo "<P>Couldn't create table!";
} else {
    echo "<P>$table_name has been created!";
}
```

From start to finish, the file `do_createtable.php` should look something like this:

```
<!DOCTYPE HTML PUBLIC "-//W3C//DTD HTML 3.2//EN">
<HTML>
<HEAD>
<TITLE>Create a Database Table: Step 3</TITLE></HEAD>
<BODY>
<h1>Adding table <?php echo "$table_name"; ?></h1>
<?php
    $sql = "CREATE TABLE $table_name (";
    for ($i = 0; $i < count($field_name); $i++) {
        $sql .= "$field_name[$i] $field_type[$i]";
        if ($field_length[$i] != "") {
            $sql .= " ($field_length[$i]),";
        } else {
            $sql .= ",";
        }
    }
```

```
  $sql = substr($sql, 0, -1);
   $sql .= ")";

// create connection
// substitute your own hostname, username and password
$connection = mysql_connect("localhost","sandman","34Nhjp") or die ("Couldn't
connect to server.");

// select database
// substitute your own database name
$db = mysql_select_db("secretDB", $connection) or die ("Couldn't select
database.");

// execute SQL query and get result
$sql_result = mysql_query($sql,$connection) or die ("Couldn't execute query.");

    if (!$sql_result) {
        echo "<P>Couldn't create table!";
    } else {
        echo "<P>$table_name has been created!";
    }
?>
</BODY>
</HTML>
```

Place this file on your Web server, and then go back to your Web browser and the form staring back at you from Step 2. You should see four sets of form fields. Create the following fields:

FIELD NAME	FIELD TYPE	FIELD SIZE
ITEM_ID	int	5
ITEM_TITLE	varchar	50
ITEM_DESC	text	
ITEM_PRICE	float	

Before you submit the form, it should look something like what is shown in Figure 4.3.

Ann Metzger-Weig

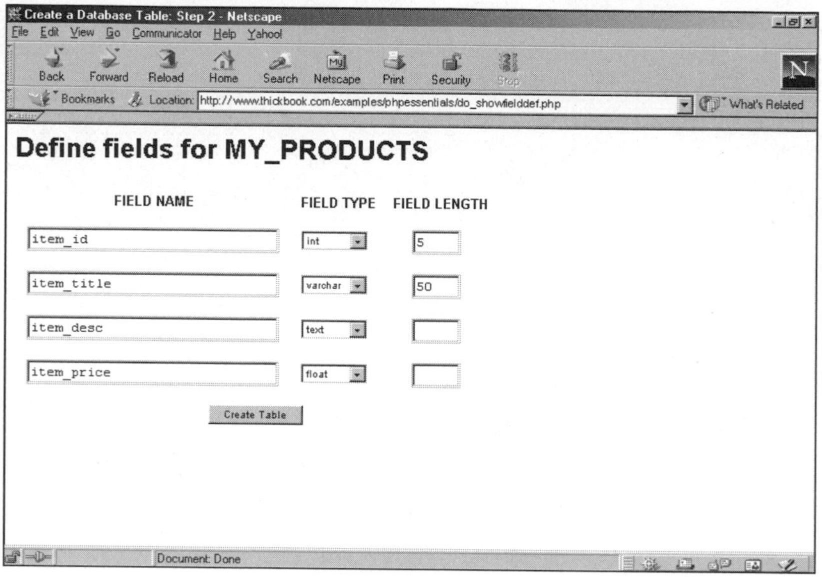

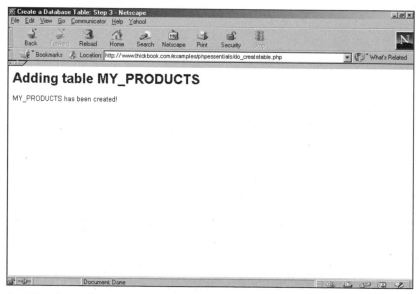

Figure 4.3 *Preparing to submit the form*

Go ahead and click on the Create Table button to execute the `do_createtable.php` script. You should see a results page like the one shown in Figure 4.4.

In the next section, you'll create a form and accompanying PHP script to populate the table. It's not much fun without any data in it!

Figure 4.4 *Successful table creation*

Inserting Data

Now it's time to add some records to the MY_PRODUCTS table. This series of forms is much simpler than the three-step table-creation forms—it has only two steps.

To begin, open your favorite text editor, create a file called show_addrecord.html, and set up an HTML "shell":

```
<!DOCTYPE HTML PUBLIC "-//W3C//DTD HTML 3.2//EN">
<HTML>
<HEAD>
<TITLE>Add a Record</TITLE>
</HEAD>
<BODY>
    <!-- your HTML form will go here -->
</BODY>
</HTML>
```

Give the page a heading so that you know what you're doing:

```
<h1>Adding a Record to MY_PRODUCTS</h1>
```

To create the form code, assume that Step 2 in the sequence will be a PHP script called do_addrecord.php and that your form will use the POST method:

```
<FORM method="POST" action="do_addrecord.php">
```

Next, create three text fields and a text area to capture the values for $item_id, $item_title, $item_desc, and $item_price—the names of the columns in MY_PRODUCTS. The following sample form uses an HTML table to display the form fields, but feel free to display the form however you'd like:

```
<FORM method="POST" action="do_addrecord.php">
<table cellspacing=5 cellpadding=5>

<tr>
<td valign=top><strong>Item ID:</strong></td>
<td valign=top><INPUT type="text" name="item_id" size=5 maxlength=5></td>
</tr>
<tr>
<td valign=top><strong>Item Title:</strong></td>
<td valign=top><INPUT type="text" name="item_title" size=30 maxlength=50></td>
</tr>
<tr>
```

```
<td valign=top><strong>Item Description:</strong></td>
<td valign=top><TEXTAREA name="item_desc" cols=30 rows=5></TEXTAREA></td>
</tr>
<tr>
<td valign=top><strong>Item Price:</strong></td>
<td valign=top>$ <INPUT type="text" name="item_price" size=10></td>
</tr>
```

Finally, add the Add Record button:

```
<tr>
<td align=center colspan=2><INPUT type="submit" value="Add Record"></td>
</tr>
```

Don't forget the closing `</FORM>` and `</TABLE>` tags!

Your HTML source code should look something like this:

```
<!DOCTYPE HTML PUBLIC "-//W3C//DTD HTML 3.2//EN">
<HTML>
<HEAD>
<TITLE>Add a Record</TITLE>
</HEAD>
<BODY>
<h1>Adding a Record to MY_PRODUCTS</h1>
<FORM method="POST" action="do_addrecord.php">
    <table cellspacing=5 cellpadding=5>
    <tr>
    <td valign=top><strong>Item ID:</strong></td>
    <td valign=top><INPUT type="text" name="item_id" size=5 maxlength=5></td>
    </tr>
    <tr>
    <td valign=top><strong>Item Title:</strong></td>
    <td valign=top><INPUT type="text" name="item_title" size=30 maxlength=50></td>
    </tr>
    <tr>
    <td valign=top><strong>Item Description:</strong></td>
    <td valign=top><TEXTAREA name="item_desc" cols=30 rows=5></TEXTAREA></td>
    </tr>
    <tr>
    <td valign=top><strong>Item Price:</strong></td>
    <td valign=top>$ <INPUT type="text" name="item_price" size=10></td>
```

```
        </tr>
        <tr>
        <td align=center colspan=2><INPUT type="submit" value="Add Record"></td>
        </tr>
        </table>
        </FORM>
</BODY>
</HTML>
```

Place this file on your Web server, and access it with your browser at its URL, http://www.yourserver.com/show_addrecord.html. In your browser window, you should now see something like what is shown in Figure 4.5.

Next, you'll create the PHP script that takes your form input, creates a proper SQL statement, creates the record, and displays the record for you as a confirmation. It's not as difficult as it sounds. Since the form action in show_addrecord.html is do_addrecord.php, open your favorite text editor and create a file called do_addrecord.php.

Before your script does anything else, you'll want to check that values were actually entered in the form. Set up a statement that looks for these values. If they don't exist, redirect the user to the form:

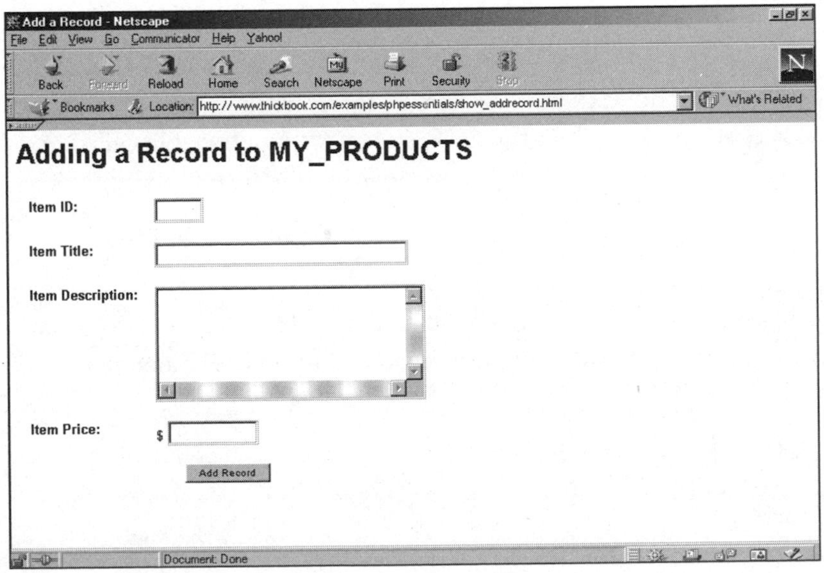

Figure 4.5 *The form to add a record*

```php
<?php
    if ((!$item_id) || (!$item_title) || (!$item_desc) || (!$item_price)) {
        header("Location: http://www.yourserver.com/show_addrecord.html");
        exit;
    }
?>
```

Next, add the HTML "shell" after the `if` statement:

```html
<!DOCTYPE HTML PUBLIC "-//W3C//DTD HTML 3.2//EN">
<HTML>
<HEAD>
<TITLE>Add a Record</TITLE>
</HEAD>
<BODY>
    <!-- your HTML form will go here -->
</BODY>
</HTML>
```

Give the page a heading so that you know what you're doing:

```html
<h1>Adding a record to MY_PRODUCTS</h1>
```

The next section of PHP code will build the SQL statement that will be sent to MySQL. Remember, the `INSERT` syntax is

```
INSERT INTO [table name] (column1, column2) VALUES ('value1', 'value2');
```

When you initially created the `MY_PRODUCTS` table, the field order was `ITEM_ID`, `ITEM_TITLE`, `ITEM_DESC`, and `ITEM_PRICE`. Use this same order in the `INSERT` statement used to create a record. Hold the SQL statement in a variable called `$sql`, and build the `VALUES` list using the variable names from the form:

```php
$sql = "INSERT INTO MY_PRODUCTS (ITEM_ID, ITEM_TITLE, ITEM_DESC, ITEM_PRICE) VALUES ('$item_id', '$item_title', '$item_desc', '$item_price')";
```

Now use the basic connection code described earlier in this chapter to connect to and query the MySQL database using your record-addition SQL statement:

```php
// create connection
// substitute your own hostname, username and password
$connection = mysql_connect("localhost","sandman","34Nhjp") or die ("Couldn't connect to server.");

// select database
```

```
// substitute your own database name
$db = mysql_select_db("secretDB", $connection) or die ("Couldn't select database.");

// execute SQL query and get result
$sql_result = mysql_query($sql,$connection) or die ("Couldn't execute query.");
```

Add an if...else statement to print a warning if the query failed, or to print the full text of the record that was successfully added:

```
if (!$sql_result) {
echo "<P>Couldn't add record!";
} else {
echo "
    <P>Record added!</p>
    <table cellspacing=5 cellpadding=5>

    <tr>
    <td valign=top><strong>Item ID:</strong></td>
    <td valign=top>$item_id</td>
    </tr>
    <tr>
    <td valign=top><strong>Item Title:</strong></td>
    <td valign=top>$item_title</td>
    </tr>
    <tr>
    <td valign=top><strong>Item Description:</strong></td>
    <td valign=top>$item_desc</td>
    </tr>

    <tr>
    <td valign=top><strong>Item Price:</strong></td>
    <td valign=top>\$ $item_price</td>
    </tr>
    </table>
";
}
?>
```

That's all there is to it. Your source code should look something like this:

```
<?php
    if ((!$item_id) || (!$item_title) || (!$item_desc) || (!$item_price)) {
```

```
        header("Location: http://www.yourserver.com/show_addrecord.html");
            exit;
    }
?>
<!DOCTYPE HTML PUBLIC "-//W3C//DTD HTML 3.2//EN">
<HTML>
<HEAD>
<TITLE>Add a Record</TITLE>
</HEAD>
<BODY>

<h1>Adding a Record to MY_PRODUCTS</h1>
<?php
$sql = "INSERT INTO MY_PRODUCTS (ITEM_ID, ITEM_TITLE, ITEM_DESC, ITEM_PRICE) VALUES
('$item_id', '$item_title', '$item_desc', '$item_price')";

// create connection
// substitute your own hostname, username and password
$connection = mysql_connect("localhost","sandman","34Nhjp") or die ("Couldn't
connect to server.");

// select database
// substitute your own database name
$db = mysql_select_db("secretDB", $connection) or die ("Couldn't select
database.");

// execute SQL query and get result
$sql_result = mysql_query($sql,$connection) or die ("Couldn't execute query.");

    if (!$sql_result) {
        echo "<P>Couldn't add record!";
    } else {

    echo "
    <P>Record added!</p>
    <table cellspacing=5 cellpadding=5>
    <tr>
    <td valign=top><strong>Item ID:</strong></td>
    <td valign=top>$item_id</td>
    </tr>
```

```
        <tr>
        <td valign=top><strong>Item Title:</strong></td>
        <td valign=top>$item_title</td>
        </tr>
        <tr>
        <td valign=top><strong>Item Description:</strong></td>
        <td valign=top>$item_desc</td>
        </tr>
        <tr>
        <td valign=top><strong>Item Price:</strong></td>
        <td valign=top>\$ $item_price</td>
        </tr>
        </table>
        ";
        }
?>
</BODY>
</HTML>
```

Place this file on your Web server, and go back to the form at http://www.yourserver.com/show_addrecord.html. Create a sample product such as the one shown in Figure 4.6.

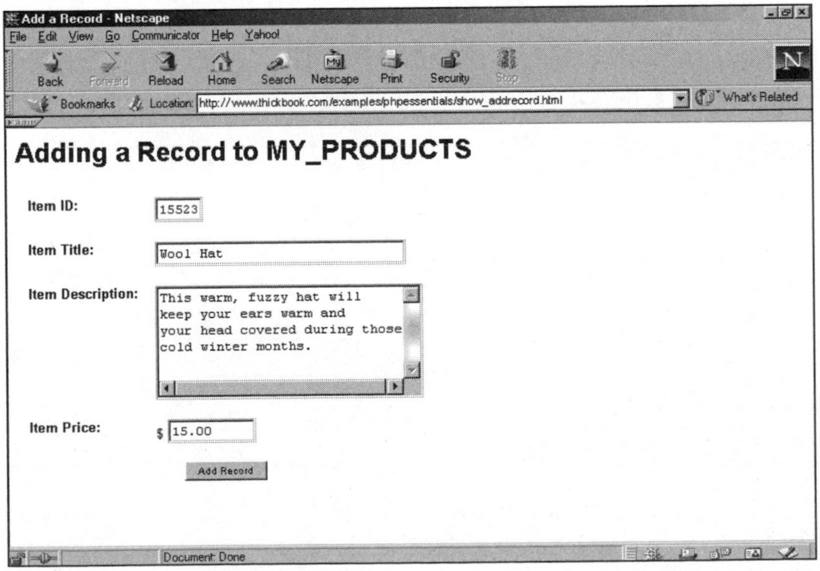

Figure 4.6 *Adding a sample product*

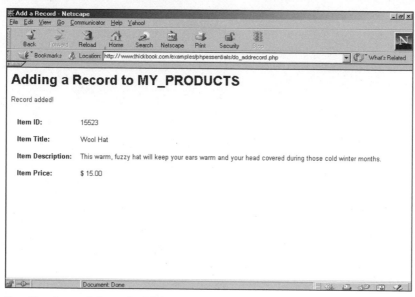

Figure 4.7   *Successful record addition*

Go ahead and click on the Add Record button to execute the `do_addrecord.php` script. If the query is successful, you should see a results page like the one shown in Figure 4.7.

Use this form to add several more products to the `MY_PRODUCTS` table. In the next section, you'll select some records to display (it won't be any fun with just one record!).

Select and Display Data

The most difficult part of selecting and displaying data is deciding the order in which you want to see it! Remember, the `SELECT` syntax is

```
SELECT [field names]
FROM [table names]
WHERE [some expression]
ORDER BY [field names];
```

To view all the records in the `MY_PRODUCTS` table, ordered by `ITEM_ID`, the SQL statement would look something like this:

```
$sql = "SELECT ITEM_ID, ITEM_TITLE, ITEM_DESC, ITEM_PRICE
    FROM MY_PRODUCTS
    ORDER BY ITEM_ID ASC";
```

To view the records in MY_PRODUCTS ordered by ITEM_PRICE, from highest price to lowest, use this SQL statement:

```
$sql = "SELECT ITEM_ID, ITEM_TITLE, ITEM_DESC, ITEM_PRICE
    FROM MY_PRODUCTS
    ORDER BY ITEM_PRICE DESC";
```

To view all the records in MY_PRODUCTS that have a price greater than $10.00, use a WHERE clause in your SQL statement:

```
$sql = "SELECT ITEM_ID, ITEM_TITLE, ITEM_DESC, ITEM_PRICE
    FROM MY_PRODUCTS
    WHERE ITEM_PRICE > 10.00
    ORDER BY ITEM_ID ASC ";
```

Using the basic connection code found earlier in this chapter, create a PHP script called display_products.php and use any of the sample SQL statements just shown as the value of the variable $sql.

Here's a complete sample script, using an SQL statement that shows all records in the MY_PRODUCTS table, ordered by ITEM_ID:

```php
<?php
// create connection
// substitute your own hostname, username and password
$connection = mysql_connect("localhost","sandman","34Nhjp") or die ("Couldn't
connect to server.";

// select database
// substitute your own database name
$db = mysql_select_db("secretDB", $connection) or die ("Couldn't select
database.");

// create SQL statement
$sql = "SELECT ITEM_ID, ITEM_TITLE, ITEM_DESC, ITEM_PRICE
        FROM MY_PRODUCTS
        ORDER BY ITEM_ID ASC";

// execute SQL query and get result
$sql_result = mysql_query($sql,$connection) or die ("Couldn't execute query.");

// start results formatting
echo "<TABLE BORDER=1>";
```

```
echo "<TR><TH>Item ID</TH><TH>Item Title</TH><TH>Item Description</TH><TH>Item
Price</TH></TR>";

// format results by row
while ($row = mysql_fetch_array($sql_result)) {
$item_id = $row["ITEM_ID"];
$item_title = $row["ITEM_TITLE"];
$item_desc = $row["ITEM_DESC"];
$item_price = $row["ITEM_PRICE"];
echo "<TR><TD>$item_id</TD><TD>$item_title</TD><TD>$item_desc</TD><TD
align=right>$item_price</TD></TR>";
}
echo "</TABLE>";

// free resources and close connection
mysql_free_result($sql_result);
mysql_close($connection);
?>
```

Some sample results are shown in Figures 4.8 through 4.10. Your results will differ, depending on the products you inserted into your table.

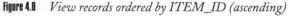

Figure 4.8   *View records ordered by ITEM_ID (ascending)*

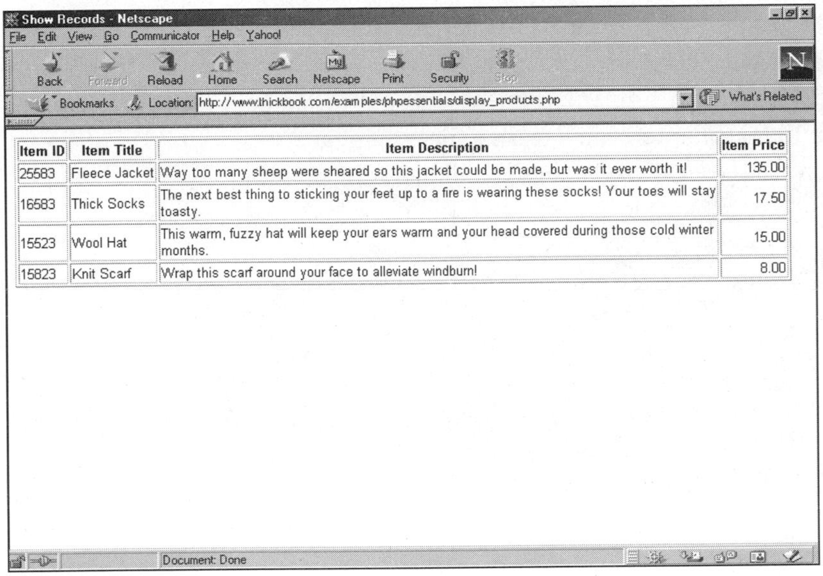

Item ID	Item Title	Item Description	Item Price
25583	Fleece Jacket	Way too many sheep were sheared so this jacket could be made, but was it ever worth it!	135.00
16583	Thick Socks	The next best thing to sticking your feet up to a fire is wearing these socks! Your toes will stay toasty.	17.50
15523	Wool Hat	This warm, fuzzy hat will keep your ears warm and your head covered during those cold winter months.	15.00
15823	Knit Scarf	Wrap this scarf around your face to alleviate windburn!	8.00

Figure 4.9 *View records ordered by ITEM_PRICE (descending)*

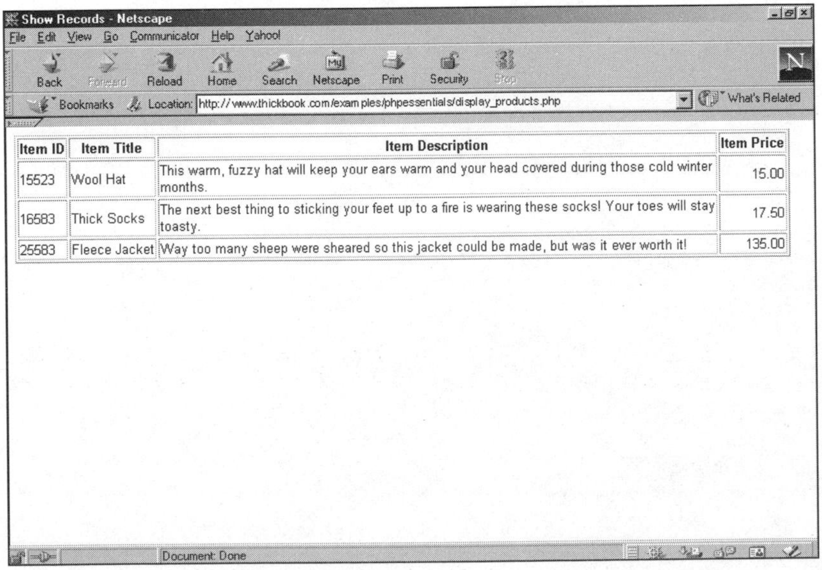

Item ID	Item Title	Item Description	Item Price
15523	Wool Hat	This warm, fuzzy hat will keep your ears warm and your head covered during those cold winter months.	15.00
16583	Thick Socks	The next best thing to sticking your feet up to a fire is wearing these socks! Your toes will stay toasty.	17.50
25583	Fleece Jacket	Way too many sheep were sheared so this jacket could be made, but was it ever worth it!	135.00

Figure 4.10 *View records with ITEM_PRICE greater than $10.00*

This chapter has provided you with the basics of database connectivity, table and record creation, and record display. Part of Chapter 7, "Advanced PHP Techniques: Web-Based Database Administration," is devoted to taking these processes one step further. In that chapter, you'll learn to insert, update, and delete records in the context of creating your own database administration system.

Chapter 5: User Authentication

Basic HTTP Authentication

Database-Driven Authentication

Limit by IP Address

U ser authentication schemes verify that a user has permission to access certain content on a Web site. When initially developing a Web site, you may want to restrict access to only certain members of your development team. Or, if your corporate Web site contains sensitive financial data, you may want to restrict your financial statements to a particular list of investors.

Web developers usually employ one of the following types of user authentication for reasons ranging from ease of installation and ease of maintenance, to how the authentication scheme works within their overall application development:

- **Basic HTTP.** This is the most popular type of authentication. It uses the built-in functions of the Web server to limit access to documents and whole directories. The popularity of this scheme stems from the fact that any site developer, whether he controls his own server or houses his site with an Internet Service Provider, has the ability to use Basic HTTP authentication within his document directories.

- **Database-driven.** Usernames and passwords are kept in a database table and accessed via a script.

- **Limit by IP address.** Access is limited to a specific IP or IP range.

In this section, you'll learn how to use various forms of user authentication in your PHP-enabled Web sites.

Basic HTTP Authentication

HTTP authentication uses a *challenge/response scheme* to authenticate users. The process begins when the user requests a file from a Web server. If the file is within a protected area, the server responds with a 401 (Unauthorized User) error and the browser displays the familiar username/password dialog box. The user then enters a username and password and clicks OK, which sends the information to the server for authentication. If the username and password pair is valid, the server displays the requested file. Otherwise, the dialog box appears and prompts the user to try again.

To use basic HTTP authentication, you must have available two elements: an authentication-enabled Web server and a list of usernames and passwords. However, authentication configuration varies among Web servers. Although the Netscape and Microsoft families of Web servers have a graphical user interface for creating and administering a username and password list, the Apache Web server uses the "old school" method that requires a user to manually modify the server configuration and password files. Because of these differences, be sure to read your Web server documentation before diving headfirst into password-protecting your Web site!

Configuring HTTP Authentication on Apache

The first step in configuring basic HTTP authentication is to create the file containing usernames and passwords. This file contains a list of all valid users for a particular protected area (or *realm*), along with the matching password for each user. You can place this file anywhere on your Web server, preferably in a private directory, above the /usr/local/apache/htdocs document root. If your password file is kept under the document root (/usr/local/apache/htdocs/), anyone with Web access can access your password file via a URL. If your file is called passwordfile and it is located in the document root directory, its URL is http://www.yourserver.com/passwordfile. This is not a good idea. A good location for a private password file is /usr/local/apache/.

Creating the Users and Groups Files

Use the htpasswd program included in the Apache distribution to create the username/password file. To create a username/password file called users with an entry for the user jane, do the following in the /usr/local/apache/ directory:

1. Type htpasswd -c /usr/local/apache/users jane. The -c flag alerts the program that the file /usr/local/apache/users must be created.
2. You are prompted to add a password for user jane. Enter the password and press Enter.
3. You are prompted to confirm the password. Type the password again, exactly as before, and press Enter.

Open the /usr/local/apache/users file to see the username you just entered, followed by a colon, followed by the encrypted version of the password you just entered. For example:

```
jane:Hsyn78/dQdr9
```

To add additional users, such as joe, bob, and mary, follow the preceding steps, omitting the -c flag because the /usr/local/apache/users file already exists.

Categorizing your users into groups makes your life much easier, because you'll be able to grant access rights to an entire group rather than to 10 or 12 (or 200!) individual users. By granting access to an entire group, you won't have to manually list each individual member of that group in the corresponding access file.

To create a group file, manually create the file `/usr/local/apache/groups`. To define the group friends, containing the users jane, joe, bob, and mary (who are already defined in your `users` file), type the following in the `/usr/local/apache/groups` file:

```
friends: jane joe bob mary
```

In the next section, you'll learn to configure Apache to allow members of the friends group to access a protected directory.

Configuring the Web Server

Configuration directives can be inserted either in the Apache `httpd.conf` file (usually in `/usr/local/apache/conf/`) or in a separate `.htaccess` file, placed in the protected directory. For example:

- To protect http://www.yourdomain.com/privatestuff/ using an `.htaccess` file, place the file in `/usr/local/apache/htdocs/privatestuff/`.
- To protect http://www.yourdomain.com/privatestuff/ using `httpd.conf`, create a section in `httpd.conf` beginning with `<Directory /usr/local/apache/htdocs/privatestuff/>` and ending with `</Directory>`.

One drawback of using multiple `.htaccess` files is that you must keep track of all of them! When issuing directives in the `httpd.conf` file, all of the directives are in one constant place and are easier to maintain. Whether you put the directives in an `.htaccess` file or within a `<Directory> </Directory>` section of the `httpd.conf` file, the information is the same:

- `AuthName`. The name of the protected area, or realm, such as "My Private Stuff" or "Jane's Development Area".
- `AuthType`. The authentication protocol in use, usually Basic. Digest authentication also exists, in which the usernames and passwords are encrypted as they pass between browser and server. Digest authentication is unsupported by some older browsers, therefore limiting its use in applications.
- `AuthUserFile`. The full path to the file containing the usernames and passwords.
- `AuthGroupFile`. The full path to the file containing the list of groups, if any.
- `require`. Specifies which users and/or groups have access to the protected area. Can be valid-users, just jane, just the group friends, or a combination.

A sample set of directives might look like this:

```
AuthName "My Private Stuff"
AuthType Basic
```

```
AuthGroup /usr/local/apache/groups
require friends
```

In this example, anyone accessing the "privatestuff" directory is faced with the username/password dialog box. If the user is a member of the friends group and enters the correct username and password, the protected information is displayed.

However, imagine the amount of server processing that is necessary for a Web site that has more visitors than just your friends. As your user base increases and Web server performance begins to erode, think about moving the usernames and passwords to a separate database table (which can be parsed by the Web server faster than a simple text file) and creating your own authentication systems.

Working with PHP Authentication Variables

A custom PHP script can mimic the HTTP authentication challenge/response system by setting HTTP headers that cause the automatic display of the username/password dialog box. PHP stores the information entered in the dialog box in three variables ($PHP_AUTH_USER, $PHP_AUTH_PW, and $PHP_AUTH_TYPE) that can be used to validate input.

> HTTP authentication variables in PHP are available only when PHP is installed as a module. If the CGI version of PHP is installed, you are limited to normal .htaccess-based authentication or database-driven authentication using HTML forms to input the username and password.

To become familiar with sending authorization headers via the header() function, first create a PHP script that pops up the username/password dialog box without validating a username/password pair.

The following code checks for the existence of a value for $PHP_AUTH_USER and displays the username/password dialog box if a value does not exist, then exits the script:

```php
<?php //authorize1.php
// Check to see if $PHP_AUTH_USER already contains info
    if (!isset($PHP_AUTH_USER)) {
        // If empty, send header causing dialog box to appear
        header('WWW-Authenticate: Basic realm="My Private Stuff"');
        header('HTTP/1.0 401 Unauthorized');
        echo 'Authorization Required.';
```

```
        exit;
    }

    // If not empty, display values for variables
    else {
        echo "<P>You have entered this username: $PHP_AUTH_USER<br>";
        echo "You have entered this password: $PHP_AUTH_PW<br>";
        echo "The authorization type is: $PHP_AUTH_TYPE</P>";
    }
?>
```

In this case, if any value exists, the script assumes that the username and password are valid and returns the value of the three PHP authorization variables as directed in the `else` statement. Absolutely no authentication is performed in this example because the script does not check the values against a master list of allowable users.

The `header()` function is key to this script; the HTTP header is the first output from the script to the browser. When a user enters a username and password in the dialog box and clicks on OK, the page reloads and sends another HTTP header to the server, this time with the variables populated.

Since `$PHP_AUTH_USER` now contains a value, the `if` statement returns false, and the script skips to the `else` statement, which contains code to print the variable information to the screen.

Now that you know how to create the dialog box, write some code that validates these values. The easiest method is to hard-code acceptable values in the script:

```
<?php //authorize2.php
// Check to see if $PHP_AUTH_USER already contains info
    if (!isset($PHP_AUTH_USER)) {
        // If empty, send header causing dialog box to appear
        header('WWW-Authenticate: Basic realm="My Private Stuff"');
        header('HTTP/1.0 401 Unauthorized');
        echo 'Authorization Required.';
        exit;
    }

    // If not empty, do something else
    else {
        // Try to validate the values of $PHP_AUTH_USER and
// $PHP_AUTH_PW against hard-coded values
        if (($PHP_AUTH_USER == "jane") && ($PHP_AUTH_PW == "mypassword")) {
            echo "<P>You have entered this username: $PHP_AUTH_USER<br>";
```

```
            echo "You have entered this password: $PHP_AUTH_PW<br>";
            echo "The authorization type is: $PHP_AUTH_TYPE</P>";
        }
        else {
            echo "You are not authorized!";
        }
    }
?>
```

But who wants to hard-code all valid usernames and passwords into their authentication script? It's an awful lot of work. Furthermore, if you carry your authentication routine through numerous pages, each of those pages must contain the entire list. If you have to make a change in the list, you have to make it on every single page containing the list. It's better to carry through only an authorization routine, which accesses a database containing all the usernames and passwords.

Database-Driven Authentication

Validating against a database alleviates the need for additional Web server configuration and increases Web server response times. Using the PHP authentication variables, you can still present the familiar username/password dialog box. Or, create a short HTML login form that requests a username and password. Whichever method you choose, you need to have access to a users table that holds username and password information.

Your table can be as simple or as complex as you want to make it. For the following examples, I've created a four-field users table in a MySQL database. The fields are `id`, `real_name`, `username`, and `password`.

| You can use any database type to create and access a users table. See Chapter 3, "Working with Databases," for instructions on creating a table and accessing it via PHP for your specific database type. |

Using PHP Authentication Variables to Validate Users

With a few minor additions to the `authorize2.php` script, you can validate the dialog box input against usernames and passwords in the users table. Assume that the users table has been populated with the following information, where the username is a unique field:

```
+------+------------+----------+------------+
| id   | real_name  | username | password   |
+------+------------+----------+------------+
| 1    | Jane Smith | jane     | mypassword |
| 2    | Mary Smith | mary     | passme     |
| 3    | John Smith | john     | gopass     |
+------+------------+----------+------------+
```

The goals of the `authorize3.php` script are to display the username/password dialog box, accept the values, open the database connection, validate the values, and display the appropriate information.

```php
<?php //authorize3.php
// Check to see if $PHP_AUTH_USER already contains info
    if (!isset($PHP_AUTH_USER)) {
        // If empty, send header causing dialog box to appear
        header('WWW-Authenticate: Basic realm="My Private Stuff"');
        header('HTTP/1.0 401 Unauthorized');
        echo 'Authorization Required.';
        exit;
    }
        // If not empty, do something else
    else {
        // Open the database connnection
        mysql_connect("localhost", "sandman", "34NhjP")
        or die ("Unable to connect to database.");
        mysql_select_db("secretDB")
        or die ("Unable to select database.");
        // Formulate the query
        $sql = "SELECT id
          FROM users
          WHERE username='$PHP_AUTH_USER' and password='$PHP_AUTH_PW'";

        // Execute the query and put results in $result
        $result = mysql_query($sql) or die ("Couldn't get results.");

        // Get number of rows in $result. Should be 0 if invalid, 1 if valid.
        $num = mysql_numrows($result);

        // Present results based on validity.
        if ($num == 1) {
            echo "<P>You are a valid user!<br>";
```

```
        echo "Your username is $PHP_AUTH_USER<br>";
            echo "Your password is $PHP_AUTH_PW</P>";
        }
        else if ($num == 0)  {
            echo "You are not authorized!";
        }
    }
?>
```

There are drawbacks when sending and receiving HTTP headers and PHP authentication variables. For example, once a user is authorized, a different user can't attempt to authorize himself or herself within the current browser session. After processing the script and validating a user within the current browser session, the browser will not display the username/password dialog box again, because the browser doesn't know if a different person is sitting in front of the machine or not. You must end the browser session, then restart the browser and access the protected area again, in order to validate a different user. An additional problem is that no "global" authentication directive exists, such as exists when you use an .htaccess file in a protected directory or create a <Directory></Directory> block in the Apache configuration file. When using PHP-based authentication, the authentication routine must be included at the beginning of each file you want to protect.

If you are querying a database for valid users, these additional requests will cause some slowdown in your server response times. Using an HTML form as a front-end to an authentication system has proven to be the most successful in my own commercial applications. The database is queried on-demand, which provides accurate results as well as a consistently speedy server connection.

Using HTML Forms to Validate Users

Instead of sending HTTP authorization headers and displaying the username/password dialog box, create a simple form that asks for a username and password:

```
<!-- Name this file login.html -->
<HTML>
<HEAD>
<TITLE>My Login Form</TITLE>
</HEAD>
<!-- Configure the form -->
<FORM ACTION="login.php" METHOD="post">
<!-- Create the form fields in a pretty table -->
    <table border=0>
```

```
        <tr>
        <td><strong>Username</strong></td>
        <td><input type="text" name="username" size="10" maxsize="10"></td>
        </tr>
        <tr>
        <td><strong>Password</strong></td>
        <td><input type="password" name="password" size="10" maxsize="10"></td>
        </tr>
        <tr>
        <td colspan="2" align="center">
        <input type="submit" value="Validate Me">
        </td>
        </tr>
        </table>
</FORM>
</BODY>
</HTML>
```

When the user types values in the form fields and clicks on the Validate Me button, the values are sent to the login.php script. This script must hold the values, connect to the database, validate the user, and display the appropriate information. Essentially, only a few variable names will change from the authorize3.php script used earlier in this chapter. Instead of storing the username and password in $PHP_AUTH_USER and $PHP_AUTH_PW, the values are stored in $username and $password, as named by the form field names.

```
<?php //login.php
// When submitting a form, PHP automatically assigns values to
// variables with names matching the form fields.  In this case, $username
// and $password have already been created and are available for our use.
    // Open the database connnection
    mysql_connect("localhost", "sandman", "34NhjP")
        or die ("Unable to connect to database.");
    mysql_select_db("secretDB")
        or die ("Unable to select database.");
    // Formulate the query
    $sql = "SELECT id
        FROM users
        WHERE username='$username' and password='$password'";

    // Execute the query and put results in $result
```

```
$result = mysql_query($sql) or die ("Couldn't get results.");

// Get number of rows in $result. Should be 0 if invalid, 1 if valid.
$num = mysql_numrows($result);

// Present results based on validity.
if ($num == 1) {
    echo "<P>You are a valid user!<br>";
    echo "Your username is $username<br>";
    echo "Your password is $password</P>";
}
else if ($num == 0)  {
    echo "You are not authorized!";
}
?>
```

To take this process a step further, you can combine the HTML form and PHP script into one file using the `include()` function. By telling the script when to include the file containing the login form, you can display the form again, should a user enter invalid entries (or none at all), all without leaving this one script.

First, create a file called `login_form.inc` containing the following code:

```
<!-- Configure the form -->
<FORM ACTION="login2.php?do=authenticate" METHOD="post">
<!-- Create the form fields in a pretty table -->
<table border=0>
<tr>
<td><strong>Username</strong></td>
<td><input type="text" name="username" size="10" maxlength="10"></td>
</tr>
<tr>
<td><strong>Password</strong></td>
<td><input type="password" name="password" size="10" maxlength="10"></td>
</tr>
<tr>
<td colspan="2" align="center">
<input type="submit" value="Validate Me">
</td>
</tr>
</table>
</form>
```

This code is simply the snippet of HTML that displays the form fields. The surrounding HTML will already be in the login2.php file, since you can intertwine HTML and PHP code in the same file.

```
<!-- Call this file login2.php -->
<!-- This file begins like any normal HTML file -->
<HTML>
<HEAD>
<TITLE>My Login Form</TITLE>
</HEAD>
<!-- Now we start our PHP code -->
<?php
// Continue a process, depending on the value of the $do variable.
// If this is the first time to access this script, the $do variable
// has no value.

switch ($do) {
    // if the value of $do is "authenticate", continue this process
    case "authenticate":
        // When submitting a form, PHP automatically assigns values to
        // variables with names matching the form fields.  In this case, $username
        // and $password have already been created, transparently.

        // Open the database connection
        mysql_connect("localhost", "sandman", " 34NhjP")
            or die ("Unable to connect to database.");
        mysql_select_db("secretDB")
            or die ("Unable to select database.");

        // Formulate the query
        $sql = "SELECT id
                FROM users
                WHERE username='$username' and password='$password'";

        // Execute the query and put results in $result
        $result = mysql_query($sql) or die ("Couldn't get results.");

        // Get number of rows in $result. Should be 0 if invalid, 1 if valid.
        $num = mysql_numrows($result);
        // Present results based on validity.
```

```
        if ($num == 1) {
            echo "<P>You are a valid user!<br>";
            echo "Your username is $username<br>";
            echo "Your password is $password</P>";
        }
        else if ($num == 0)  {
            unset($do);
            echo "<P>You are not authorized! Please try again.</P>";
            // The next command automatically places the contents of
            // login_form.inc at this position; the HTML form fields will display.
            include("login_form.inc");
        }
        break;


        default:
        // The default case, in this instance, means "if no value
        // exists for $do, or if no other case matches a value for $do,
        // display the login form."
        // We only send a value for $do in the action of the form, i.e.
        // <form action=login2.php?do=authenticate" … >
            include("login_form.inc");
    }
?>
<!-- We have exited out of PHP code and are back in HTML -->
</BODY>
</HTML>
```

It's that simple to combine PHP and HTML into one comprehensive file that contains all the routines for querying a database, displaying error messages to unauthorized users, and providing custom content to valid users.

If you need to indicate to a subsequent script whether or not a user has been authenticated, it's not a good idea to pass the username and password in the URL using the GET method. Using the GET method would create a URL such as http://www.yourcompany.com/login2.php?username=jane&password=mypassword.

If a friend or coworker (or a random person off the street) looks over the user's shoulder at the browser, he will see the full URL in the Location area and will then know a valid username and password pair. Similarly, if the user bookmarks the page after a successful login, he will have bookmarked the complete URL, with the username and password. If that user shares a terminal, or if a friend or coworker (or random person off the street) opens the browser and uses that bookmark, that person will have access to everything that a correct username and password pair grants him.

In the next chapter, you'll learn to use cookies, those powerful little bits of text stored on a user's hard drive, which you can use to set and store variables and values you may need later, such as authentication variables.

Limit by IP Address

Another method of protecting sensitive data is to limit the display to a specific IP or IP range. Although this is a very simple process, it's not the most effective. Most users do not have static IP addresses, and those who do are usually behind a firewall and access the World Wide Web via a proxy. When you access via a proxy, a kind of gateway that filters traffic out to the Internet, the remote address is always the same value, because it belongs to the proxy and not the specific user attempting to access a Web site.

However, if you're creating a site in a closed environment, adding these few lines at the beginning of your PHP script will determine the remote IP address and limit access based on the result it finds.

```php
<?php //limitbyIP.php
    $userIP = getenv("REMOTE_ADDR");
    if ($userIP != "127.0.0.1") {
        echo "It's not local…";
    } else {
        echo "User is authorized!";
    }
?>
```

You can use regular expressions to match a block of IP addresses, in this case, any IP address that begins with 208.56.5.

```php
<?php //limitbyIP_range.php
    $userIP = getenv("REMOTE_ADDR");
    if (preg_match("/208.56.5./", "$userIP")) {
        echo "You're not in my neighborhood…";
    } else {
        echo "User is authorized!";
    }
?>
```

REMOTE_ADDR is a standard HTTP environment variable that is always sent by the machine making the request. The limitbyIP.php script uses 127.0.0.1, or the default value for localhost, as the only authorized IP address. In this script, if the remote address *is not* 127.0.0.1 or localhost, the user *is not* shown any content, and instead the message "It's not local…" is displayed in the browser.

Although this is a neat trick, and quite speedy since the script doesn't connect to a database to validate specific users, it loses its value in a production environment given the prevalence of non-static IPs and proxy servers.

In the next chapter, you'll learn the value of storing information in cookies and retrieving that information to provide customized user environments. We'll also take a look at the new session-handling functions available in PHP4, and we'll see how to create your own quasi-session variables in PHP3.

Chapter 6: User Tracking and Session Management

Cookies

PHP4 Session Handling

You can't effectively track visitors on a Web site without a little intervention. Every Web server tracks basic accesses, meaning that for each "hit," it keeps a log of at least the date and time, the IP or domain name of the user making the request, and the name of the file that was sent. This type of log isn't very helpful when you want to track buying trends or user preferences, and it doesn't give you any real insight into your user base. The solution to this problem requires definite planning but is easy to implement—use cookies!

However, there are limits to the number of elements you can hold in cookies, and some people can't or don't want to accept them. Alternative measures can be put in place by using the session management functions in PHP4. In this chapter, you'll learn how to develop a system that manages user information using both cookies and sessions.

Cookies

Cookies are little pieces of text that are sent to a user's browser along with the pretty pictures and well-worded content of a good Web site. They can help you create shopping carts, user communities, and personalized sites. Say you've planned to assign an identification variable to a user so that you can track what he does when he visits your site. First, the user logs in, and you send a cookie with variables designed to say "This is Joe, and Joe is allowed to be here." While Joe is surfing around your site, you can say "Hello, Joe!" on each and every page. If Joe clicks through your catalog and chooses 14 different items to buy, you can keep track of these items and display them all in a bunch when Joe clicks on Checkout. But what happens when a user doesn't accept cookies? Are your well-laid plans all for naught? Will Joe ever get to buy those 14 items?

These sorts of identification cookies are valuable in e-commerce sites, when you're creating a shopping system that allows the user to store selected items until he's ready to pay for them. You can use cookies for all sorts of things, but because e-commerce sites are popular, we'll go with that example.

Setting Cookies

Before you go around setting cookies, determine how you will use them and at what point you will set them. Do you want to check for a cookie on every page of your site, and set one if it doesn't exist? How will you use the cookie data? Whatever cookies you decide to use, remember that you absolutely must set a cookie before sending any other content to the browser. If you remember this, you won't spend hours wondering why you're getting "Can't send additional information, header already sent" errors!

In this example, pretend you're building an online coffee shop. Obviously, you can't buy a triple-shot super-size latte, but you *can* order bags of coffee. When I build an e-commerce site, I usually check for and set a cookie on every page in the site, because I usually display a shopping cart icon and the number of items in the user's cart on every page. That's just a personal preference, however, and it does require every page to be parsed by the PHP engine.

Assume that our online coffee store checks for a cookie on every page. The first time a user accesses any page on the site, he is assigned a random value as his user identification number. From that point forward, the user holds a valid cookie. The PHP code at the beginning of each page checks for a cookie and sends one only if one doesn't already exist. This method keeps cookie values from being overwritten. Every page in the site starts off something like this:

```php
<?php
    // set cookie if not already set
if (!isset($id)) {
        srand((double)microtime()*1000000);
        $randval = rand();
        setcookie("id",$randval,time()+14400,"/",".mycoffeeshop.com",0);
}
?>
```

That's all well and good, you say, but what does it all mean? The first two lines after the `if` statement, just seed the random number generator and produce a value to use for the ID. This random number is usually something like 1404291115.

Next, we set the cookie:

```php
setcookie("id",$randval,time()+14400,"/",".mycoffeeshop.com",0);
```

Here's the syntax of the `setcookie()` function in PHP:

```
setcookie("name", "value", "expiration", "path", "domain", "security");
```

- `Name.` The `name` parameter holds the name of the variable which will be kept in the global`$HTTP_COOKIE_VARS`, and will be accessible in subsequent scripts.

- `Value.` The `value` parameter is the value of the variable passed in the name parameter.

- `Expiration.` The `expiration` parameter sets a specific time at which the cookie value will no longer be accessible. Cookies without a specific expiration time will expire with the current user session (when the browser closes).

- `Path.` The `path` parameter determines for which directories the cookie is valid. If a single slash is in the `path` parameter, the cookie is valid for all files and directories on the Web server. If a specific directory is named, this cookie is only valid for pages within that directory.

- `Domain.` Cookies are only valid for the host and domain that set them, and if no domain is specified then the default value is the host name of the server that generated the cookie. The `domain` parameter must have at least 2 periods in the string in order to be valid.

- `Security.` If the `security` parameter is 1, then the cookie will only be transmitted via HTTPS.

In our cookie example, we are calling the cookie "id" and assigning to it the value of `$randval`. This particular cookie will expire in four hours (the current time plus 14,400 seconds). The cookie is valid for any page below the document root on the domain mycoffeeshop.com.

To ensure that your cookie can be set and accepted by a wide variety of browsers, use some sort of value for each part of the cookie. Don't just skip the expiration or the path and hope it works out. You know that the minute you skip something "optional," the one browser that it won't work with will belong to the user who wants to buy $10,000 worth of stuff from your fledgling e-commerce site. A good place to learn about the ins and outs of cookies is Netscape's preliminary cookie specification page, at http://www.netscape.com/newsref/std/cookie_spec.html.

Reading Cookies

Now you have a cookie called "id," accessible from every page in the mycoffeeshop.com domain. To use that value in subsequent pages, you can get it from the global PHP variable `$HTTP_COOKIE_VARS`. In our example, we extract the value of the ID from the cookie using this code:

```
$id = $HTTP_COOKIE_VARS["id"];
```

You can use the value of `$id` as a unique identifier in a database table, in which you track a user's purchases. For example, suppose you have a database table that holds all users' shopping cart items:

```
+-------------+----------+-----------------------+----------+
| id          | item_id  | item_desc             | item_qty |
+-------------+----------+-----------------------+----------+
| 1404291115  | CAF-0122 | Really Strong Coffee  | 5        |
+-------------+----------+-----------------------+----------+
```

Using this type of database table, you can easily get an ongoing count of the number of items in a user's shopping cart, with an SQL statement like this:

```
$sql = "select sum(item_qty) from db_table where id='$id'";
```

Somewhere in your PHP code, get the count:

```php
<?php
    $id = $HTTP_COOKIE_VARS["id"];
    // connect to MySQL
    // substitute your own hostname, username and password
    mysql_connect("localhost", "sandman", "34Nhjp")
        or die ("Unable to connect to database.");


    // select database on MySQL server
    // substitute your own database name
    mysql_select_db("secretDB")
    or die ("Unable to select database.");


    // prepare SQL statement
    $sql = "select sum(sel_item_qty) from db_table where id='$id'";


    // query DB using SQL statement
    $item_result = mysql_query($sql) or die ("Can't perform query");


    // assign value to variable called $item_count
    $item_count = mysql_result($item_result,0,"sum(item_qty)");
?>
```

When you're ready to display the number of items in this particular user's shopping cart, just echo the value of `$item_count`:

```php
<?php
    echo "Cart contains: $item_count items.";
?>
```

Or, to be grammatically correct about it:

```php
<?php
    if ($item_count == "1") {
        echo "Cart contains: $item_count item.";
    } else {
        echo "Cart contains: $item_count items.";
    }
?>
```

In Chapter 8, "Advanced PHP Techniques: e-Commerce," this shopping cart example will be greatly expanded, showing checkout procedures, cart item modification and removal, and so on.

In this cookie-setting example, we set a cookie that expired after four hours. If you don't want your cookies to expire at any particular time, but rather when a user explicitly logs out of your system (via a Logout button, for example), you can effectively delete a cookie by sending a cookie of the same name but with a blank value.

Say you've set a cookie such as this:

```php
setcookie("valid_user","yes",time()+14400,"/",".yourdomain.com",0);
```

The name of this cookie is `valid_user`, and the value is "yes". To delete this cookie, have your script send an identical cookie to the user—identical except for the value, which is now blank:

```php
setcookie("valid_user","",time()+14400,"/",".yourdomain.com",0);
```

This process effectively deletes the cookie by assigning a null value to it. No more valid user!

PHP4 Session Handling

NOTE

PHP4, beta 3 and higher, is recommended.

In terms of time, a *session* is the amount of time during which a user visits a site. In the programming world, a session is kind of like a big blob that can hold all sorts of variables and values. This blob of stuff, also known as a session *object,* has an identification string. This identification string, such as `940f8b05a40d5119c030c9c7745aead9`, is automatically sent to the user when a session is initiated, via a cookie called `PHPSESSID`. On the server side, a matching temporary file is created with the same name— `940f8b05a40d5119c030c9c7745aead9`.

New Feature

If the question is "How do I maintain user-specific information without setting multiple cookies and making numerous calls to a database?", the answer is to use the session management functions in PHP4.

Understanding Session Variables

Each session object has variables registered with it, such as `count` or `valid`. Inside the session file on the server, the registered variables and their values are kept safe and sound. Since these values and variables are not kept in a database, no additional system resources are required to connect to and extract information from database tables.

For example, the session file might look like this:

```
count|s:7:"76";
valid|s:7:"yes";
```

where `count` and `valid` are the names of the registered variables and "76" and "yes" are their respective values.

When you register a session variable, you eliminate the need to send additional cookies to the user. To assign values for `count` and `valid` to a user without using sessions, you'd have to send two separate cookies, like so:

```
setcookie("count","1",time()+14400,"/",".yourdomain.com",0);
setcookie("valid","yes",time()+14400,"/",".yourdomain.com",0);
```

To access session variables, just call the variable name, such as `$count` or `$valid`. PHP will perform a magic trick when you say something like this:

```
echo "<P>$count</p>";
```

The PHP engine takes the value of `$PHPSESSID` (the unique user session ID, stored in a cookie), matches it to a temporary session file, looks for `count`, finds its value (say, "76"), and returns it to you:

```
<P>76</p>
```

The only cookie that is sent to the user is the cookie that holds the value of `$PHPSESSID`.

Starting a Session and Registering Variables

We'll use a simple access counter to get used to the idea of sessions and session variables. At the beginning of your page, call the `session_start()` function. This function serves two purposes. First, it checks to see if a session has been started for this user and starts one if necessary. Second, it alerts the PHP engine that session variables and other session-related functions will be used within the specific script.

Open your favorite text editor, create a file called `count_me.php`, and type the following:

```php
<?php
    // count_me.php
    // if a session does not yet exist for this user, start one
    session_start();
?>
```

Next, register the `count` variable inside your session object:

```php
Session_register('count');
```

Now, for as long as this session exists, a variable called `count` also exists. Currently, the variable has no value. However, if you increment it, it will have a value of "1":

```php
$count++;
```

Put these pieces together, and you'll have done the following: started a session if it hasn't already been started, assigned a session ID to a user if one doesn't exist, and registered the variable called `count` and incremented it by 1 to represent the initial time the user has accessed the page.

Next, to display the value of the `$count` session variable and show the user how many times he has accessed this page in his current session, just print the value of `$count`:

```php
echo "<P>You've been here $count times.  Thanks!</p>";
```

The entire access count code should look something like this:

```php
<?php
    // count_me.php
    // if a session does not yet exist for this user, start one
    session_start();
    session_register('count');
    $count++;
    echo "<P>You've been here $count times.  Thanks!</p>";
?>
```

Reload the page a number of times, and watch the value of `$count` increment by 1 each time.

Managing User Preferences with Sessions

Moving beyond the simple access counter, you can use sessions to manage your users' preferences when they visit your site. For example, you can have your users select a background color, text color, and their favorite font for displaying site content. In this three-step example, you'll start a session, ask a user for his display preferences, display those preferences on subsequent pages, and allow the user to change his mind and reset the values.

For the first step, create a file called `session1.php`. In this step, start the session if it doesn't exist and register the variables we'll use later: `$body_color`, `$text_color`, and `$font_family`:

```php
<?php
    // File name: session1.php
    // if a session does not yet exist for this user, start one
    session_start();
    if (!$PHPSESSID) {
        session_register('body_color');
        session_register('text_color');
        session_register('font_family');
    } else if ((!$body_color) || (!$text_color) || (!$font_family)) {
        session_register('body_color');
        session_register('text_color');
        session_register('font_family');
    }
?>
```

In this example, the `if…else…if` loop is important. This loop registers the session variables only if a value for `$PHPSESSID` does not exist, or if the `$body_color`, `$text_color`, and `$font_family` variables have not yet been created or registered with a session. Since the user will come back to this screen to reset his display preferences, we have to take into account the fact that the values of the variables must always be extracted from the session itself. If we just said this:

```php
session_start();
session_register('body_color');
session_register('text_color');
session_register(font_family);
```

at the top of the page, then each time the page were loaded, the value of these variables would be overwritten as an empty string, or a newly-registered, empty variable.

Next, create a simple HTML form that asks the user to select his color preferences:

```
<HTML>
<HEAD>
<TITLE>My Display Preferences</TITLE>
<style type="text/css">
P {font-family:Arial;font-size:10pt;font-weight:normal;}
H1 {font-family:Arial;font-size:16pt;font-weight:bold;}
</style>
</HEAD>
<BODY BGCOLOR="#FFFFFF" TEXT="#000000">
<H1>Set Your Color and Font Preferences</h1>
<FORM METHOD="POST" ACTION="session2.php">
    <P>Pick a Background Color:<br>
    <input type="radio" name="sel_body_color" value="#FFFFFF">white
    <input type="radio" name="sel_body_color" value="#000000">black
    <input type="radio" name="sel_body_color" value="#0000FF">blue
    <input type="radio" name="sel_body_color" value="#FF0000">red
    <input type="radio" name="sel_body_color" value="#FFFF00">yellow
    </p>

    <P>Pick a Text Color:<br>
    <input type="radio" name="sel_text_color" value="#FFFFFF">white
    <input type="radio" name="sel_text_color" value="#000000">black
    <input type="radio" name="sel_text_color" value="#0000FF">blue
    <input type="radio" name="sel_text_color" value="#FF0000">red
    <input type="radio" name="sel_text_color" value="#FFFF00">yellow
    </p>

    <P>Pick a Font:<br>
    <input type="radio" name="sel_font_family" value="Arial">Arial
    <input type="radio" name="sel_font_family" value="Times">Times
    <input type="radio" name="sel_font_family" value="Courier">Courier
    </p>

    <P><input type="submit" name="submit" value="Set Display Preferences"></p>

</FORM>
```

```
</BODY>
</HTML>
```

But wait! Since the user will be coming back to this page to modify his preferences at some point, you'll also want to show this page using his preferences. Before the opening `<HTML>` tag, add the following code to determine the user's preferred colors, if any, or to define the defaults if preferences have yet to be set:

```
if (!$body_color) {
    $body_color = "#FFFFFF";
}
if (!$text_color) {
    $text_color = "#000000";
}
if (!$font_family) {
    $font_family = "Arial";
}
```

If this is the first time the user has been to this page, the session variables `$body_color`, `$text_color`, and `$font_family` will be registered, but they won't have values because we haven't given them any. Since we have to display some colors and a font even on this first screen, we assign temporary values via these `if` statements.

To make your code dynamic, replace the original style sheet code with this code:

```
<style type="text/css">
P {font-family:<? echo "$font_family"; ?>;font-size:10pt;font-weight:normal;}
H1 {font-family:<? echo "$font_family"; ?>;font-size:16pt;font-weight:bold;}
</style>
```

Also, replace the original HTML `<BODY>` tag with this code:

```
<BODY BGCOLOR="<? echo "$body_color"; ?>" TEXT="<? echo "$text_color"; ?>">
```

Your code should look something like this:

```
<?php
    // File name: session1.php
    // if a session does not yet exist for this user, start one
    session_start();

    if (!$PHPSESSID) {
        session_register('body_color');
        session_register('text_color');
        session_register('font_family');
```

```
        } else if ((!$body_color) || (!$text_color) || (!$font_family)) {
            session_register('body_color');
            session_register('text_color');
            session_register('font_family');
        }


    if (!$body_color) {
        $body_color = "#FFFFFF";
    }
    if (!$text_color) {
        $text_color = "#000000";
    }
    if (!$font_family) {
        $font_family = "Arial";
    }
?>
<HTML>
<HEAD>
<TITLE>My Display Preferences</TITLE>
<style type="text/css">
P {font-family:<? echo "$font_family"; ?>;font-size:10pt;font-weight:normal;}
H1 {font-family:<? echo "$font_family"; ?>;font-size:16pt;font-weight:bold;}
</style>
</HEAD>
<BODY BGCOLOR="<? echo "$body_color"; ?>" TEXT="<? echo "$text_color"; ?>"
<H1>Set Your Color and Font Preferences</h1>
<FORM METHOD="POST" ACTION="session2.php">
    <P>Pick a Background Color:<br>
    <input type="radio" name="sel_body_color" value="#FFFFFF">white
    <input type="radio" name="sel_body_color" value="#000000">black
    <input type="radio" name="sel_body_color" value="#0000FF">blue
    <input type="radio" name="sel_body_color" value="#FF0000">red
    <input type="radio" name="sel_body_color" value="#FFFF00">yellow
    </p>

    <P>Pick a Text Color:<br>
    <input type="radio" name="sel_text_color" value="#FFFFFF">white
    <input type="radio" name="sel_text_color" value="#000000">black
```

```
<input type="radio" name="sel_text_color" value="#0000FF">blue
<input type="radio" name="sel_text_color" value="#FF0000">red
<input type="radio" name="sel_text_color" value="#FFFF00">yellow
</p>

<P>Pick a Font:<br>
<input type="radio" name="sel_font_family" value="Arial">Arial
<input type="radio" name="sel_font_family" value="Times">Times
<input type="radio" name="sel_font_family" value="Courier">Courier
</p>

<P><input type="submit" name="submit" value="Set Display Preferences"></P>

</FORM>
</BODY>
</HTML>
```

In the next step, the form action (session2.php), we'll assign to the appropriate session variables the values selected by the user. Open your text editor and create a file called session2.php. In your code, create a session if one doesn't exist, and register the $body_color, $text_color, and $font_family session variables, if they don't exist.

Remember, since we assigned temporary values to $body_color, $text_color, and $font_family in Step 1, they aren't considered "empty" and thus won't be reregistered with the session.

Your code should begin like this:

```php
<?php
    // File name: session2.php
    // if a session does not yet exist for this user, start one
    session_start();
    if (!$PHPSESSID) {
        session_register('body_color');
        session_register('text_color');
        session_register('font_family');
    } else if ((!$body_color) || (!$text_color) || (!$font_family)) {
        session_register('body_color');
        session_register('text_color');
        session_register('font_family');
    }
```

Next, assign the selected values to the session variables:

```
// do something with POST vars
$body_color = $sel_body_color;
$text_color = $sel_text_color;
$font_family = $sel_font_family;
```

You might wonder why we didn't just name the form input elements `body_color`, `text_value`, and `font_family`. That way, we would automatically have the new values, right? Wrong. For very important security reasons, you can't directly change the value of a registered session variable using `POST` or `GET`. You must, in your script, explicitly reassign the values as we have done here.

Finish the script by checking for the value of the three variables and assigning default values if they're still empty (if, for example, the user accessed Step 2 before Step 1 for some reason). Print the value of the variables in the body of the page, just to show the user that the values have indeed changed:

```
// continue PHP code
if (!$body_color) {
    $body_color = "#FFFFFF";
}
if (!$text_color) {
    $text_color = "#000000";
}
if (!$font_family) {
    $font_family = "Arial";
}
?>
<HTML>
<HEAD>
<TITLE>My Display Preferences</TITLE>
<style type="text/css">
    P {font-family:<? echo "$font_family"; ?>;font-size:10pt;font-weight:normal;}
    H1 {font-family:<? echo "$font_family"; ?>;font-size:16pt;font-weight:bold;}
</style>
</HEAD>
<BODY BGCOLOR="<? echo "$body_color"; ?>" TEXT="<? echo "$text_color"; ?>">
<H1>Your Preferences Have Been Set</h1>
<P>As you can see, your BODY color is now <strong><? echo "$body_color"; ?></
strong> and your TEXT color is now <strong><? echo "$text_color"; ?></strong>.</p>
<P>You have selected the <? echo "$font_family" ?> font.</p>
```

```
<P>Please feel free to <a href="session1.php">change your preferences</a> </p>
</BODY>
</HTML>
```

The entire `session2.php` script should look something like this:

```php
<?php
    // File name: session2.php
    // if a session does not yet exist for this user, start one
    session_start();
    if (!$PHPSESSID) {
        session_register('body_color');
        session_register('text_color');
        session_register('font_family');
    } else if ((!$body_color) || (!$text_color) || (!$font_family)) {
        session_register('body_color');
        session_register('text_color');
        session_register('font_family');
    }

    // do something with POST vars
    $body_color = $sel_body_color;
    $text_color = $sel_text_color;
    $font_family = $sel_font_family;

    if (!$body_color) {
        $body_color = "#FFFFFF";
    }
    if (!$text_color) {
        $text_color = "#000000";
    }
    if (!$font_family) {
        $font_family = "Arial";
    }
?>
<HTML>
<HEAD>
<TITLE>My Display Preferences</TITLE>

<style type="text/css">
    P {font-family:<? echo "$font_family"; ?>;font-size:10pt;font-weight:normal;}
```

```
    H1 {font-family:<? echo "$font_family"; ?>;font-size:16pt;font-weight:bold;}
</style>
</HEAD><BODY BGCOLOR="<? echo "$body_color"; ?>" TEXT="<? echo "$text_color"; ?>">
<H1>Your Preferences Have Been Set</h1>
<P>As you can see, your BODY color is now <strong><? echo "$body_color"; ?></
strong> and your TEXT color is now <strong><? echo "$text_color"; ?></strong>.</p>
<P>You have selected the <? echo "$font_family" ?> font.</p>
<P>Please feel free to <a href="session1.php">change your preferences</a> again.</
p>
</BODY>
</HTML>
```

Place these files on your Web server and go back and forth between `session1.php` and `session2.php`, changing your preferences as much as you like. Add additional values to the form, such as purple colors and strange fonts, to see that you too can make a dynamic, user-based Web site using sessions!

A Word of Advice

Although the built-in session support of PHP4 does provide greater flexibility and security than storing every user variable in a cookie, there are a few places for improvement. As PHP4 matures, session management functions will mature as well.

There's also the cookie aspect of session management: what if a user doesn't accept your `PHPSESSID` cookie? How will PHP know which session file to use if it can't extract a session ID from a cookie? In this case, it becomes your responsibility to send the value of `PHPSESSID` via the `GET` method.

For example, the `session2.php` file contains this line:

```
<P>Please feel free to <a href="session1.php">change your preferences</a> </p>
```

As part of the link, add `?PHPSESSID=[value]`, like this:

```
<P>Please feel free to <a href="session1.php?PHPSESSID=<? echo "$PHPSESSID";
?>">change your preferences</a> </p>
```

It's a little more work, but it ensures that a session ID of some sort always follows the user as he moves through your site.

Chapter 7: Advanced PHP Techniques: Web-Based Database Administration

Planning Your Product Catalog

The previous chapters were designed to give you a solid foundation for developing applications with PHP. Many dynamic, user-friendly, e-commerce Web sites are simply several basic concepts put together to form one cohesive unit. For example, a successful shopping system needs a product catalog, a method for maintaining the contents, some sort of item order tracking, a method to order products securely, and a way for you to tell your boss what a wonderful job you're doing. In the next two chapters, you'll learn the basics of most of these tasks (except dealing with your boss).

While the term "Web-Based Database Administration" might seem daunting, don't be afraid—it's just a fancy label for "data goes in, data comes out." The goal of this section is to create a product catalog for an online shopping system, which will be fully functional by the end of this chapter. By breaking down the elements piece by piece, before you know it you'll have created a graphical user interface to a product catalog in a MySQL database. You can repeat the same steps for any type of database-driven system you want to develop: news articles, address books, your mother's recipe collection. If you're not using the MySQL database, just substitute the functions for your particular database for the MySQL database functions. You can also find database-specific source code in the "Code" section at http://www.thickbook.com/.

Planning Your Product Catalog

This sample shopping site will be called XYZ Company, and it will sell books. The first step in creating this sample shopping site is developing the product catalog. It's up to you to determine if you want to create multiple tables to hold your product information or if you want to keep your product information in one big table. Because we're creating only a simple example catalog, we'll use one large table called MASTER_PRODUCTS.

Let's sell some books. Think about all the information you'll need to know in order to give the user an accurate description of a product:

- ISBN (a standard publishing identification number)
- Book title
- Author's name
- Publisher
- Category
- Type (hardcover or paperback)
- A paragraph of information about the book

- Number of pages
- Price

It's time to create the database table. Chapter 3, "Working with Databases," contains a section on creating a Web front-end to creating a database table. You can use the three-step process in that section to create the MASTER_PRODUCTS table for XYZ Company. Start by loading the HTML form in show_createtable1.html, and use it to create a nine-field table called MASTER_PRODUCTS, as shown in Figure 7.1.

After submitting the form, you'll see nine rows containing empty form fields. Use these rows to define the fields in MASTER_PRODUCTS. In this example, we'll use the following:

Field Name	Field Type	Field Length
ISBN	varchar	25
TITLE	varchar	150
AUTHOR	varchar	75
PUBLISHER	varchar	75
CATEGORY	varchar	50
TYPE	varchar	25
INFO_BLURB	text	
PAGE_NUM	int	5
PRICE	float	

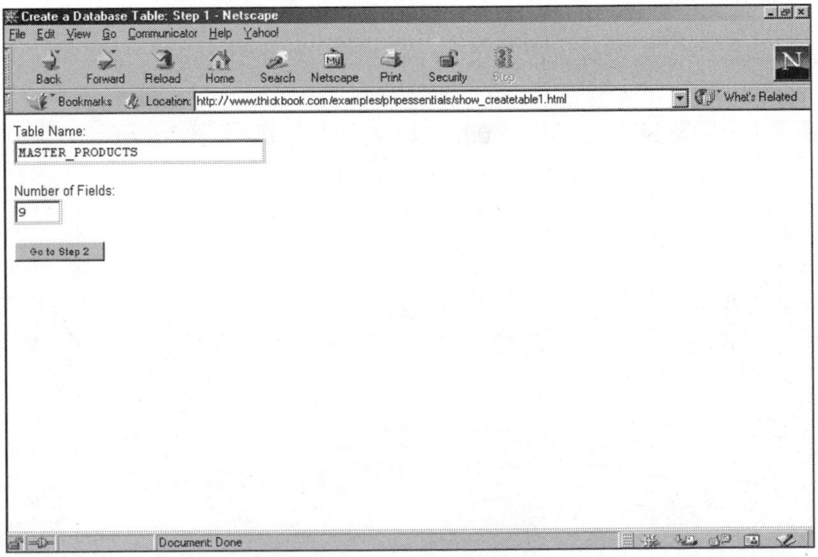

Figure 7.1   *Name Your Table and the Number of Fields*

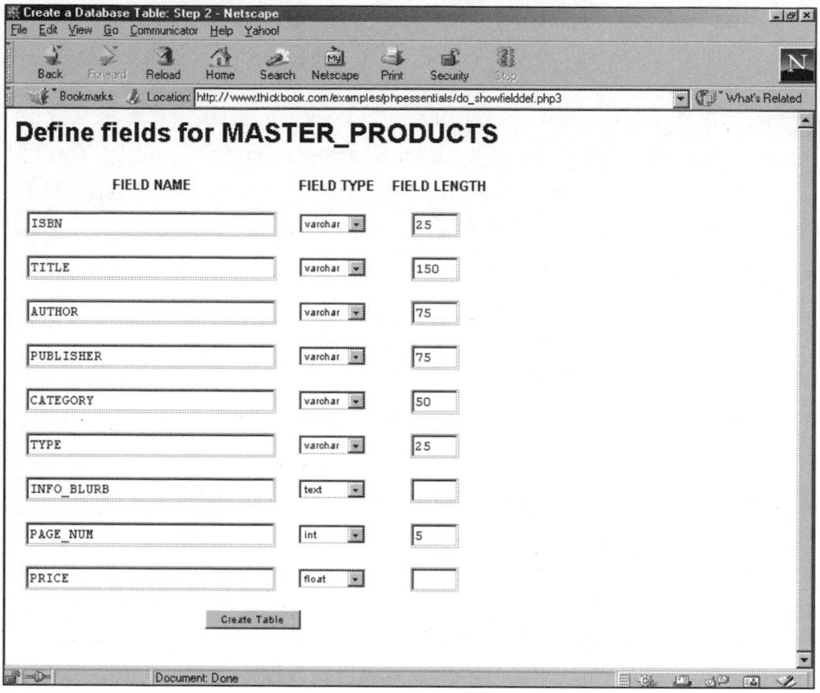

Figure 7.2   *Define the fields in* MASTER_PRODUCTS

Before you submit the form, it should look something like what is shown in Figure 7.2.

After you click on the Create Table button, the table will be created in your database, and a confirmation screen will appear (see Figure 7.3).

For your reference, here is the SQL statement created by the PHP script:

```
CREATE TABLE MASTER_PRODUCTS (
    ISBN varchar(25),
    TITLE varchar(150),
    AUTHOR varchar(75),
    PUBLISHER varchar(75),
    CATEGORY varchar(50),
    TYPE varchar(25),
    INFO_BLURB text,
    PAGE_NUM int(5),
    PRICE float
);
```

Figure 7.3 *Successful table creation!*

If you don't insert a field length for the PAGE_NUM and PRICE fields, MySQL will use the default values for the field type. The default field length for an int field is (11), while a float field defaults to (10,2), or the ability to hold numbers such as 0000000000.00.

In the next sections, you'll create sequences of HTML forms and PHP scripts to add, modify, and delete records in your MASTER_PRODUCTS table.

Developing an Administration Menu

Somewhere on the Web site for XYZ Company, you'll want to have a special series of "admin" pages, which only you (or whomever has the correct password) can access to make changes to the product catalog. The main elements of the administration menu will be as follows:

- Add a New Product
- Modify an Existing Product
- Delete an Existing Product

We'll use a PHP-based authentication scheme, which you learned about in Chapter 5, "User Authentication." If you are using the CGI version of PHP, you must substitute this authentication scheme with another type from Chapter 5, such as .htaccess-based authentication.

The XYZ Company administration area will be accessible by anyone who knows the username and password pair—in this case, "admin" and "abc123." At the top of every page in the administration sequence, use the following code, which should look very familiar to you if you read Chapter 5:

```php
<?php
    // Check to see if $PHP_AUTH_USER already contains info
    if (!isset($PHP_AUTH_USER)) {
        // If empty, send header causing dialog box to appear
        header('WWW-Authenticate: Basic realm="XYZ Company Admin"');
        header('HTTP/1.0 401 Unauthorized');
        echo 'Authorization Required.';
        exit;
    } else if (isset($PHP_AUTH_USER)) {
        if (($PHP_AUTH_USER != "admin") || ($PHP_AUTH_PW != "abc123")) {
            header('WWW-Authenticate: Basic realm="XYZ Company Admin"');
            header('HTTP/1.0 401 Unauthorized');
            echo 'Authorization Required.';
            exit;
        } else {
            // Display code here
        }
    }
?>
```

If you add this to the top of every page in the XYZ Company administration area, the PHP script will always look for a valid entry for `$PHP_AUTH_USER` and `$PHP_AUTH_PW`. You will need to enter the login information only the first time you see the pop-up box. From that point forward, the proper values will exist for `$PHP_AUTH_USER` and `$PHP_AUTH_PW` and will be carried along wherever you go, until you exit your browser. The code comment "`// Display code here`" will be replaced by the content you want to display to the valid user. For the first screen, the administration menu, this content can be three bullet items, linking to `admin_addrecord1.php`, `admin_modrecord1.php`, and `admin_delrecord1.php`, like this:

```html
<HTML>
<HEAD>
<TITLE>XYZ Company Administration Menu</TITLE>
</HEAD>
<BODY>
```

```
<h1>XYZ Company Administration Menu</h1>
<p>Select an option:</p>
<ul>
<li><a href="admin_addrecord1.php">Add a New Product</a>
<li><a href="admin_modrecord1.php">Modify an Existing Product</a>
<li><a href="admin_delrecord1.php">Delete an Existing Product</a>
</ul>
</BODY>
</HTML>
```

When you put this section of HTML within an `echo` statement, be sure to escape the quotation marks! The entire administration menu code should look something like this:

```php
<?php
    // File name: admin_menu.php
    // Check to see if $PHP_AUTH_USER already contains info
    if (!isset($PHP_AUTH_USER)) {
        // If empty, send header causing dialog box to appear
        header('WWW-Authenticate: Basic realm="XYZ Company Admin Area"');
        header('HTTP/1.0 401 Unauthorized');
        echo 'Authorization Required.';
        exit;
    } else if (isset($PHP_AUTH_USER)) {
        if (($PHP_AUTH_USER != "admin") || ($PHP_AUTH_PW != "abc123")) {
            header('WWW-Authenticate: Basic realm="XYZ Company Admin Area"');
            header('HTTP/1.0 401 Unauthorized');
            echo 'Authorization Required.';
            exit;
        } else {
            // start echo statement
            echo "
<HTML>
<HEAD>
<TITLE>XYZ Company Administration Menu</TITLE>
</HEAD>
<BODY>
<h1>XYZ Company Administration Menu</h1>
<p>Select an option:</p>
```

```
<ul>
<li><a href=\"admin_addrecord1.php\">Add a New Product</a>
<li><a href=\"admin_modrecord1.php\">Modify an Existing Product</a>
<li><a href=\"admin_delrecord1.php\">Delete an Existing Product</a>
</ul>
    </BODY>
</HTML>
";

            // finished with the echo statement

    }
    }
?>
```

Save this file and place it on your Web server. Access it at its URL, something like http://www.yourcompany.com/admin_menu.php, and enter the correct username and password when prompted. If you are authorized, you should see a menu such as the one shown in Figure 7.4.

Now that you've built the menu, it's time to build the pages behind it, starting with "Add a New Product."

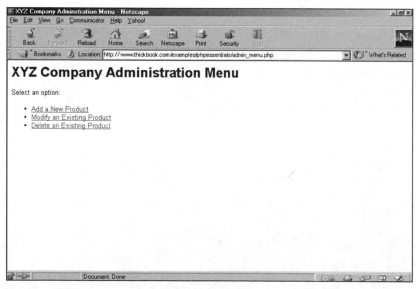

Figure 7.4   *XYZ company administration menu*

Adding Records to the Product Catalog

Of the three menu options, adding a product is the simplest to execute. Using a two-step system, you'll create the addition form, and then you'll create the PHP script to insert the contents into the MASTER_PRODUCTS table. The link in the administration menu says admin_addrecord1.php, so create a file with that name and add your PHP authentication code:

```php
<?php
    // File name: admin_addrecord1.php
    // Check to see if $PHP_AUTH_USER already contains info
    if (!isset($PHP_AUTH_USER)) {
        // If empty, send header causing dialog box to appear
        header('WWW-Authenticate: Basic realm="XYZ Company Admin Area"');
        header('HTTP/1.0 401 Unauthorized');
        echo 'Authorization Required.';
        exit;
    } else if (isset($PHP_AUTH_USER)) {
        if (($PHP_AUTH_USER != "admin") || ($PHP_AUTH_PW != "abc123")) {
            header('WWW-Authenticate: Basic realm="XYZ Company Admin Area"');
            header('HTTP/1.0 401 Unauthorized');
            echo 'Authorization Required.';
            exit;
        } else {
            // Display code here
        }
    }
?>
```

The code comment "// Display code here" will be replaced by the HTML used to create the product addition form. Start by echoing the title and main topic heading:

```php
echo "
<HTML>
<HEAD>
<TITLE>XYZ Company: Add a Product</TITLE>
</HEAD>
<BODY>
<h1>Add a product to the XYZ Company Catalog</h1>
```

Assume that the PHP script for the next step is called `admin_addrecord2.php`, and add this file name to the form action:

```
<FORM method=\"POST\" action=\"admin_addrecord2.php\">
```

Next, create the text fields, drop-down menus, and a text area to capture the values needed to populate the nine fields in the MASTER_PRODUCTS table: `$isbn`, `$title`, `$author`, `$publisher`, `$category`, `$type`, `$info_blurb`, `$page_num`, and `$price`. The following sample form uses an HTML table to display the form fields, but feel free to display the form however you'd like:

```
<table cellspacing=5 cellpadding=5>
<tr>
<td valign=top><strong>ISBN:</strong></td>
<td valign=top><INPUT type=\"text\" name=\"isbn\" size=35 maxlength=25></td>
</tr>

<tr>
<td valign=top><strong>Title of the Book:</strong></td>
<td valign=top><INPUT type=\"text\" name=\"title\" size=35 maxlength=150></td>
</tr>

<tr>
<td valign=top><strong>Author's Name:</strong></td>
<td valign=top><INPUT type=\"text\" name=\"author\" size=35 maxlength=75></td>
</tr>

<tr>
<td valign=top><strong>Publisher:</strong></td>
<td valign=top>
<SELECT name=\"publisher\">
<OPTION value=\"\">-- Select One --</OPTION>
<OPTION value=\"Prima-Tech\">Prima-Tech</OPTION>
<OPTION value=\"Prima Games\">Prima Games</OPTION>
<OPTION value=\"Prima Lifestyles\">Prima Lifestyles</OPTION>
</SELECT>
</td>
</tr>

<tr>
<td valign=top><strong>Category:</strong></td>
<td valign=top>
```

```
<SELECT name=\"category\">
<OPTION value=\"\">-- Select One --</OPTION>
<OPTION value=\"Applications\">Applications</OPTION>
<OPTION value=\"Cooking\">Cooking</OPTION>
<OPTION value=\"Operating Systems\">Operating Systems</OPTION>
<OPTION value=\"Pets\">Pets</OPTION>
<OPTION value=\"Programming\">Programming</OPTION>
<OPTION value=\"Strategy Guides\">Strategy Guides</OPTION>
</SELECT>
</td>
</tr>

<tr>
<td valign=top><strong>Type:</strong></td>
<td valign=top>
<SELECT name=\"type\">
<OPTION value=\"\">-- Select One --</OPTION>
<OPTION value=\"hardcover\">hardcover</OPTION>
<OPTION value=\"paperback\">paperback</OPTION>
</SELECT>
</td>
</tr>

<tr>
<td valign=top><strong>Paragraph about this book:</strong></td>
<td valign=top>
<TEXTAREA name=\"info_blurb\" cols=35 rows=5></TEXTAREA>
</td>
</tr>

<tr>
<td valign=top><strong>Number of Pages:</strong></td>
<td valign=top><INPUT type=\"text\" name=\"page_num\" size=5 maxlength=5></td>
</tr>

<tr>
<td valign=top><strong>Retail Price:</strong></td>
<td valign=top><INPUT type=\"text\" name=\"price\" size=5 maxlength=5></td>
</tr>
```

Finally, add the Add New Product button and the necessary closing tags:

```
<tr>
<td align=center colspan=2><INPUT type=\"submit\" value=\"Add New Product\"></td>
</tr>

</table>
</FORM>
</BODY>
</HTML>
    ";
    // finished with the echo statement
```

In this example, the values of the drop-down menus are hard-coded into the HTML. You could also put these values in separate PUBLISHER, CATEGORY, and TYPE tables, and use PHP to extract the data and dynamically create your drop-down menus. Visit the "Tutorials" section at http://www.thickbook.com/ for examples of this functionality. The entire admin_addrecord1.php script should look something like this (be sure to escape the quotation marks within the echo statement):

```
<?php
    // File name: admin_addrecord1.php
    // Check to see if $PHP_AUTH_USER already contains info
    if (!isset($PHP_AUTH_USER)) {
        // If empty, send header causing dialog box to appear
        header('WWW-Authenticate: Basic realm="XYZ Company Admin Area"');
        header('HTTP/1.0 401 Unauthorized');
        echo 'Authorization Required.';
        exit;
    } else if (isset($PHP_AUTH_USER)) {
        if (($PHP_AUTH_USER != "admin") || ($PHP_AUTH_PW != "abc123")) {
            header('WWW-Authenticate: Basic realm="XYZ Company Admin Area"');
            header('HTTP/1.0 401 Unauthorized');
            echo 'Authorization Required.';
            exit;
        } else {
            echo "
<HTML>
<HEAD>
<TITLE>XYZ Company: Add a Product</TITLE>
</HEAD>
```

```
<BODY>
<h1>Add a product to the XYZ Company Catalog</h1>
    <FORM method=\"POST\" action=\"admin_addrecord2.php\">
    <table cellspacing=5 cellpadding=5>
    <tr>
    <td valign=top><strong>ISBN:</strong></td>
    <td valign=top><INPUT type=\"text\" name=\"isbn\" size=35 maxlength=25></td>
    </tr>

    <tr>
    <td valign=top><strong>Title of the Book:</strong></td>
    <td valign=top><INPUT type=\"text\" name=\"title\" size=35 maxlength=150></td>
    </tr>

    <tr>
    <td valign=top><strong>Author's Name:</strong></td>
    <td valign=top><INPUT type=\"text\" name=\"author\" size=35 maxlength=75></td>
    </tr>

    <tr>
    <td valign=top><strong>Publisher:</strong></td>
    <td valign=top>
    <SELECT name=\"publisher\">
    <OPTION value=\"\">-- Select One --</OPTION>
    <OPTION value=\"Prima-Tech\">Prima-Tech</OPTION>
    <OPTION value=\"Prima Games\">Prima Games</OPTION>
    <OPTION value=\"Prima Lifestyles\">Prima Lifestyles</OPTION>
    </SELECT>
    </td>
    </tr>

    <tr>
    <td valign=top><strong>Category:</strong></td>
    <td valign=top>
    <SELECT name=\"category\">
    <OPTION value=\"\">-- Select One --</OPTION>
    <OPTION value=\"Applications\">Applications</OPTION>
    <OPTION value=\"Cooking\">Cooking</OPTION>
    <OPTION value=\"Operating Systems\">Operating Systems</OPTION>
```

```
<OPTION value=\"Pets\">Pets</OPTION>
<OPTION value=\"Programming\">Programming</OPTION>
<OPTION value=\"Strategy Guides\">Strategy Guides</OPTION>
</SELECT>
</td>
</tr>

<tr>
<td valign=top><strong>Type:</strong></td>
<td valign=top>
<SELECT name=\"type\">
<OPTION value=\"\">-- Select One --</OPTION>
<OPTION value=\"hardcover\">hardcover</OPTION>
<OPTION value=\"paperback\">paperback</OPTION>
</SELECT>
</td>
</tr>

<tr>
<td valign=top><strong>Paragraph about this book:</strong></td>
<td valign=top>
<TEXTAREA name=\"info_blurb\" cols=35 rows=5></TEXTAREA>
</td>
</tr>

<tr>
<td valign=top><strong>Number of Pages:</strong></td>
<td valign=top><INPUT type=\"text\" name=\"page_num\" size=5 maxlength=5></td>
</tr>

<tr>
<td valign=top><strong>Retail Price:</strong></td>
<td valign=top><INPUT type=\"text\" name=\"price\" size=5 maxlength=5></td>
</tr>

<tr>
<td align=center colspan=2>
<INPUT type=\"submit\" value=\"Add New Product\"></td>
</tr>
</table>
```

```
</FORM>
</BODY>
</HTML>
            ";
            // finished with the echo statement
        }
    }
?>
```

Place this file on your Web server, and click on the Add a New Product link on the initial administration menu. If you are authorized, you should see the product addition form shown in Figure 7.5.

Next, you'll create the PHP script that takes your form input, creates a proper SQL statement, creates the record, and displays the record to you as a confirmation. It's not as difficult as it sounds. Since the form action in admin_addrecord1.php is admin_addrecord2.php, open your favorite text editor and create a file called admin_addrecord2.php. Add the PHP authentication code, as you've done in the

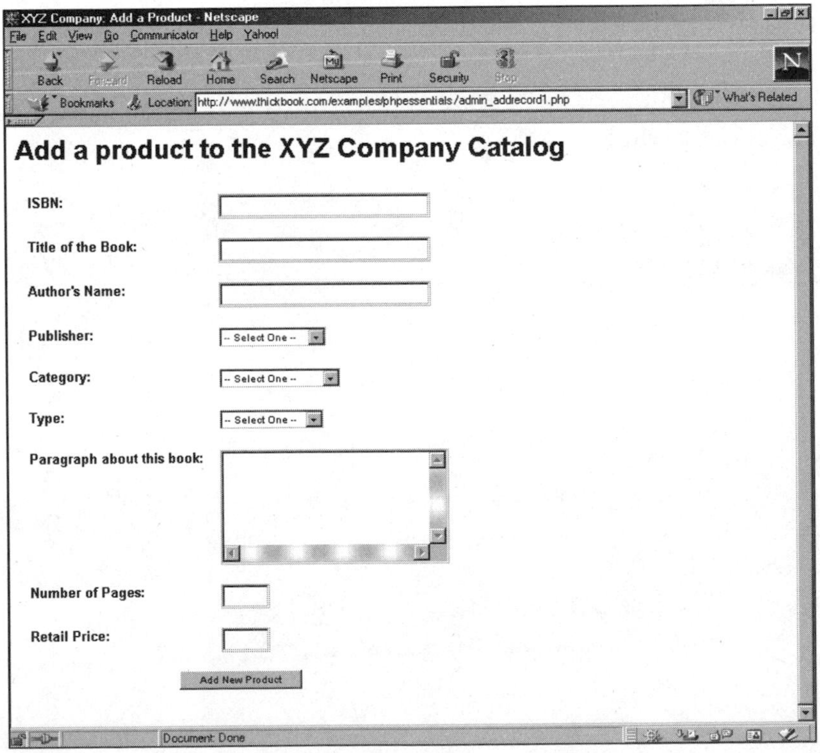

Figure 7.5 *Add a new product to the XYZ company product catalog*

previous scripts. However, in this script, you'll want to do a bit more than just echo HTML back to the browser. First, you'll want to check for some required fields. Then you'll redirect the user to the form if all the necessary fields aren't complete.

In this catalog, the required fields are ISBN, book title, and book price. Check that a value has been entered for their matching variable names: $isbn, $title, and $price:

```
if ((!$isbn) || (!$title) || (!$price)) {
    header("Location: http://www.yourserver.com/admin_addrecord1.php");
    exit;
}
```

If your script makes it past the required-field check, the next step is to build the SQL statement used to insert the data into the MASTER_PRODUCTS table. Hold the SQL statement in a variable called $sql, and build the VALUES list using the variable names from the form:

```
$sql = "INSERT INTO MASTER_PRODUCTS VALUES (\"$isbn\", \"$title\", \"$author\",
\"$publisher\", \"$category\", \"$type\", \"$info_blurb\", \"$page_num\",
\"$price\")";
```

Use the basic connection code described in Chapter 3, "Working with Databases," to connect to and query the MySQL database using the SQL statement just shown. Be sure to echo your HTML after your error-checking database connectivity code, because the code is told to exit upon error. You wouldn't want to display a half-formed HTML page to the browser!

```
// create connection
$connection = mysql_connect("localhost","sandman","34Nhjp") or die ("Couldn't
connect to the database.");

// select database
$db = mysql_select_db("secretDB", $connection) or die ("Couldn't select database.);

// execute SQL query and get result
$sql_result = mysql_query($sql,$connection) or die ("Couldn't execute query");

if (!$sql_result) {
echo "<P>Couldn't add record!";
} else {
echo "
<HTML>
<HEAD>
```

```
<TITLE>XYZ Company: Add a Product</TITLE>
</HEAD>
<BODY>
<h1>Product Added to XYZ Company Catalog:</h1>
    <table cellspacing=5 cellpadding=5>

    <tr>
    <td valign=top><strong>ISBN:</strong></td>
    <td valign=top>$isbn</td>
    </tr>

    <tr>
    <td valign=top><strong>Title of the Book:</strong></td>
    <td valign=top>$title</td>
    </tr>

    <tr>
    <td valign=top><strong>Author's Name:</strong></td>
    <td valign=top>$author</td>
    </tr>

    <tr>
    <td valign=top><strong>Publisher:</strong></td>
    <td valign=top>$publisher</td>
    </tr>

    <tr>
    <td valign=top><strong>Category:</strong></td>
    <td valign=top>$category</td>
    </tr>

    <tr>
    <td valign=top><strong>Type:</strong></td>
    <td valign=top>$type</td>
    </tr>

    <tr>
    <td valign=top><strong>Paragraph about this book:</strong></td>
    <td valign=top>$info_blurb</td>
    </tr>
```

```
    <tr>
    <td valign=top><strong>Number of Pages:</strong></td>
    <td valign=top>$page_num</td>
    </tr>

    <tr>
    <td valign=top><strong>Retail Price:</strong></td>
    <td valign=top>$price</td>
    </tr>
    </table>
<p align=center><a href=\"admin_menu.php\">Return to Menu</a></p>
</BODY>
</HTML>
        ";
        // finished with the echo statement
    }
}
}
?>
```

That's all there is to it! The entire code for `admin_addrecord2.php` should look something like this:

```php
<?php
    // File name: admin_addrecord2.php
    // Check to see if $PHP_AUTH_USER already contains info
    if (!isset($PHP_AUTH_USER)) {
        // If empty, send header causing dialog box to appear
        header('WWW-Authenticate: Basic realm="XYZ Company Admin Area"');
        header('HTTP/1.0 401 Unauthorized');
        echo 'Authorization Required.';
        exit;
    } else if (isset(PHP_AUTH_USER)) {
        if (($PHP_AUTH_USER != "admin") || ($PHP_AUTH_PW != "abc123")) {
            header('WWW-Authenticate: Basic realm="XYZ Company Admin Area"');
            header('HTTP/1.0 401 Unauthorized');
            echo 'Authorization Required.';
            exit;
        } else {
            if ((!$isbn) || (!$title) || (!$price)) {
```

```
                header("Location: http://www.yourcompany.com/
admin_addrecord1.php");
                exit;
            }

            // prepare SQL statement
            $sql = "INSERT INTO MASTER_PRODUCTS VALUES (\"$isbn\", \"$title\",
\"$author\", \"$publisher\", \"$category\", \"$type\", \"$info_blurb\",
\"$page_num\", \"$price\")";

            // create connection
            $connection = mysql_connect("localhost","sandman","34Nhjp") or die
            ("Couldn't connect to the database.");

            // select database
            $db = mysql_select_db("secretDB", $connection) or die
            ("Couldn't select database.);

            // execute SQL query and get result
            $sql_result = mysql_query($sql,$connection) or die
            ("Couldn't execute query");

            if (!$sql_result) {
                echo "<P>Couldn't add record!";
            } else {
echo "
<HTML>
<HEAD>
<TITLE>XYZ Company: Add a Product</TITLE>
</HEAD>
<BODY>
<h1>Product Added to XYZ Company Catalog:</h1>
<table cellspacing=5 cellpadding=5>
<tr>
<td valign=top><strong>ISBN:</strong></td>
<td valign=top>$isbn</td>
</tr>

    <tr>
    <td valign=top><strong>Title of the Book:</strong></td>
```

```
        <td valign=top>$title</td>
        </tr>

        <tr>
        <td valign=top><strong>Author's Name:</strong></td>
        <td valign=top>$author</td>
        </tr>

        <tr>
        <td valign=top><strong>Publisher:</strong></td>
        <td valign=top>$publisher</td>
        </tr>

        <tr>
        <td valign=top><strong>Category:</strong></td>
        <td valign=top>$category</td>
        </tr>

        <tr>
        <td valign=top><strong>Type:</strong></td>
        <td valign=top>$type</td>
        </tr>

        <tr>
        <td valign=top><strong>Paragraph about this book:</strong></td>
        <td valign=top>$info_blurb</td>
        </tr>

        <tr>
        <td valign=top><strong>Number of Pages:</strong></td>
        <td valign=top>$page_num</td>
        </tr>

        <tr>
        <td valign=top><strong>Retail Price:</strong></td>
        <td valign=top>$price</td>
        </tr>
        </table>
        <p align=center><a href=\"admin_menu.php\">Return to Menu</a></p>
</BODY>
```

```
</HTML>
        ";
        // finished with the echo statement
    }
  }
}
?>
```

Place this file on your Web server, and go back to the form at http://www.yourserver.com/admin_addrecord1.php. Complete the form to add a product such as the one shown in Figure 7.6.

Go ahead and click on the Add New Product button to execute the `admin_addrecord2.php` script. If the query is successful, you should see a results page like the one shown in Figure 7.7.

Use this sequence of forms to continue adding several more products to the MASTER_PRODUCTS table. In the next sections, you'll modify and delete some of these records. In the next chapter, you'll use the MASTER_PRODUCTS table to create a functioning online bookstore.

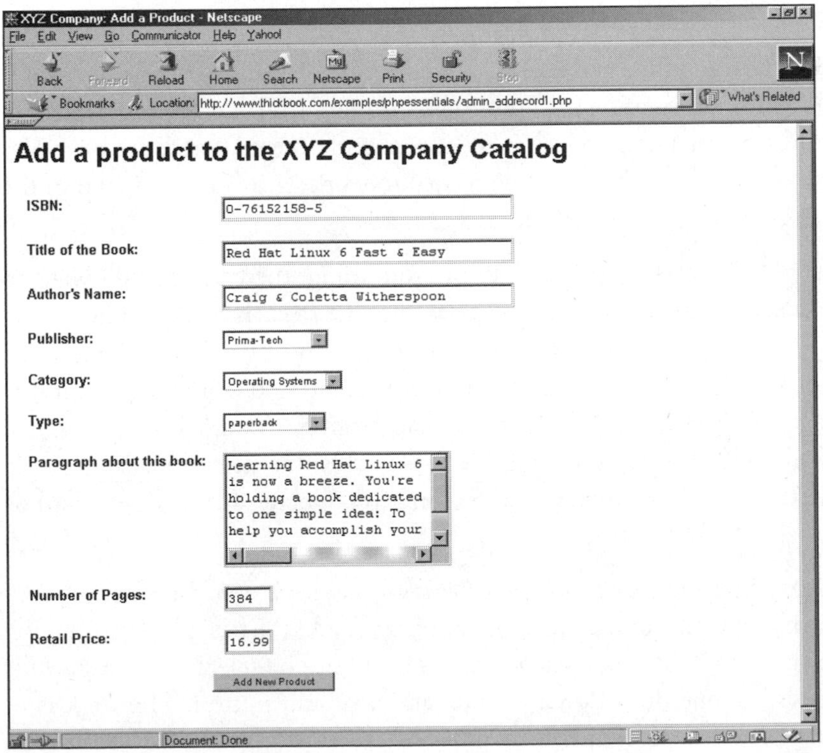

Figure 7.6 *Adding a sample product*

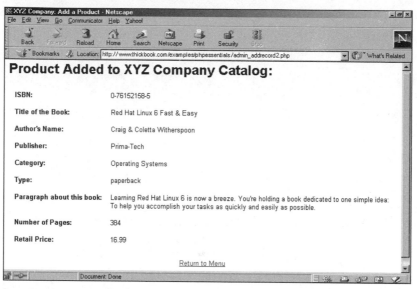

Figure 7.7   *Successful record addition*

Modifying Records in the Product Catalog

If you really were an online bookseller, it's quite likely that at some point you'd want to modify the information in your product catalog. You've already got the link in your administration menu, so let's make it active! Before you modify a product's information, you need to select a single record to work with. The first step in the modification sequence is to select a record to modify.

As with just about everything related to programming, there are several ways to display the selection screen. You could display the title of each book in a list, along with a radio button, to select the record you want to edit. If you have a long list of products, you could limit the display to groups of 10 or 15 or some other number and use Next and Previous links to display each group. The goal is to pick one record whose modifiable contents will be displayed in the next step. My sample product catalog has only six items, so I'm going to populate a drop-down list box with each book's ISBN and title.

Open your text editor and create a file called `admin_modrecord1.php`. Since the product selection form is also part of the administration area, add the basic PHP authentication code you used in previous scripts in this chapter. The selection form itself is quite basic: it's just one drop-down list box and a submit button. The trick is to populate that list box with elements in the `MASTER_PRODUCTS` table. As you'll soon see, it's not that tricky!

All you really need in order to populate the <OPTION> elements of the <SELECT> box are the book's ISBN and title. You can order the results any way you'd like, but I've chosen to order the books alphabetically, in ascending order (numbers first, then A, B, C, and so on). You'll use the basic connection code described in Chapter 3, "Working with Databases," to connect to and query the MySQL database. Be sure to echo your HTML after your error-checking database connectivity code.

```
// create connection
$connection = mysql_connect("localhost","sandman","34Nhjp") or die ("Couldn't
connect to the database.");
// select database
$db = mysql_select_db("secretDB", $connection) or die ("Couldn't select database.);

//SQL statement to select just ISBN and title
$sql = "SELECT ISBN, TITLE FROM MASTER_PRODUCTS ORDER BY TITLE ASC";

// execute SQL query and get result
$sql_result = mysql_query($sql,$connection) or die ("Couldn't execute query");

if (!$sql_result) {
    echo "<P>Couldn't get list!";
} else {
    // Display code here
}
```

The code comment "// Display code here" will be replaced by the HTML used to create the product addition form. Start by echoing the title and main topic heading:

```
echo "
<HTML>
<HEAD>
<TITLE>XYZ Company: Modify a Product</TITLE>
</HEAD>
<BODY>
<h1>Select a Product from the XYZ Company Catalog</h1>
```

Assume that the PHP script for the next step is called admin_modrecord2.php and add this file name to the form action:

```
<FORM method=\"POST\" action=\"admin_modrecord2.php\">
```

Next, start the table that will hold the single form element: the drop-down list box. Go so far as to open the <SELECT> tag, which will have a name of sel_record, and add an empty Select an Item <OPTION> tag:

```
<table cellspacing=5 cellpadding=5>
<tr>
<td align=right><strong>Product ID/Title:</strong></td>
<td valign=top>
<select name=\"sel_record\">
<option value=\"\"> -- Select an Item -- </option>
";
```

This particular `echo` statement ends because the next section of code will dynamically create additional `<OPTION>` elements based on the number of rows in the `MASTER_PRODUCTS` table. The following `while` loop continues to execute for as long as there are rows waiting for retrieval, as a result of the SQL query. For each row that is retrieved, the value of the `ISBN` column is assigned to the variable `$isbn`, and the value of the `TITLE` column is assigned to the variable `$title`. The loop then creates the `<OPTION>` element for the product retrieved, placing the value of `$isbn` in the value attribute of the `<OPTION>` field.

```
while ($row = mysql_fetch_array($sql_result)) {
    $isbn = $row["ISBN"];
    $title = $row["TITLE"];
    echo "
    <option value=\"$isbn\">$isbn : $title</option>
    ";
}
```

After the `while` loop runs its course, begin another `echo` statement and print the rest of the page, closing all open tags and sticking in a form submission button where appropriate:

```
echo "
</select>
</td>
</tr>

<tr>
<td align=center colspan=2><INPUT type=\"submit\" value=\"Select Product\"></td>
</tr>

</table>
</FORM>
```

```
</BODY>
</HTML>
";
    }
  }
}
?>
```

That's all that's involved in dynamically populating a <SELECT> list as part of a form. The entire admin_addrecord1.php script should look something like this (be sure to escape the quotation marks within the echo statement):

```
<?php
    // File name: admin_modrecord1.php
    // Check to see if $PHP_AUTH_USER already contains info
    if (!isset($PHP_AUTH_USER)) {
        // If empty, send header causing dialog box to appear
        header('WWW-Authenticate: Basic realm="XYZ Company Admin Area"');
        header('HTTP/1.0 401 Unauthorized');
        echo 'Authorization Required.';
        exit;
    } else if (isset($PHP_AUTH_USER)) {
        if (($PHP_AUTH_USER != "admin") || ($PHP_AUTH_PW != "abc123")) {
            header('WWW-Authenticate: Basic realm="XYZ Company Admin Area"');
            header('HTTP/1.0 401 Unauthorized');
            echo 'Authorization Required.';
            exit;
        } else {
// create connection
$connection = mysql_connect("localhost","sandman","34Nhjp") or die ("Couldn't
connect to the database.");

// select database
$db = mysql_select_db("secretDB", $connection) or die ("Couldn't select database.);

//SQL statement to select just ISBN and title
$sql = "SELECT ISBN, TITLE FROM MASTER_PRODUCTS ORDER BY TITLE ASC";

// execute SQL query and get result
```

```php
$sql_result = mysql_query($sql,$connection) or die ("Couldn't execute query");

        if (!$sql_result) {
            echo "<P>Couldn't get list!";
        } else {

echo "
<HTML>
<HEAD>
<TITLE>XYZ Company: Modify a Product</TITLE>
</HEAD>
<BODY>
<h1>Select a Product from the XYZ Company Catalog</h1>
<FORM method=\"POST\" action=\"admin_modrecord2.php\">
<table cellspacing=5 cellpadding=5>

<tr>
<td align=right><strong>Product ID/Title:</strong></td>
<td valign=top>
<select name=\"sel_record\">
<option value=\"\"> -- Select an Item -- </option>
";
        while ($row = mysql_fetch_array($sql_result)) {
            $isbn = $row["ISBN"];
            $title = $row["TITLE"];
            echo "
            <option value=\"$isbn\">$isbn : $title</option>
            ";
        }
echo "
</select>
</td>
</tr>

<tr>
<td align=center colspan=2><INPUT type=\"submit\" value=\"Select Product\"></td>
</tr>

</table>
</FORM>
```

```
</BODY>
</HTML>
";
        }
    }
}
?>
```

Place this file on your Web server, and click on the Modify an Existing Product link on the initial administration menu. If you are authorized, you should see the product selection form, shown in Figure 7.8.

The next step will create the PHP script used to display the selected record. The information currently in the database will be used to prepopulate the modification form. The modification form is exactly the same as the addition form, so its structure should be familiar to you.

The action of the form in step one is `admin_modrecord2.php`, so open your text editor and create a file called `admin_modrecord2.php`. Since the product modification form is also part of the administration area, add the basic PHP authentication code you used in previous scripts in this chapter. Add an `if` statement that checks for the one required field: `sel_record`. Obviously, if a record hasn't been selected, you won't get very far with the modification.

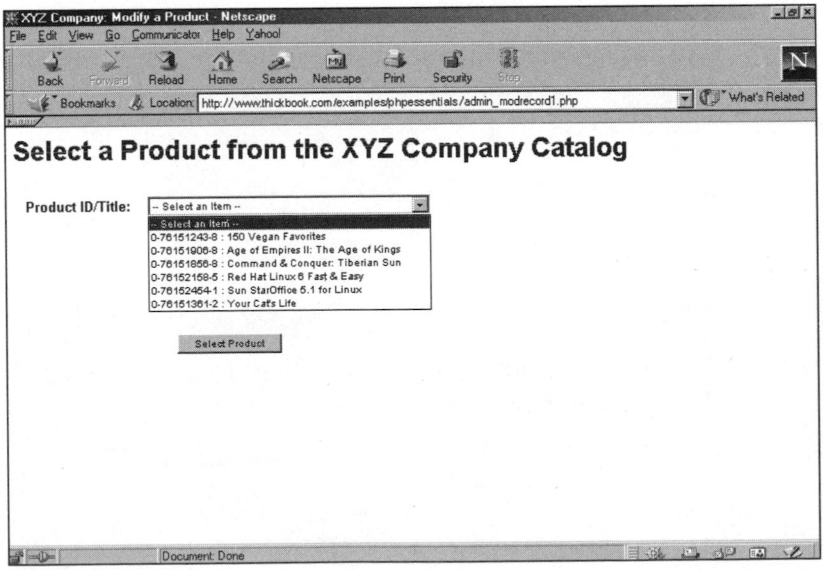

Figure 7.8   *Select the product to modify*

```
if (!$sel_record) {
    header("Location: http://www.yourcompany.com/admin_modrecord1.php");
    exit;
}
```

If your script makes it past the required-field check, the next step is to connect to the database and issue the SQL statement used to retrieve the selected record. The goal is to pull all the information for a record with a matching ISBN, so issue the following SQL statement within your basic connection code:

```
$sql = "SELECT * FROM MASTER_PRODUCTS WHERE ISBN = \"$sel_record\"";
```

Be sure to echo your HTML after your error-checking database connectivity code, as in the previous section:

```
if (!$sql_result) {
    echo "<P>Couldn't get record!";
} else {
    // Display code here
}
```

The code comment "`// Display code here`" will be replaced by a series of variable assignments as well as the HTML used to create the product modification form. Use the `mysql_fetch_array()` function to grab all the data for the selected record, and assign meaningful variable names to the columns in the table:

```
$row = mysql_fetch_array($sql_result);
$isbn = $row["ISBN"];
$title = $row["TITLE"];
$author = $row["AUTHOR"];
$publisher = $row["PUBLISHER"];
$category = $row["CATEGORY"];
$type = $row["TYPE"];
$info_blurb = $row["INFO_BLURB"];
$page_num = $row["PAGE_NUM"];
$price = $row["PRICE"];
```

Now, build the HTML form for modifying the product. Start with the basic headings and form tag, where the action of the form is `admin_modrecord3.php`:

```
echo "
<HTML>
<HEAD>
<TITLE>XYZ Company: Modify a Product</TITLE>
```

```
</HEAD>
<BODY>

<h1>You have selected the following product to modify:</h1>

<FORM method=\"POST\" action=\"admin_modrecord3.php\">
```

In the following table, you will prepopulate all text fields and text areas with their current values by placing the variable such as $isbn or $title inside the tag's value attribute:

```
<table cellspacing=5 cellpadding=5>

<tr>
<td valign=top><strong>ISBN:</strong></td>
<td valign=top><INPUT type=\"text\" name=\"isbn\" value=\"$isbn\" size=35
maxlength=25></td>
</tr>

<tr>
<td valign=top><strong>Title of the Book:</strong></td>
<td valign=top><INPUT type=\"text\" name=\"title\" value=\"$title\" size=35
maxlength=150></td>
</tr>

<tr>
<td valign=top><strong>Author's Name:</strong></td>
<td valign=top><INPUT type=\"text\" name=\"author\" value=\"$author\" size=35
maxlength=75></td>
</tr>
```

Whoa! What about drop-down list boxes? In this example, I'll show you the verbose method of displaying selected elements versus nonselected elements in a drop-down list box—by using an if…else statement for each <OPTION>. ·

Continue the echo statement and include the field title and the opened <SELECT> element, plus the empty <OPTION> element. After the empty <OPTION> element, end the echo statement, because the next chunk of code will be an if…else statement:

```
<tr>
<td valign=top><strong>Publisher:</strong></td>
<td valign=top>
```

```
<SELECT name=\"publisher\">
<OPTION value=\"\">-- Select One --</OPTION>
";
```

Before printing each <OPTION> for Publisher, check the value of the $publisher variable. If the value of the <OPTION> matches the value of $publisher, that option should have an attribute of selected. If the value of the <OPTION> does not match the value of $publisher, do not give it the selected attribute.

```
if ($publisher == "Prima-Tech") {
    echo "<OPTION value=\"Prima-Tech\" selected>Prima-Tech</OPTION>";
} else {
    echo "<OPTION value=\"Prima-Tech\">Prima-Tech</OPTION>";
}


if ($publisher == "Prima Games") {
    echo "<OPTION value=\"Prima Games\" selected>Prima Games</OPTION>";
} else {
    echo "<OPTION value=\"Prima Games\">Prima Games</OPTION>";
}


if ($publisher == "Prima Lifestyles") {
    echo "<OPTION value=\"Prima Lifestyles\" selected>Prima Lifestyles</OPTION>";
} else {
    echo "<OPTION value=\"Prima Lifestyles\">Prima Lifestyles</OPTION>";
}
```

After printing an if...else statement for each <OPTION>, start an echo statement again, to close the required tags and start a new row. Continue to use the if...else sequence for each <SELECT> element in the modification form.

```
echo "
</SELECT>
</td>
</tr>

<tr>
<td valign=top><strong>Category:</strong></td>
<td valign=top>
<SELECT name=\"category\">
<OPTION value=\"\">-- Select One --</OPTION>
```

```
";

if ($category == "Applications") {
    echo "<OPTION value=\"Applications\" selected>Applications</OPTION>";
} else {
    echo "<OPTION value=\"Applications\">Applications</OPTION>";
}

if ($category == "Cooking") {
    echo "<OPTION value=\"Cooking\" selected>Cooking</OPTION>";
} else {
    echo "<OPTION value=\"Cooking\">Cooking</OPTION>";
}

if ($category == "Operating Systems") {
    echo "<OPTION value=\"Operating Systems\" selected>Operating Systems</OPTION>";
} else {
    echo "<OPTION value=\"Operating Systems\">Operating Systems</OPTION>";
}

if ($category == "Pets") {
    echo "<OPTION value=\"Pets\" selected>Pets</OPTION>";
} else {
    echo "<OPTION value=\"Pets\">Pets</OPTION>";
}

if ($category == "Programming") {
    echo "<OPTION value=\"Programming\" selected>Programming</OPTION>";
} else {
    echo "<OPTION value=\"Programming\">Programming</OPTION>";
}

if ($category == "Strategy Guides") {
    echo "<OPTION value=\"Strategy Guides\" selected>Strategy Guides</OPTION>";
} else {
    echo "<OPTION value=\"Strategy Guides\">Strategy Guides</OPTION>";
}

echo "
</SELECT>
```

```
</td>
</tr>

<tr>
<td valign=top><strong>Type:</strong></td>
<td valign=top>
<SELECT name=\"type\">
<OPTION value=\"\">-- Select One --</OPTION>
";

if ($type == "hardcover") {
    echo "<OPTION value=\"hardcover\" selected>hardcover</OPTION>";
} else {
    echo "<OPTION value=\"hardcover\">hardcover</OPTION>";
}

if ($type == "paperback") {
    echo "<OPTION value=\"paperback\" selected>paperback</OPTION>";
} else {
    echo "<OPTION value=\"paperback\">paperback</OPTION>";
}

echo "
</SELECT>
</td>
</tr>
```

> The usage of multiple if…else statements to determine selected elements in a drop-down list box could be eliminated if the <OPTION> elements existed in a separate table. If that were the case, a loop could be constructed to print the proper values. You can find an example of this type of loop in the "Code" section at http://www.thickbook.com/.

Now the form returns to text fields. Remember that when you want to prepopulate a text area, the value goes between the <TEXTAREA></TEXTAREA> tags.

```
<tr>
<td valign=top><strong>Paragraph about this book:</strong></td>
<td valign=top>
<TEXTAREA name=\"info_blurb\" cols=35 rows=5>$info_blurb</TEXTAREA>
```

```
</td>
</tr>
```

Finish creating the table. Don't forget to add a Modify Product submit button and close all necessary HTML tags.

```
<tr>
<td valign=top><strong>Number of Pages:</strong></td>
<td valign=top><INPUT type=\"text\" name=\"page_num\" value=\"$page_num\" size=5
maxlength=5></td>
</tr>

<tr>
<td valign=top><strong>Retail Price:</strong></td>
<td valign=top><INPUT type=\"text\" name=\"price\" value=\"$price\" size=5
maxlength=5></td>
</tr>

<tr>
<td align=center colspan=2><INPUT type=\"submit\" value=\"Modify Product\"></td>
</tr>

</table>
</FORM>
</BODY>
</HTML>
";
```

The entire `admin_modrecord2.php` script should look something like this (be sure to escape the quotation marks within the echo statement):

```php
<?php
    // File name: admin_modrecord2.php
    // Check to see if $PHP_AUTH_USER already contains info
    if (!isset($PHP_AUTH_USER)) {
        // If empty, send header causing dialog box to appear
        header('WWW-Authenticate: Basic realm="XYZ Company Admin Area"');
        header('HTTP/1.0 401 Unauthorized');
        echo 'Authorization Required.';
        exit;
    } else if (isset($PHP_AUTH_USER)) {
        if (($PHP_AUTH_USER != "admin") || ($PHP_AUTH_PW != "abc123")) {
```

```php
        header('WWW-Authenticate: Basic realm="XYZ Company Admin Area"');
        header('HTTP/1.0 401 Unauthorized');
        echo 'Authorization Required.';
        exit;
    } else {
        if (!$sel_record) {
            header("Location: http://www.yourcompany.com/
admin_modrecord1.php");
            exit;
        }
    // create connection
    $connection = mysql_connect("localhost","sandman","34Nhjp") or die
    ("Couldn't connect to the database.");


    // select database
    $db = mysql_select_db("secretDB", $connection) or die
    ("Couldn't select database.);

        // SQL statement to select record
        $sql = "SELECT * FROM MASTER_PRODUCTS WHERE ISBN = \"$sel_record\"";

    // execute SQL query and get result
    $sql_result = mysql_query($sql,$connection) or die
    ("Couldn't execute query");

        if (!$sql_result) {
            echo "<P>Couldn't get record!";
        } else {
            // fetch row and assign meaningful names to variables
            $row = mysql_fetch_array($sql_result);
            $isbn = $row["ISBN"];
            $title = $row["TITLE"];
            $author = $row["AUTHOR"];
            $publisher = $row["PUBLISHER"];
            $category = $row["CATEGORY"];
            $type = $row["TYPE"];
            $info_blurb = $row["INFO_BLURB"];
            $page_num = $row["PAGE_NUM"];
```

```
                $price = $row["PRICE"];

echo "
<HTML>
<HEAD>
<TITLE>XYZ Company: Modify a Product</TITLE>
</HEAD>
<BODY>
<h1>You have selected the following product to modify:</h1>
    <FORM method=\"POST\" action=\"admin_modrecord3.php\">
    <table cellspacing=5 cellpadding=5>

    <tr>
    <td valign=top><strong>ISBN:</strong></td>
    <td valign=top><INPUT type=\"text\" name=\"isbn\" value=\"$isbn\" size=35
maxlength=25></td>
    </tr>

    <tr>
    <td valign=top><strong>Title of the Book:</strong></td>
    <td valign=top><INPUT type=\"text\" name=\"title\" value=\"$title\" size=35
maxlength=150></td>
    </tr>

    <tr>
    <td valign=top><strong>Author's Name:</strong></td>
    <td valign=top><INPUT type=\"text\" name=\"author\" value=\"$author\" size=35
maxlength=75></td>
    </tr>

    <tr>
    <td valign=top><strong>Publisher:</strong></td>
    <td valign=top>
    <SELECT name=\"publisher\">
    <OPTION value=\"\">-- Select One --</OPTION>
    ";

    if ($publisher == "Prima-Tech") {
        echo "<OPTION value=\"Prima-Tech\" selected>Prima-Tech</OPTION>";
```

```php
    } else {
        echo "<OPTION value=\"Prima-Tech\">Prima-Tech</OPTION>";
    }


    if ($publisher == "Prima Games") {
        echo "<OPTION value=\"Prima Games\" selected>Prima Games</OPTION>";
    } else {
        echo "<OPTION value=\"Prima Games\">Prima Games</OPTION>";
    }


    if ($publisher == "Prima Lifestyles") {
        echo "<OPTION value=\"Prima Lifestyles\" selected>Prima Lifestyles</
OPTION>";
    } else {
        echo "<OPTION value=\"Prima Lifestyles\">Prima Lifestyles</OPTION>";
    }

    echo "
    </SELECT>
    </td>
    </tr>

    <tr>
    <td valign=top><strong>Category:</strong></td>
    <td valign=top>
    <SELECT name=\"category\">
    <OPTION value=\"\">-- Select One --</OPTION>
";

    if ($category == "Applications") {
        echo "<OPTION value=\"Applications\" selected>Applications</OPTION>";
    } else {
        echo "<OPTION value=\"Applications\">Applications</OPTION>";
    }


    if ($category == "Cooking") {
        echo "<OPTION value=\"Cooking\" selected>Cooking</OPTION>";
    } else {
        echo "<OPTION value=\"Cooking\">Cooking</OPTION>";
    }
```

```
    if ($category == "Operating Systems") {
        echo "<OPTION value=\"Operating Systems\" selected>Operating Systems</
OPTION>";
    } else {
        echo "<OPTION value=\"Operating Systems\">Operating Systems</OPTION>";
    }

    if ($category == "Pets") {
        echo "<OPTION value=\"Pets\" selected>Pets</OPTION>";
    } else {
        echo "<OPTION value=\"Pets\">Pets</OPTION>";
    }

    if ($category == "Programming") {
        echo "<OPTION value=\"Programming\" selected>Programming</OPTION>";
    } else {
        echo "<OPTION value=\"Programming\">Programming</OPTION>";
    }

    if ($category == "Strategy Guides") {
        echo "<OPTION value=\"Strategy Guides\" selected>Strategy Guides</OPTION>";
    } else {
        echo "<OPTION value=\"Strategy Guides\">Strategy Guides</OPTION>";
    }

    echo "
    </SELECT>
    </td>
    </tr>

    <tr>
    <td valign=top><strong>Type:</strong></td>
    <td valign=top>
    <SELECT name=\"type\">
    <OPTION value=\"\">-- Select One --</OPTION>
    ";

    if ($type == "hardcover") {
        echo "<OPTION value=\"hardcover\" selected>hardcover</OPTION>";
```

```
    } else {
        echo "<OPTION value=\"hardcover\">hardcover</OPTION>";
    }

    if ($type == "paperback") {
        echo "<OPTION value=\"paperback\" selected>paperback</OPTION>";
    } else {
        echo "<OPTION value=\"paperback\">paperback</OPTION>";
    }

    echo "
    </SELECT>
    </td>
    </tr>

    <tr>
    <td valign=top><strong>Paragraph about this book:</strong></td>
    <td valign=top>
    <TEXTAREA name=\"info_blurb\" cols=35 rows=5>$info_blurb</TEXTAREA>
    </td>
    </tr>

    <tr>
    <td valign=top><strong>Number of Pages:</strong></td>
    <td valign=top><INPUT type=\"text\" name=\"page_num\" value=\"$page_num\"
size=5 maxlength=5></td>
    </tr>

    <tr>
    <td valign=top><strong>Retail Price:</strong></td>
    <td valign=top>
<INPUT type=\"text\" name=\"price\" value=\"$price\" size=5 maxlength=5></td>
    </tr>

    <tr>
    <td align=center colspan=2>
    <INPUT type=\"submit\" value=\"Modify Product\"></td>
```

```
      </tr>

      </table>
      </FORM>

</BODY>
</HTML>
";
}
}
}
?>
```

Place this file on your Web server, and choose a product by selecting an option in
`admin_modrecord1.php` and clicking on the Select Product button. The modification form should appear, prepopulating the form fields with the proper data from
your `MASTER_PRODUCTS` table. Figure 7.9 shows an example.

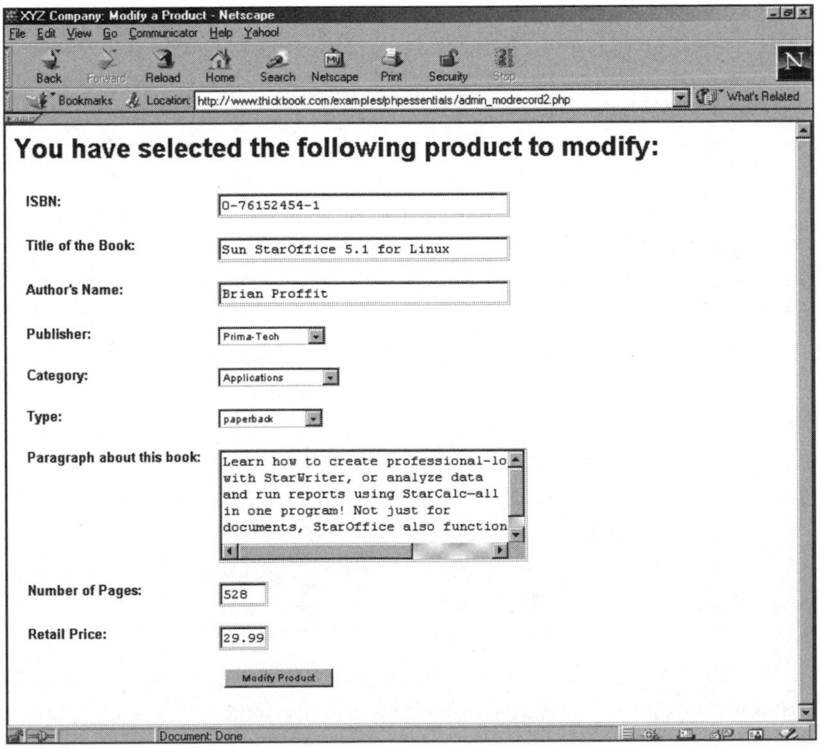

Figure 7.9   *Product information prepopulates the modification form*

The final step in the modification sequence is to update the fields in the table with their new values and return a confirmation to the user. This script, called `admin_modrecord3.php` according to the form action in the previous script, is nearly identical to the `admin_addrecord2.php` script created earlier in this section. Copy `admin_addrecord2.php` to `admin_modrecord3.php` and open it in your text editor. I'll explain the minor changes, and you'll be on your way to the next section.

The first modification is part of the `if` statement that checks required fields. The redirection that occurs if a required value is not present should look something like this:

```
if ((!$isbn) || (!$title) || (!$price)) {
    header("Location: http://www.yourcompany.com/admin_modrecord1.php");
    exit;
}
```

The next difference is in the SQL statement. The Add Product script uses the `INSERT` command. If we used the `INSERT` command in the modification sequence, a second record would be created with the new information. This isn't what we want. We want the original record to be updated with the new information. Use the `UPDATE` command, and `SET` the fields to the new values:

```
$sql = "UPDATE MASTER_PRODUCTS SET ISBN = \"$isbn\", TITLE = \"$title\", AUTHOR =
\"$author\", PUBLISHER = \"$publisher\", CATEGORY = \"$category\", TYPE =
\"$type\", INFO_BLURB = \"$info_blurb\", PAGE_NUM = \"$page_num\", PRICE =
\"$price\" where ISBN = \"$isbn\"";
```

> If one or more of the columns had an attribute of `unique`, you could use the `REPLACE` command, which will `INSERT` a record in place of a record with a matching unique field.

The next change occurs in the error statement when checking for a value of `$sql_result`. A meaningful error in this instance would be

```
if (!$sql_result) {
    echo "<P>Couldn't update record!";
} else {
// continue
}
```

The final differences are purely cosmetic. You'll want the page's title and heading to reflect your actions:

```
<TITLE>XYZ Company: Modify a Product</TITLE>
```

and

```
<h1>You have made the following modifications:</h1>
```

The entire `admin_modrecord3.php` script should look something like this (be sure to escape the quotation marks within the echo statement):

```php
<?php
    // File name: admin_modrecord3.php
    // Check to see if $PHP_AUTH_USER already contains info
    if (!isset($PHP_AUTH_USER)) {
        // If empty, send header causing dialog box to appear
        header('WWW-Authenticate: Basic realm="XYZ Company Admin Area"');
        header('HTTP/1.0 401 Unauthorized');
        echo 'Authorization Required.';
        exit;
    } else if (isset($PHP_AUTH_USER)) {
        if (($PHP_AUTH_USER != "admin") || ($PHP_AUTH_PW != "abc123")) {
            header('WWW-Authenticate: Basic realm="XYZ Company Admin Area"');
            header('HTTP/1.0 401 Unauthorized');
            echo 'Authorization Required.';
            exit;
        } else {
            if ((!$isbn) || (!$title) || (!$price)) {
                header("Location: http://www.yourcompany.com/
admin_modrecord1.php");
                exit;
            }
        // create connection
        $connection = mysql_connect("localhost","sandman","34Nhjp") or die
("Couldn't connect to the database.");

        // select database
        $db = mysql_select_db("secretDB", $connection) or die
("Couldn't select database.");

            // SQL to update record
```

```
            $sql = "UPDATE MASTER_PRODUCTS SET ISBN = \"$isbn\", TITLE =
\"$title\", AUTHOR = \"$author\", PUBLISHER = \"$publisher\", CATEGORY =
\"$category\", TYPE = \"$type\", INFO_BLURB = \"$info_blurb\", PAGE_NUM =
\"$page_num\", PRICE = \"$price\" where ISBN = \"$isbn\"";

        // execute SQL query and get result
        $sql_result = mysql_query($sql,$connection) or die
        ("Couldn't execute query");

            if (!$sql_result) {
                echo "<P>Couldn't update record!";

            } else {
echo "

<HTML>
<HEAD>
<TITLE>XYZ Company: Modify a Product</TITLE>
</HEAD>
<BODY>
<h1>You have made the following modifications:</h1>
    <table cellspacing=5 cellpadding=5>

    <tr>
    <td valign=top><strong>ISBN:</strong></td>
    <td valign=top>$isbn</td>
    </tr>

    <tr>
    <td valign=top><strong>Title of the Book:</strong></td>
    <td valign=top>$title</td>
    </tr>

    <tr>
    <td valign=top><strong>Author's Name:</strong></td>
    <td valign=top>$author</td>
    </tr>

    <tr>
    <td valign=top><strong>Publisher:</strong></td>
```

```
        <td valign=top>$publisher</td>
        </tr>

        <tr>
        <td valign=top><strong>Category:</strong></td>
        <td valign=top>$category</td>
        </tr>

        <tr>
        <td valign=top><strong>Type:</strong></td>
        <td valign=top>$type</td>
        </tr>

        <tr>
        <td valign=top><strong>Paragraph about this book:</strong></td>
        <td valign=top>$info_blurb</td>
        </tr>

        <tr>
        <td valign=top><strong>Number of Pages:</strong></td>
        <td valign=top>$page_num</td>
        </tr>

        <tr>
        <td valign=top><strong>Retail Price:</strong></td>
        <td valign=top>$price</td>
        </tr>
        </table>
        <p align=center><a href=\"admin_menu.php\">Return to Menu</a></p>
</BODY>
</HTML>
";
}
}
}
?>
```

Place this file on your Web server, and go back to the form at http://
www.yourserver.com/admin_modrecord1.php. Select a product to modify, and make
some changes to its record. If successful, you should see a verification screen such
as the one shown in Figure 7.10.

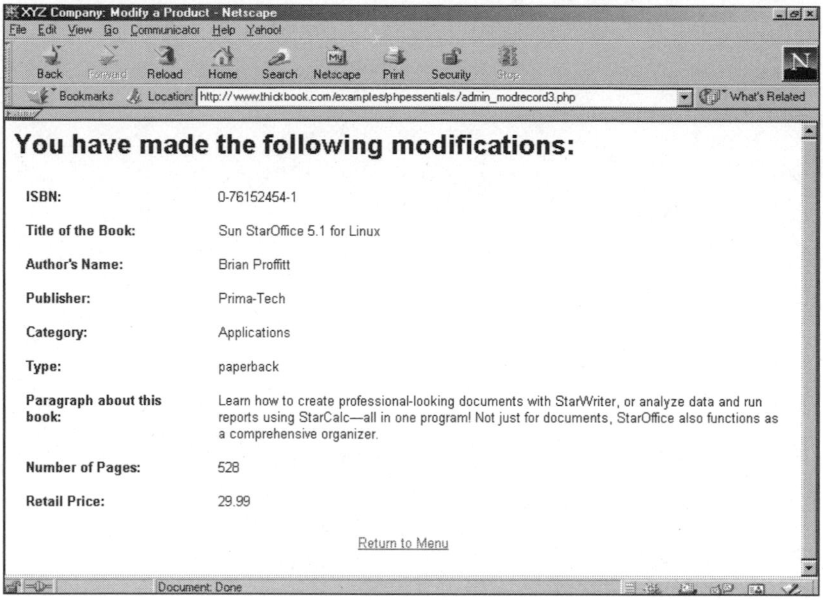

Figure 7.10   *Verification of product modifications*

Use this sequence of forms to modify any records you need to change in the MASTER_PRODUCTS table. The next section shows you the final step in the product administration menu: deleting a record.

Deleting Records from the Product Catalog

During the course of business, products are inevitably discontinued for one reason or another. A good administration menu will account for this by offering a Delete Product option. The following three-step sequence gives you that option in your administration menu.

The first step is to select a product for deletion, using virtually the same code you used to select a product for modification. Copy admin_modrecord1.php to admin_delrecord1.php, and open it in your text editor. I'll explain the minor changes, and you'll be on your way to the next section.

The only changes are in the HTML used to display the form. Change the title to

```
<TITLE>XYZ Company: Delete a Product</TITLE>
```

and change the form action to

```
<FORM method=\"POST\" action=\"admin_delrecord2.php\">
```

Those are the only changes, so the entire code should look something like this (be sure to escape the quotation marks within the echo statement):

```php
<?php
    // File name: admin_delrecord1.php
    // Check to see if $PHP_AUTH_USER already contains info
    if (!isset($PHP_AUTH_USER)) {
        // If empty, send header causing dialog box to appear
        header('WWW-Authenticate: Basic realm="XYZ Company Admin Area"');
        header('HTTP/1.0 401 Unauthorized');
        echo 'Authorization Required.';
        exit;
    } else if (isset($PHP_AUTH_USER)) {
        if (($PHP_AUTH_USER != "admin") || ($PHP_AUTH_PW != "abc123")) {
            header('WWW-Authenticate: Basic realm="XYZ Company Admin Area"');
            header('HTTP/1.0 401 Unauthorized');
            echo 'Authorization Required.';
            exit;
        } else {

        // create connection
        $connection = mysql_connect("localhost","sandman","34Nhjp") or die
        ("Couldn't connect to the database.");

        // select database
        $db = mysql_select_db("secretDB", $connection) or die
        ("Couldn't select database.);

        // SQL statement to select data
        $sql = "SELECT ISBN, TITLE FROM MASTER_PRODUCTS ORDER BY TITLE ASC";

        // execute SQL query and get result
        $sql_result = mysql_query($sql,$connection) or die
        ("Couldn't execute query");

        if (!$sql_result) {
            echo "<P>Couldn't get list!";
        } else {
echo "
<HTML>
<HEAD>
```

```
<TITLE>XYZ Company: Delete a Product</TITLE>
</HEAD>
<BODY>
<h1>Select a Product from the XYZ Company Catalog</h1>
<FORM method=\"POST\" action=\"admin_delrecord2.php\">
<table cellspacing=5 cellpadding=5>

<tr>
<td align=right><strong>Product ID/Title:</strong></td>
<td valign=top>

<select name=\"sel_record\">
<option value=\"\"> -- Select an Item -- </option>
";
        while ($row = mysql_fetch_array($sql_result)) {
            $isbn = $row["ISBN"];
            $title = $row["TITLE"];
            echo "
            <option value=\"$isbn\">$isbn : $title</option>
            ";
        }
echo "
</select>
</td>
</tr>

<tr>
<td align=center colspan=2><INPUT type=\"submit\" value=\"Select Product\"></td>
</tr>

</table>
</FORM>
</BODY>
</HTML>
";
        }
    }
}
?>
```

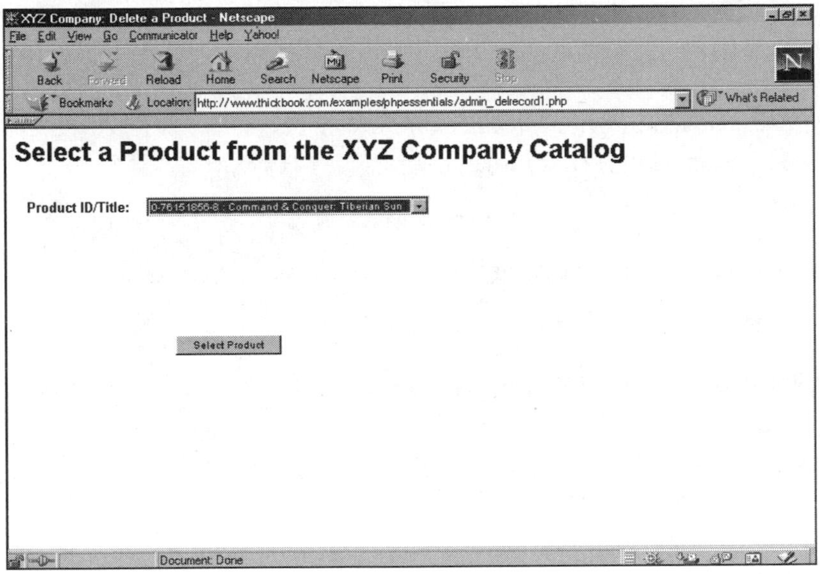

Figure 7.11   *Select a product to delete*

Place this file on your Web server, and click on the Delete an Existing Product link on the initial administration menu. If you are authorized, you should see the product selection form shown in Figure 7.11.

The next step displays the entire selected record as a confirmation before acting on a `delete` command. The script, `admin_delrecord2.php`, is very similar to `admin_modrecord2.php`, in that it selects the contents of the record and displays them to the user. The difference lies in the fact that the information does not prepopulate a form. Instead, it just displays it on the screen.

Copy `admin_modrecord2.php` to `admin_delrecord2.php`, and open it in your text editor. The first modification is part of the `if` statement that checks required fields. The redirection that occurs if a required value is not present should be something like this:

```
if (!$sel_record) {
    header("Location: http://www.yourcompany.com/admin_delrecord1.php");
    exit;
}
```

The next changes are in the HTML. Change the title to

```
<TITLE>XYZ Company: Delete a Product</TITLE>
```

and the heading to

```
<h1>Do you wish to delete this product?</h1>
```

Open a form with an action of `admin_delrecord3.php`. The `admin_delrecord3.php` script will issue the actual `DELETE` command.

```
<FORM method=\"POST\" action=\"admin_delrecord3.php\">
```

Add a hidden field to identify the record to be deleted:

```
<input type=\"hidden\" name=\"sel_record\" value=\"$isbn\">
```

Finally, add a form submission button:

```
<tr>
<td align=center colspan=2><INPUT type=\"submit\" value=\"Yes, Delete this
Product!\"></td>
</tr>
```

The entire code for `admin_delrecord2.php` should look something like this (be sure to escape the quotation marks within the echo statement):

```php
<?php
    // File name: admin_delrecord2.php
    // Check to see if $PHP_AUTH_USER already contains info
    if (!isset($PHP_AUTH_USER)) {
        // If empty, send header causing dialog box to appear
        header('WWW-Authenticate: Basic realm="XYZ Company Admin Area"');
        header('HTTP/1.0 401 Unauthorized');
        echo 'Authorization Required.';
        exit;
    } else if (isset($PHP_AUTH_USER)) {
        if (($PHP_AUTH_USER != "admin") || ($PHP_AUTH_PW != "abc123")) {

            header('WWW-Authenticate: Basic realm="XYZ Company Admin Area"');
            header('HTTP/1.0 401 Unauthorized');
            echo 'Authorization Required.';
            exit;
        } else {
            if (!$sel_record) {
                header("Location: http://www.yourcompany.com/
admin_delrecord1.php");
                exit;
```

```
            }

        // create connection
        $connection = mysql_connect("localhost","sandman","34Nhjp") or die
        ("Couldn't connect to the database.");

        // select database
        $db = mysql_select_db("secretDB", $connection) or die
        ("Couldn't select database.);

        // SQL statement to retrieve record
        $sql = "SELECT * FROM MASTER_PRODUCTS WHERE ISBN = \"$sel_record\"";

        // execute SQL query and get result
        $sql_result = mysql_query($sql,$connection) or die
        ("Couldn't execute query");

            if (!$sql_result) {
                echo "<P>Couldn't get record!";
            } else {
            // fetch row and assign meaningful names to variables
            $row = mysql_fetch_array($sql_result);
            $isbn = $row["ISBN"];
            $title = $row["TITLE"];
            $author = $row["AUTHOR"];
            $publisher = $row["PUBLISHER"];
            $category = $row["CATEGORY"];
            $type = $row["TYPE"];
            $info_blurb = $row["INFO_BLURB"];
            $page_num = $row["PAGE_NUM"];
            $price = $row["PRICE"];
echo "
<HTML>
<HEAD>
<TITLE>XYZ Company: Delete a Product</TITLE>
</HEAD>
<BODY>
<h1>Do you wish to delete this product?</h1>
    <FORM method=\"POST\" action=\"admin_delrecord3.php\">
```

```
<input type=\"hidden\" name=\"sel_record\" value=\"$isbn\">

<table cellspacing=5 cellpadding=5>

<tr>
<td valign=top><strong>ISBN:</strong></td>
<td valign=top>$isbn</td>
</tr>

<tr>
<td valign=top><strong>Title of the Book:</strong></td>
<td valign=top>$title</td>
</tr>

<tr>
<td valign=top><strong>Author's Name:</strong></td>
<td valign=top>$author</td>
</tr>

<tr>
<td valign=top><strong>Publisher:</strong></td>
<td valign=top>$publisher</td>
</tr>

<tr>
<td valign=top><strong>Category:</strong></td>
<td valign=top>$category</td>
</tr>

<tr>
<td valign=top><strong>Type:</strong></td>
<td valign=top>$type</td>
</tr>

<tr>
<td valign=top><strong>Paragraph about this book:</strong></td>
<td valign=top>$info_blurb</td>
</tr>

<tr>
```

```
        <td valign=top><strong>Number of Pages:</strong></td>
        <td valign=top>$page_num</td>
        </tr>

        <tr>
        <td valign=top><strong>Retail Price:</strong></td>
        <td valign=top>$price</td>
        </tr>

        <tr>
        <td align=center colspan=2><INPUT type=\"submit\" value=\"Yes, Delete this
Product!\"></td>
        </tr>

        </table>
        </FORM>

</BODY>
</HTML>
";
}
}
}
?>
```

Place this file on your Web server, and choose a product by selecting an option in
`admin_delrecord1.php` and clicking on the Select Product button. The confirmation should appear, as shown in Figure 7.12.

The final step in the deletion sequence is to actually issue the DELETE command and
return a confirmation to the user. This script, called `admin_delrecord3.php` according
to the form action in the previous script, is nearly identical to the previous step. The
only difference lies in the SQL statement and the HTML displayed on the screen.

Copy `admin_delrecord1.php` to `admin_delrecord3.php`, and open it in your text editor. The first modification is the SQL statement. Instead of using the SELECT
command, you'll DELETE:

```
$sql = "DELETE FROM MASTER_PRODUCTS WHERE ISBN = \"$sel_record\"";
```

The next change occurs in the error statement, when checking for a value of
`$sql_result`. A meaningful error in this instance would be

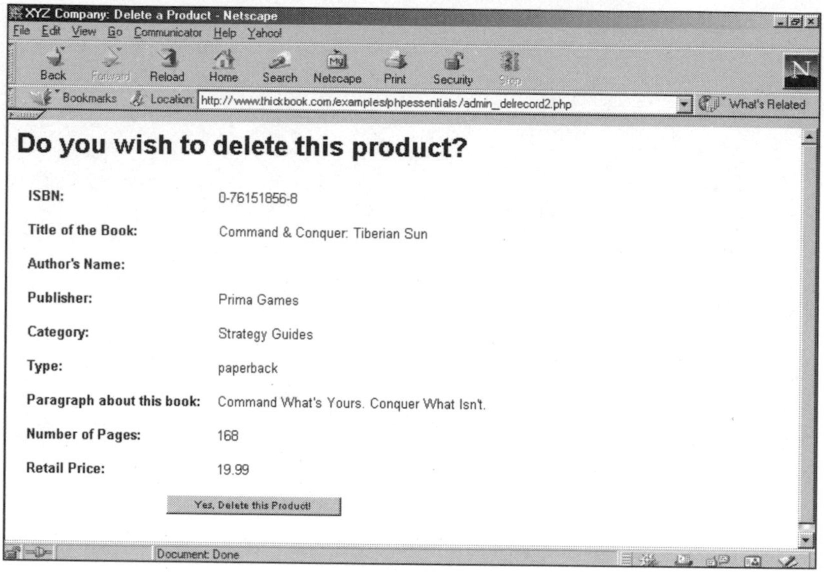

Figure 7.12   *Display product information to verify deletion*

```
if (!$sql_result) {
    echo "<P>Couldn't update record!";
} else {
// continue
}
```

The final difference is the confirmation that's returned to the user. Change the heading to something like this:

```
<h1>You have deleted ISBN $sel_record from the XYZ Product Catalog</h1>
```

Those are the only changes, so the entire code should look something like this (be sure to escape the quotation marks within the echo statement):

```
<?php
    // File name: admin_delrecord3.php
    // Check to see if $PHP_AUTH_USER already contains info
    if (!isset($PHP_AUTH_USER)) {
        // If empty, send header causing dialog box to appear
        header('WWW-Authenticate: Basic realm="XYZ Company Admin Area"');
        header('HTTP/1.0 401 Unauthorized');
        echo 'Authorization Required.';
        exit;
    } else if (isset($PHP_AUTH_USER)) {
        if (($PHP_AUTH_USER != "admin") || ($PHP_AUTH_PW != "abc123")) {
            header('WWW-Authenticate: Basic realm="XYZ Company Admin Area"');
```

```
                header('HTTP/1.0 401 Unauthorized');
                echo 'Authorization Required.';
                exit;
          } else {
                if (!$sel_record) {
                    header("Location: http://www.yourcompany.com/
admin_delrecord1.php");
                    exit;
                }

// create connection
$connection = mysql_connect("localhost","sandman","34Nhjp") or die ("Couldn't
connect to the database.");

// select database
$db = mysql_select_db("secretDB", $connection) or die ("Couldn't select database.);

                //SQL statement to delete record
                $sql = "DELETE FROM MASTER_PRODUCTS WHERE ISBN = \"$sel_record\"";

// execute SQL query and get result
$sql_result = mysql_query($sql,$connection) or die ("Couldn't execute query");

                if (!$sql_result) {
                    echo "<P>Couldn't delete record!";
                } else {
echo "
<HTML>
<HEAD>
<TITLE>XYZ Company: Delete a Product</TITLE>
</HEAD>
<BODY>
<h1>You have deleted ISBN $sel_record from the XYZ Product Catalog</h1>

</BODY>
</HTML>
";
}
}
}
?>
```

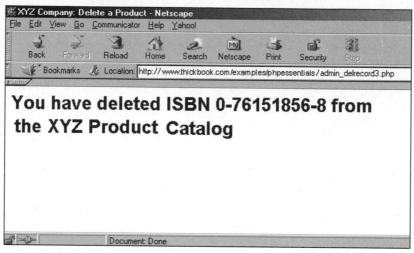

Figure 7.13   *Deletion confirmed!*

Place this file on your Web server, and go back to the form at http://www.yourserver.com/admin_delrecord1.php. Select a product to delete, and confirm your action. You should see a result screen such as the one shown in Figure 7.13.

Whew! You now have the ability to perform basic administration tasks within a product catalog. The next chapter takes the product catalog and creates a functioning e-commerce Web site out of it.

Chapter 8: Advanced PHP Techniques: e-Commerce

Data Encryption, or Safe and Secure Shopping

Creating a Shopping System

More Advanced Techniques

The previous chapter showed you how to build the product catalog of an online store. In this chapter, you'll finish putting together the pieces, and by the time you're through, you will have created a fully-functioning online store.

Data Encryption, or Safe and Secure Shopping

It would be a very bad idea to develop an insecure shopping mechanism. No matter how large or small your site might be, if it's insecure, it's open season for crackers. The legal liability aspects differ from country to country, but without a doubt, the bulk of the responsibility lies with you, the site designer, to develop a safe and secure application. Unless you are doing real-time credit card processing and never store credit card data on your system, you must utilize some sort of data encryption so that sensitive information safely finds its way to the recipient.

The majority of small-to-midsize e-commerce applications do not utilize real-time payment processing. Usually, the customer completes an order form on a secure server and an encrypted e-mail is sent to a designated customer service representative. The representative uses software to decrypt the e-mail message, from that point handling the order based on the company's internal procedures. Usually, the customer's credit card is charged and the customer is notified via e-mail that the order was placed, when it will be shipped, and so forth.

This type of e-commerce solution is not difficult to implement. Besides purchasing an SSL (secure socket layer) certificate for your server, which encrypts data between a Web browser and your Web server, you are left with only the problem of encrypting the e-mail that is sent to the customer service representative. As you'll learn in the next sections, two common types of encryption software are available, both of which work perfectly well in a PHP-based e-commerce application.

A Brief Glance at Data Encryption

Author Neal Stephenson wrote an amazing novel called *Cryptonomicon*, which manages to tell a good story while giving an incredible amount of insight into modern cryptography. The book is over 900 pages long, so you can see I'm not kidding when I say this section is a brief glance at data encryption.

For the purpose of understanding how you can easily encrypt and decrypt data (files, e-mail, and so on), I'll tell you about public-key cryptography. Feel free to visit crypto Web sites to learn about other cryptosystems and determine if other methods will be of use to you. A good place to start is the RSA Labs Crypto FAQ, found at http://www.rsasecurity.com/rsalabs/faq/.

When using public-key cryptography, a user has a pair of keys: public and private. As their names suggest, the private key is kept private, and the public key is distributed to other users. The public and private keys of a particular user are linked via complex mathematical structures in a way that is beyond my comprehension but that is crucial to establishing the key relationship. The public key is used as the basis for encrypting a message, and the private key is necessary for the recipient to decrypt the encrypted message.

For example, suppose that Joe User has a pair of keys. Jane User also has a pair of keys. Joe and Jane want to send encrypted messages to each other, so they exchange public keys. Keys are kept on key rings—one for private keys and one for public keys—which are essentially files containing key information, just like a real key ring is an object that holds your car, house, and other keys together. On Joe's public key ring, he has Jane's public key. On Jane's public key ring, she has Joe's public key. Both Joe and Jane also have private key rings that hold only their own private keys.

When Joe wants to send an encrypted message to Jane, he uses his encryption software to scramble the message based on Jane's public key. Jane receives the message and uses her encryption software to decrypt the message with her secret decoder ring—I mean, her private key. Only Jane can decrypt a message that has been encrypted using her public key.

In the early 1990s, Phil Zimmerman developed PGP, or Pretty Good Privacy, which quickly became a very popular piece of software for e-mail and file encryption. However, due to United States export regulations and the import regulations of other countries with regards to encryption algorithms, the OpenPGP standard was developed, and the GNUPG software was built around it. Unlike PGP software, GNUPG does not use patented or restricted encryption algorithms, so it has become a popular alternative to PGP.

Although U.S. export laws were recently modified, both PGP and GNUPG will likely continue to coexist in the developer community. After determining which encryption software you want to use, follow the steps outlined in either of the following sections to learn how to encrypt and send e-mail to specific recipients.

Using PGP

If you decide to use the PGP family of software, there are two parts to the puzzle: PGP on your Web server (to encrypt) and PGP on the recipient's machine (to decrypt). The best place to start is http://www.pgp.com, where you can follow the links to either download for free or purchase the pieces of the PGP puzzle. If you're using PGP for noncommercial purposes, it's free. If you're using PGP for commercial purposes, you must pay for it.

Most ISPs have PGP installed on their Web servers, and you may very well have access to it for the encryption side of the equation. Be sure to check with your system administrator about the availability of PGP and how to add keys to the PHP user's key ring if you do not have direct control over the server.

The next sections assume that you have followed the installation and key-creation procedures outlined in the PGP documentation, and that you have created a valid public key for the person who is to receive the encrypted data.

Adding a Public Key to the Key Ring

After PGP has been installed on the server and on the recipient's machine, and the necessary key pair for the recipient has been created, that recipient's public key must be added to the PHP user's public key ring. If PHP runs as user "www" on your Web server, that's the user whose key ring must contain the recipient's public key. The following steps add a public key to a user's key ring:

1. Export an ASCII version of a user's public key, following the steps in the PGP documentation.

2. Upload the public key text file to the PHP user's directory on the server (`/home/www/`, for example).

3. Log in to your Web server via telnet or SSH, or walk over to it and type at the keyboard if you are so lucky.

4. Become the PHP user. This might involve the `su` command, such as `su www`.

5. Add the key to the key ring: `pgpk -a /path/to/keyfile`

   You will see a confirmation that the key was added to your key ring. At this point, you can delete the text file containing the public key.

6. Assign a trust level to the key: `pgpk -e [keyname]`

7. Select `always trust`.

8. Test this process by creating an input file containing something unimportant, such as the line "I want to test this encryption sequence."

9. Manually issue the command to encrypt the test file: `pgpe -r [keyname] -o [output file] -a [input file]`

10. When prompted to trust the key file, answer `Y`.

11. The output file will contain the encrypted version of the text in the input file.

If you've made it through these steps, you're ready to encrypt data with PGP, using your PHP scripts to issue the commands. If you're stuck on any of these steps, or if you don't have access to the PHP user's key ring, contact your system administrator.

Encrypting Data with PGP

Before you encrypt any data, you must figure out where the data will come from. In this example, we'll create an HTML form to accept data, and the PHP script will encrypt and e-mail the results to a specified recipient.

> The recipient's public key must already be on the PHP user's key ring.

NOTE

To begin, open your favorite text editor, create a file called `secret_form.html`, and set up an HTML "shell":

```
<!DOCTYPE HTML PUBLIC "-//W3C//DTD HTML 3.2//EN">
<HTML>
<HEAD>
<TITLE>Secret Form</TITLE>
</HEAD>
<BODY>
    <!-- your HTML form will go here -->
</BODY>
</HTML>
```

Give the page a heading so that you know what you're doing:

```
<h1>Form to Send Secret Stuff</h1>
```

To create the form code, assume that step two in the sequence will be a PHP script called `do_sendsecret.php` and that your form will use the `POST` method:

```
<FORM method="POST" action="do_sendsecret.php">
```

Next, create two text fields and a text area to capture the message:

```
<p>Your Name:<br>
<INPUT type="text" name="sender_name" size=25>
```

```
</p>
<p>Your E-Mail Address:<br>
<INPUT type="text" name="sender_email" size=25>
</p>
<p>The Secret Message:<br>
<TEXTAREA name="secret_msg" cols=35 rows=5></TEXTAREA>
</p>
```

Finally, add the Send Secret Message button:

```
<p>
<INPUT type="submit" value="Send Secret Message">
</p>
```

Don't forget the closing `</FORM>` tag!

Your HTML source code should look something like this:

```
<HTML>
<HEAD>
<TITLE>Secret Form</TITLE>
</HEAD>
<BODY>

<h1>Form to Send Secret Stuff</h1>
<FORM method="POST" action="do_sendsecret.php">
<p>Your Name:<br>
<INPUT type="text" name="sender_name" size=25>
</p>
<p>Your E-Mail Address:<br>
<INPUT type="text" name="sender_email" size=25>
</p>
<p>The Secret Message:<br>
<TEXTAREA name="secret_msg" cols=35 rows=5></TEXTAREA>
</p>

<p>
<INPUT type="submit" value="Send Secret Message">
</p>
</BODY>
</HTML>
</FORM>
```

Here's a very important point to remember: Unless your form is located on a secure server (a Web server with an SSL certificate), the information transmitted from the form in the user's Web browser to the script on your Web server is insecure, since there's no encryption going on. Bear that in mind when you need to create forms that send credit card information rather than "secret messages."

Now that your form is ready to go, open your text editor and create a file called `do_sendsecret.php`. Before anything else in the script, place the plain-text contents of the form submission into a variable called `$msg`:

```
<?php
$msg = "Sender's Full Name:\t$sender_name\n";
$msg .= "Sender's E-Mail:\t$sender_email\n";
$msg .= "Secret Message?\t$secret_msg\n\n";
```

Next, set the `PGPPATH` environment variable so that the form uses the proper key ring. This value of `PGPPATH` should be the directory containing the PHP user's key ring:

```
putenv("PGPPATH=/homedir/of/PHP/user/.pgp");
```

The next step creates a temporary file on your Web server and writes the contents of the form submission to this new file. The PHP user must have write permissions in this directory. After the contents of `$msg` are written to the file, the file is closed.

```
$fp = fopen("/path/to/temp/input/data", "w+");
fputs($fp, $msg);
fclose($fp);
```

> If you think users will send encrypted mail via a form concurrently, you should assign a unique file name to the input and output data files. Examples include using the `time()` function to get a long integer, or using a user ID or session variable kept in a cookie. If you don't use unique file names, and if two users access the PHP script at exactly the same time, one file will overwrite the other.

At this point, you're ready to encrypt the data you just placed in the temporary file. This example uses the `system()` function to invoke the PGP program on your Web server. If you are unsure of its location, contact your system administrator.

To encrypt the contents of a file, PGP needs a user ID (corresponding to a public key on the key ring), an input file, and a path and file name for the output file. The following example encrypts the file using the key for `Julie Meloni <julie@thickbook.com>`, which is on a key ring on my server. Substitute the ID of a key on your server.

```
system("/usr/local/bin/pgpe -r 'Julie Meloni <julie@thickbook.com>' -o /path/to/
temp/output/data -a /path/to/temp/input/data");
```

This command should output a file containing an encrypted message. Now, use the `unlink()` function to remove the original plain-text file:

```
unlink("/path/to/temp/input/data");
```

The next step is to place the contents of the output file in a variable, which will be used later to populate the e-mail message you'll be sending to the target recipient.

Assign the value of the encrypted data path to a variable called `$crypted`:

```
$crypted = "/path/to/temp/output/data";
```

Open the encrypted file for reading, and read the entire contents of the file to a variable called `$mail_cont`. Close the file when finished reading:

```
$fd = fopen($crypted, "r");
$mail_cont = fread($fd, filesize($crypted));
fclose($fd);
```

Remove the encrypted file from the system:

```
unlink("$crypted");
```

Finally, create the remainder of the e-mail and send it to the target recipient:

```
$recipient = "julie@thickbook.com";
$subject = "Secret Message";

$mailheaders = "From: My Web Site\n";
$mailheaders .= "Reply-To: $sender_email\n\n";

mail("$recipient", "$subject", $mail_cont, $mailheaders);
```

After your mail is sent, return a confirmation to the user by adding a few echo statements. You can even include the sender's name, since you have access to the variable `$sender_name`:

```
echo "<H1 align=center>Thank You, $sender_name</h1>";
echo "<p align=center>Your secret message has been sent.</p>";
```

Your entire PHP script should look something like this:

```
<?php
// build the message string
$msg = "Sender's Full Name:\t$sender_name\n";
```

```
$msg .= "Sender's E-Mail:\t$sender_email\n";
$msg .= "Secret Message?\t$secret_msg\n\n";

// set the environment variable for PGPPATH
putenv("PGPPATH=/homedir/of/PHP/user/.pgp");

// Create a file for writing temporary data.
// Put contents of message string into the file
// created above, then close the file.
$fp = fopen("/path/to/temp/input/data", "w+");
fputs($fp, $msg);
fclose($fp);

// Invoke PGP to encrypt data and output to new file.
system("/usr/local/bin/pgpe -r 'Julie Meloni <julie@thickbook.com>' -o /path/to/
temp/output/data -a /path/to/temp/input/data");

// remove unencrypted file from system
unlink("/path/to/temp/input/data");

// Assign the value of the encrypted data path to a
// variable called $crypted.
$crypted = "/path/to/temp/output/data";

// Open encrypted file for reading, put entire
// contents of encrypted file into variable
// called $mail_cont, then close file.
$fd = fopen($crypted, "r");
$mail_cont = fread($fd, filesize($crypted));
fclose($fd);

// Remove encrypted file from system.
unlink("$crypted");

// Build mail message and send it to target recipient.
$recipient = "julie@thickbook.com";
$subject = "Secret Message";

$mailheaders = "From: My Web Site\n";
```

```
$mailheaders .= "Reply-To: $sender_email\n\n";

mail("$recipient", "$subject", $mail_cont, $mailheaders);

// Print confirmation to screen.
echo "<H1 align=center>Thank You, $sender_name</h1>";
echo "<p align=center>Your secret message has been sent.</p>";
?>
```

After the form is sent, the target recipient should receive an e-mail that looks something like this:

> ----BEGIN PGP MESSAGE----
>
> Version: PGP for Personal Privacy 5.0
>
> MessageID: ruVxzGiwNH9hJMbhAt5mEfUmWtozI3/4
>
> qANQR1DBwk4DJoa8eforpr0QDAC2QHWlBYRTGKepMDcFXqyO1vrXlTh1p7yB0Wo4
>
> lqYoZ9FippFCJddmLbZkvBRpEBceODLg+gEf5hrtXl3b5NO7Q6xUyMiPnF/71M9v
>
> hdUvhJD/2gPnVZmq5qm0HhrjYLwQv9/2+z3sRN70NqohaWMjMR7kTcCAus/eZGS0
>
> 7ZWbyWc8x1c6qWU8EyDIw1nqfF62s4WTixx6BCve5m0A4xUXHncWZhDLvC/a47x5
>
> C6oX5C7Dv+KpyROl++1aPOfFfZ+38fEZC5+E4IgPVYvxyLRVgDoeJbZ7QlDyxkVh
>
> 6Qe/bTI9CpP5kAb6uxCywgpaecj6P8ABg4ONR6xu0uYC1lG9UhNg5a/KzNyJNpTe
>
> SYPx+1jS1q5285v3kF4ptDFQdLML/i4LTx9oE68WksAzVaqBE/zVRmGQaaczf+gx
>
> fWjQZGbU4l11TImfpO16vZ21CkbobD6AZOaG0B3a1df4GqQwIK3Jf+hWWnXNQ514
>
> DUWzW5puY6VHiEb60cztvds0/KsHNVZUAQ4VYm4R+Ahyb0M44MS4UpzILbH3HbV9
>
> GpvfxeIZ/aUNOOSpJjhn8hzjEALZP1habVZKFJV6sVRtnCadoSV2gSQNQg0kfEY1
>
> vxmbvxBAQRDga6CS8oHaFb45LJo2gVlLhiShDdp2eDR8X4KtUA6MdtO66w56qAy0
>
> UWNKKwsqv0UP3jMHvQl1eb0rHWayxMmSfYw69zo56CjnUWNJN6Rh0y1g54Bl0afA
>
> bt2D7FkQwGNPSm7e5HGcMVLocQ/XV5NTUOmX+s2DqvFT4h9/bAoBkxmR8hf2C7el
>
> v8AJ4Ya/6D139cogzfDQtCy4Bo07vqz79lXfQYSGmk5f2c4LqvtKPhmDAWmSgUsW
>
> ----END PGP MESSAGE----

The recipient will then be able to decrypt the message using the PGP tools installed on his or her machine. If you don't want to pay to use PGP encryption, or if you are in a country to which PGP cannot be exported, you can use the open source GNUPG software, detailed in the next section.

Using GNUPG

If you decide to use the open source GNUPG software, there are two parts to the puzzle: GNUPG on your Web server (to encrypt) and GNUPG on the recipient's machine (to decrypt). The best place to start is http://www.gnupg.org/, where you can follow the links to download the proper version based on your operating system.

The next sections assume that you have followed the installation and key-creation procedures outlined in the GNUPG documentation and have created a valid public key for the person who is to receive the encrypted data.

Adding a Public Key to the Key Ring

After GNUPG has been installed on the server and on the recipient's machine, and the necessary key pair for the recipient has been created, that recipient's public key must be added to the PHP user's public key ring. If PHP runs as user "www" on your Web server, that's the user whose key ring must contain the recipient's public key. The following steps add a public key to a user's key ring:

1. Export an ASCII version of a user's public key, following the steps in the GNUPG documentation.

2. Upload the public key text file to the PHP user's directory on the server (`/home/www/`, for example).

3. Log in to your Web server via telnet or SSH, or walk over to it and type at the keyboard if you are so lucky.

4. Become the PHP user. This might involve the `su` command, such as `su www`.

5. Add the key to the key ring: `gpg --import /path/to/keyfile`

   You will see a confirmation that the key was added to your key ring. At this point, you can delete the text file containing the public key.

6. Edit the key to assign a trust level: `gpg --edit-key [keyname]`

7. At the `gpg` command prompt, type `trust`.

8. Select `I trust fully`.

If you've made it through these steps, you're ready to encrypt data with GNUPG, using your PHP scripts to issue the commands. If you're stuck on any of these steps, or if you don't have access to the PHP user's key ring, contact your system administrator.

Encrypting Data with GNUPG

Before you encrypt any data, you must figure out where the data will come from. In this example, we'll create an HTML form to accept data, and the PHP script will encrypt and e-mail the results to a specified recipient.

> The recipient's public key must already be on the PHP user's key ring.

To begin, open your favorite text editor, create a file called `secret_form.html`, and set up an HTML "shell":

```
<!DOCTYPE HTML PUBLIC "-//W3C//DTD HTML 3.2//EN">
<HTML>
<HEAD>
<TITLE>Secret Form</TITLE>
</HEAD>
<BODY>
     <!-- your HTML form will go here -->
</BODY>
</HTML>
```

Give the page a heading so that you know what you're doing:

```
<h1>Form to Send Secret Stuff</h1>
```

To create the form code, assume that step two in the sequence will be a PHP script called `do_sendsecret.php` and that your form will use the POST method:

```
<FORM method="POST" action="do_sendsecret.php">
```

Next, create two text fields and a text area to capture the message.

```
<p>Your Name:<br>
<INPUT type="text" name="sender_name" size=25>
</p>
<p>Your E-Mail Address:<br>
<INPUT type="text" name="sender_email" size=25>
</p>
<p>The Secret Message:<br>
<TEXTAREA name="secret_msg" cols=35 rows=5></TEXTAREA>
</p>
```

Finally, add the Send Secret Message button:

```
<p>
<INPUT type="submit" value="Send Secret Message">
</p>
```

Don't forget the closing `</FORM>` tag!

Your HTML source code should look something like this:

```
<HTML>
<HEAD>
<TITLE>Secret Form</TITLE>
</HEAD>
<BODY>

<h1>Form to Send Secret Stuff</h1>
<FORM method="POST" action="do_sendsecret.php">

<p>Your Name:<br>
<INPUT type="text" name="sender_name" size=25>
</p>
<p>Your E-Mail Address:<br>
<INPUT type="text" name="sender_email" size=25>
</p>
<p>The Secret Message:<br>
<TEXTAREA name="secret_msg" cols=35 rows=5></TEXTAREA>
</p>
<p>
<INPUT type="submit" value="Send Secret Message">
</p>

</BODY>
</HTML>
```

Here's a very important point to remember: Unless your form is located on a secure server (a Web server with an SSL certificate), the information transmitted from the form in the user's Web browser to the script on your Web server is insecure, since there's no encryption going on. Bear that in mind when you need to create forms that send credit card information rather than "secret messages."

Now that your form is ready to go, open your text editor and create a file called `do_sendsecret.php`. Before anything else in the script, place the plain-text contents of the form submission into a variable called `$msg`:

```php
<?php
$msg = "Sender's Full Name:\t$sender_name\n";
$msg .= "Sender's E-Mail:\t$sender_email\n";
$msg .= "Secret Message?\t$secret_msg\n\n";
```

Next, set the GNUPGHOME environment variable so that the form uses the proper key ring. This value of GNUPGHOME should be the directory containing the PHP user's key ring:

```php
putenv("GNUPGHOME=/homedir/of/PHP/user/.gnupg");
```

The next step creates a temporary file on your Web server and writes the contents of the form submission to this new file. The PHP user must have write permissions in this directory. After the contents of `$msg` are written to the file, the file is closed.

```php
$fp = fopen("/path/to/temp/input/data", "w+");
fputs($fp, $msg);
fclose($fp);
```

> If you think users will send encrypted mail via a form concurrently, you should assign a unique file name to the input and output data files. Examples include using the `time()` function to get a long integer, or using a user ID or session variable kept in a cookie. If you don't use unique file names, and if two users access the PHP script at exactly the same time, one file will overwrite the other.

At this point, you're ready to encrypt the data you just placed in the temporary file. This example uses the `system()` function to invoke the GNUPG program on your Web server. If you are unsure of its location, contact your system administrator.

To encrypt the contents of a file, GNUPG needs a user ID (corresponding to a public key on the key ring), an input file, and a path and file name for the output file. The following example encrypts the file using the key for Julie Meloni <julie@thickbook.com>, which is on a key ring on my server. Substitute the ID of a key on your server.

```
system("/path/to/gpg --encrypt -ao /path/to/temp/output/data -r 'Julie Meloni
<julie@thickbook.com>' /path/to/temp/input/data ");
```

This command should output a file containing an encrypted message. Now, use the unlink() function to remove the original plain-text file:

```
unlink("/path/to/temp/input/data");
```

The next step is to place the contents of the output file in a variable, which will be used later to populate the e-mail message you'll be sending to the target recipient.

Assign the value of the encrypted data path to a variable called $crypted:

```
$crypted = "/path/to/temp/output/data";
```

Open the encrypted file for reading, and read the entire contents of the file to a variable called $mail_cont. Close the file when finished reading:

```
$fd = fopen($crypted, "r");
$mail_cont = fread($fd, filesize($crypted));
fclose($fd);
```

Remove the encrypted file from the system:

```
unlink("$crypted");
```

Finally, create the remainder of the e-mail and send it to the target recipient:

```
$recipient = "julie@thickbook.com";
$subject = "Secret Message";


$mailheaders = "From: My Web Site\n";
$mailheaders .= "Reply-To: $sender_email\n\n";


mail("$recipient", "$subject", $mail_cont, $mailheaders);
```

After your mail is sent, return a confirmation to the user by adding a few echo statements. You can even include the sender's name, since you have access to the variable $sender_name:

```
echo "<H1 align=center>Thank You, $sender_name</h1>";
echo "<p align=center>Your secret message has been sent.</p>";
```

Your entire PHP script should look something like this:

```
<?php
// build the message string
$msg = "Sender's Full Name:\t$sender_name\n";
```

```
$msg .= "Sender's E-Mail:\t$sender_email\n";
$msg .= "Secret Message?\t$secret_msg\n\n";

// set the environment variable for GNUPGHOME
putenv("GNUPGHOME=/homedir/of/PHP/user/.gnupg");

// Create a file for writing temporary data.
// Put contents of message string into the file
// created above, then close the file.
$fp = fopen("/path/to/temp/input/data", "w+");
fputs($fp, $msg);
fclose($fp);

// Invoke GNUPG to encrypt data and output to new file.
system("/path/to/gpg --encrypt -ao /path/to/temp/output/data -r 'Julie Meloni
<julie@thickbook.com>' /path/to/temp/input/data ");

// remove unencrypted file from system
unlink("/path/to/temp/input/data");

// Assign the value of the encrypted data path to a
// variable called $crypted.
$crypted = "/path/to/temp/output/data";

// Open encrypted file for reading, put entire
// contents of encrypted file into variable
// called $mail_cont, then close file.
$fd = fopen($crypted, "r");
$mail_cont = fread($fd, filesize($crypted));
fclose($fd);

// Remove encrypted file from system.
unlink("$crypted");
// Build mail message and send it to target recipient.
$recipient = "julie@thickbook.com";
$subject = "Secret Message";

$mailheaders = "From: My Web Site\n";
```

```
$mailheaders .= "Reply-To: $sender_email\n\n";

mail("$recipient", "$subject", $mail_cont, $mailheaders);

// Print confirmation to screen.
echo "<H1 align=center>Thank You, $sender_name</h1>";
echo "<p align=center>Your secret message has been sent.</p>";
?>
```

After the form is sent, the target recipient should receive an e-mail that looks
something like this:

----BEGIN PGP MESSAGE----

Version: GnuPG v1.0.1a (MingW32)

Comment: For info see http://www.gnupg.org

hQIOA7hAqKZWjd30EAf8D4xjHG+QUt9RIbE1VEKCyl6iNmhoh7laR2HkFWitRWnZ

MPwyZ6AqJKXLqzorKcRaA8TEifRC/Ec7ZmPqShByH0KBrsUGc95dX6YVLikJ70fS

81bwwjvbd4273u9MWVK8NvaJuEFvdEob4vBzkkh8Dsbw4s03jKdpAaBTC9gPyycf

hBypw/blnkHJOeNE1n+caW1itY385PsR9HmmzlY8kCK4LC+dZEgxwdlCwqROLB4F

zm8RSKmC4gxL5Dd3UiuJFwjWjO+gH3dAuEXsbI5k70c29v/P8+vyoeV51jmJTDHo

loBGV42bJBnELBwTmaeDfC9RM32LrPOnd/R8XfQtX52rOnnTFw2uIuMZzXDmjmWV

c0UI3/Xul8k6nB+i6kIfHYtT+gJPTEEz53y/f1YZ7yN9l969np1z8Z6TqLwruI3F

Gx33u/gZhCy/iPTMVpDKfjNPTA9mGTabnl2YkifPjPcpCaUD86UBRh19VjXP4+5W

----END PGP MESSAGE----

The recipient will then be able to decrypt the message using the GNUPG tools
installed on his or her own machine.

Creating a Shopping System

Since you spent all that time in the previous chapter creating a product catalog, it's
only fair that you learn how to display your products and allow people to purchase
them online. The next section takes you through the step-by-step process of creating
storefront menus. Subsequent sections will show you how to track the items selected
by shoppers, calculate the orders, and send encrypted orders to your e-mail account.

The storefront pages used in the examples have a very basic design, but by this
point you should be able to put the PHP code inside beautifully-designed, colorful
layout templates of your own.

Displaying Your Product Catalog

Unlike the administration menu created in the previous chapter, you don't have to worry about PHP authentication code at the beginning of every page of your store. However, later you will have to take into account some sort of user tracking. So, at the top of each page, you should check for an identification string and, if one isn't found, set one with a cookie.

> This is a perfect use of PHP4 sessions. If you are using PHP4, and you want the session-enabled version of the code in this chapter, go to the "Code" section of http://www.thickbook.com/ for a complete set.

Use the following code snippet to check for and set a cookie called `user_id`. Be prepared to paste this code at the top of each script created in this section:

```
<?
// set cookie if not already set
if (!isset($user_id)) {
    $token = md5(uniqid(rand()));
    setcookie("user_id",$token,time()+86400,"/",".yourcompany.com");
}
?>
```

This code sends a cookie called `user_id` with a value something like `cf2b2e6714e0bb9748a2d8f6be2c19e9`, valid for any page on the domain yourcompany.com. The cookie expires 24 hours after it was set.

Let's jump right into creating the storefront menu. Because my `MASTER_PRODUCTS` database contains only six products, I don't have that many options for categorizing my menu selections. So, let's go with two:

- View Products by Category
- View All Products Alphabetically

Open your text editor, create a file called `shop_menu.php`, and add the cookie code to the top of it. Next, create a basic HTML menu containing the two menu items. Use the file name `shop_viewbycat.php` for the first link and `shop_viewall.php` for the second link.

The code for this little menu should look something like this:

```
<?
// File name: shop_showmenu.php
```

```
// set cookie if not already set
if (!isset($user_id)) {
    $token = md5(uniqid(rand()));
    setcookie("user_id",$token,time()+86400,"/",".yourcompany.com");
}
?>
<!DOCTYPE HTML PUBLIC "-//W3C//DTD HTML 3.2//EN">
<HTML>
<HEAD>
<TITLE>XYZ Company Shopping Menu</TITLE>
</HEAD>
<BODY>
<h1>XYZ Company Shopping Menu</h1>
<p>Select an option:</p>
<ul>
<li><a href="shop_viewbycat.php">View Products by Category</a>
<li><a href="shop_viewall.php">View All Products Alphabetically</a>
</ul>
</BODY>
</HTML>
```

Save this file and place it on your Web server. Access it at its URL, such as http://www.yourcompany.com/shop_menu.php. You should see something like what is shown in Figure 8.1.

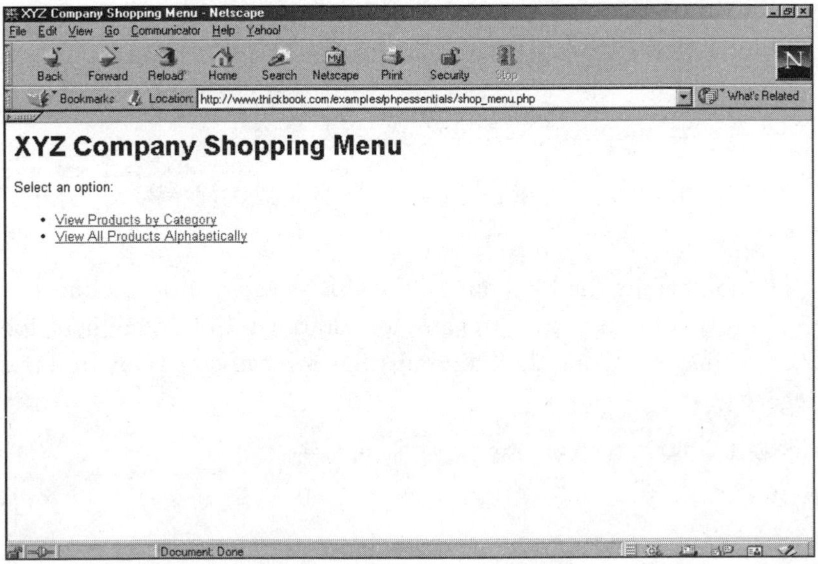

Figure 8.1 *XYZ company shopping menu*

Now that you've built the menu, it's time to build the pages behind it, starting with View Products by Category. This is a fun script, because you get to use your database to do all sorts of counting for you. For someone like me, whose mathematical skills are suspect, the SQL count() function is a wonderful thing.

Create a file called shop_viewbycat.php and add the cookie code to the beginning. Next, add the basic MySQL connection code:

```
// create connection
$connection = mysql_connect("localhost","sandman","34Nhjp") or die ("Couldn't
connect to the database.");
// select database
$db = mysql_select_db("secretDB", $connection) or die ("Couldn't select database.);
```

In previous scripts, you might have used only one SQL statement at a time. In this example, you'll use numerous database queries to get values for variables. The goal is to count the number of items within each category so that you can display the number to the user. For each category used in your MASTER_PRODUCTS table, prepare a separate SQL statement. For example, my MASTER_PRODUCTS table uses six categories: Applications, Cooking, Operating Systems, Pets, Programming, and Strategy Guides. So, here are my six SQL statements:

```
$sql_count1 = "SELECT COUNT(ISBN) FROM MASTER_PRODUCTS WHERE CATEGORY =
\"Applications\"";
$sql_count2 = "SELECT COUNT(ISBN) FROM MASTER_PRODUCTS WHERE CATEGORY =
\"Cooking\"";
$sql_count3 = "SELECT COUNT(ISBN) FROM MASTER_PRODUCTS WHERE CATEGORY = \"Operating
Systems\"";
$sql_count4 = "SELECT COUNT(ISBN) FROM MASTER_PRODUCTS WHERE CATEGORY = \"Pets\"";
$sql_count5 = "SELECT COUNT(ISBN) FROM MASTER_PRODUCTS WHERE CATEGORY =
\"Programming\"";
$sql_count6 = "SELECT COUNT(ISBN) FROM MASTER_PRODUCTS WHERE CATEGORY = \"Strategy
Guides\"";
```

The count() function counts the total number of ISBNs assigned to products in the specified category. The next step prepares an additional SQL statement for each category, this time extracting the ISBN and TITLE for every record within the specified category:

```
$sql_info1 = "SELECT ISBN, TITLE FROM MASTER_PRODUCTS WHERE CATEGORY =
\"Applications\"";
```

```
$sql_info2 = "SELECT ISBN, TITLE FROM MASTER_PRODUCTS WHERE CATEGORY =
\"Cooking\"";
$sql_info3 = "SELECT ISBN, TITLE FROM MASTER_PRODUCTS WHERE CATEGORY = \"Operating
Systems\"";
$sql_info4 = "SELECT ISBN, TITLE FROM MASTER_PRODUCTS WHERE CATEGORY = \"Pets\"";
$sql_info5 = "SELECT ISBN, TITLE FROM MASTER_PRODUCTS WHERE CATEGORY =
\"Programming\"";
$sql_info6 = "SELECT ISBN, TITLE FROM MASTER_PRODUCTS WHERE CATEGORY = \"Strategy
Guides\"";
```

Further into the script, the ISBN and TITLE of each product will be used to create the link to the template designed to show specific product information.

Now that all the SQL statements are formulated, query the database using each one, and use the die() function to exit the script if an error occurs:

```
$sql_result_count1 = mysql_query($sql_count1,$connection) or die ("Couldn't get
count!");
$sql_result_count2 = mysql_query($sql_count2,$connection) or die ("Couldn't get
count!");
$sql_result_count3 = mysql_query($sql_count3,$connection) or die ("Couldn't get
count!");
$sql_result_count4 = mysql_query($sql_count4,$connection) or die ("Couldn't get
count!");
$sql_result_count5 = mysql_query($sql_count5,$connection) or die ("Couldn't get
count!");
$sql_result_count6 = mysql_query($sql_count6,$connection) or die ("Couldn't get
count!");
$sql_result_info1 = mysql_query($sql_info1,$connection) or die ("Couldn't get
records!");
$sql_result_info2 = mysql_query($sql_info2,$connection) or die ("Couldn't get
records!");
$sql_result_info3 = mysql_query($sql_info3,$connection) or die ("Couldn't get
records!");
$sql_result_info4 = mysql_query($sql_info4,$connection) or die ("Couldn't get
records!");
$sql_result_info5 = mysql_query($sql_info5,$connection) or die ("Couldn't get
records!");
$sql_result_info6 = mysql_query($sql_info6,$connection) or die ("Couldn't get
records!");
```

If the script makes it through the queries without die()-ing, you can extract the specific results. Start with the results of the counting queries, and assign the value of each result to a variable with a meaningful name:

```
$count1 = mysql_result($sql_result_count1,0,"count(ISBN)");

$count2 = mysql_result($sql_result_count2,0,"count(ISBN)");

$count3 = mysql_result($sql_result_count3,0,"count(ISBN)");

$count4 = mysql_result($sql_result_count4,0,"count(ISBN)");

$count5 = mysql_result($sql_result_count5,0,"count(ISBN)");

$count6 = mysql_result($sql_result_count6,0,"count(ISBN)");
```

Now begin to format the HTML page. Start with the basic HTML heading, and begin a display table:

```
<!DOCTYPE HTML PUBLIC "-//W3C//DTD HTML 3.2//EN">

<HTML>

<HEAD>

<TITLE>XYZ Company Shopping Menu: View by Category</TITLE>

</HEAD>

<BODY>

<h1>XYZ Company Shopping : Category List</h1>

<div align=center>

<table border=0 cellspacing=5 cellpadding=5 width=100%>
```

For each category heading, print the value of the $countn variable for that category, next to the category label:

```
<tr>

<td valign=top width=50%><strong>APPLICATIONS</strong> (<?php echo "$count1"; ?>)</
td>

<td valign=top width=50%><strong>COOKING</strong> (<?php echo "$count2"; ?>)</td>

</tr>
```

On the next row, use a while loop within the table cell to produce a list of titles. These titles will be clickable, linked to the product details template file, shop_showbook.php. Add the value of the ISBN as an argument within the link:

```
<tr>

<td valign=top>

<?

    echo "<ul>";

    while ($row1 = mysql_fetch_array($sql_result_info1)) {
```

```
            $isbn1 = $row1["ISBN"];
            $title1 = $row1["TITLE"];
            echo "
            <li><a href=\"shop_showbook.php?isbn=$isbn1\">$title1</a>
            ";
        }
        echo "</ul>";
?>
</td>
<td valign=top>
<?
        echo "<ul>";

        while ($row2 = mysql_fetch_array($sql_result_info2)) {
            $isbn2 = $row2["ISBN"];
            $title2 = $row2["TITLE"];
            echo "
            <li><a href=\"shop_showbook.php?isbn=$isbn2\">$title2</a>
            ";
        }
        echo "</ul>";
?>
</td>
</tr>
```

Continue this process for each category. Depending on how many categories you have, the entire shop_viewbycat.php code should look something like this:

```
<?
// File name: shop_viewbycat.php
// set cookie if not already set
if (!isset($user_id)) {
    $token = md5(uniqid(rand()));
    setcookie("user_id",$token,time()+86400,"/",".yourcompany.com");
}


// create connection
$connection = mysql_connect("localhost","sandman","34Nhjp") or die ("Couldn't
connect to the database.");

// select database
```

```php
$db = mysql_select_db("secretDB", $connection) or die ("Couldn't select database.);

    // prepare SQL counting queries: count for number of books
    // in each category; also get isbn, title for books
    $sql_count1 = "SELECT COUNT(ISBN) FROM MASTER_PRODUCTS WHERE CATEGORY =
\"Applications\"";
    $sql_count2 = "SELECT COUNT(ISBN) FROM MASTER_PRODUCTS WHERE CATEGORY =
\"Cooking\"";
    $sql_count3 = "SELECT COUNT(ISBN) FROM MASTER_PRODUCTS WHERE CATEGORY =
\"Operating Systems\"";
    $sql_count4 = "SELECT COUNT(ISBN) FROM MASTER_PRODUCTS WHERE CATEGORY =
\"Pets\"";
    $sql_count5 = "SELECT COUNT(ISBN) FROM MASTER_PRODUCTS WHERE CATEGORY =
\"Programming\"";
    $sql_count6 = "SELECT COUNT(ISBN) FROM MASTER_PRODUCTS WHERE CATEGORY =
\"Strategy Guides\"";
    $sql_info1 = "SELECT ISBN, TITLE FROM MASTER_PRODUCTS WHERE CATEGORY =
\"Applications\"";
    $sql_info2 = "SELECT ISBN, TITLE FROM MASTER_PRODUCTS WHERE CATEGORY =
\"Cooking\"";
    $sql_info3 = "SELECT ISBN, TITLE FROM MASTER_PRODUCTS WHERE CATEGORY =
\"Operating Systems\"";
    $sql_info4 = "SELECT ISBN, TITLE FROM MASTER_PRODUCTS WHERE CATEGORY =
\"Pets\"";
    $sql_info5 = "SELECT ISBN, TITLE FROM MASTER_PRODUCTS WHERE CATEGORY =
\"Programming\"";
    $sql_info6 = "SELECT ISBN, TITLE FROM MASTER_PRODUCTS WHERE CATEGORY =
\"Strategy Guides\"";

    // execute SQL queries and exit if failure at any query
    $sql_result_count1 = mysql_query($sql_count1,$connection) or die ("Couldn't get
count!");
    $sql_result_count2 = mysql_query($sql_count2,$connection) or die ("Couldn't get
count!");
    $sql_result_count3 = mysql_query($sql_count3,$connection) or die ("Couldn't get
count!");
    $sql_result_count4 = mysql_query($sql_count4,$connection) or die ("Couldn't get
count!");
    $sql_result_count5 = mysql_query($sql_count5,$connection) or die ("Couldn't get
count!");
```

```
    $sql_result_count6 = mysql_query($sql_count6,$connection) or die ("Couldn't get
count!");
    $sql_result_info1 = mysql_query($sql_info1,$connection) or die ("Couldn't get
records!");
    $sql_result_info2 = mysql_query($sql_info2,$connection) or die ("Couldn't get
records!");
    $sql_result_info3 = mysql_query($sql_info3,$connection) or die ("Couldn't get
records!");
    $sql_result_info4 = mysql_query($sql_info4,$connection) or die ("Couldn't get
records!");
    $sql_result_info5 = mysql_query($sql_info5,$connection) or die ("Couldn't get
records!");
    $sql_result_info6 = mysql_query($sql_info6,$connection) or die ("Couldn't get
records!");

    // assign variable names to counting results
    $count1 = mysql_result($sql_result_count1,0,"count(ISBN)");
    $count2 = mysql_result($sql_result_count2,0,"count(ISBN)");
    $count3 = mysql_result($sql_result_count3,0,"count(ISBN)");
    $count4 = mysql_result($sql_result_count4,0,"count(ISBN)");
    $count5 = mysql_result($sql_result_count5,0,"count(ISBN)");
    $count6 = mysql_result($sql_result_count6,0,"count(ISBN)");

?>

<!DOCTYPE HTML PUBLIC "-//W3C//DTD HTML 3.2//EN">
<HTML>
<HEAD>
<TITLE>XYZ Company Shopping Menu: View by Category</TITLE>
</HEAD>
<BODY>

<h1>XYZ Company Shopping : Category List</h1>

<div align=center>
<table border=0 cellspacing=5 cellpadding=5 width=100%>
<tr>
<td valign=top width=50%><strong>APPLICATIONS</strong> (<?php echo "$count1"; ?>)</
td>
```

```
<td valign=top width=50%><strong>COOKING</strong> (<?php echo "$count2"; ?>)</td>
</tr>

<tr>
<td valign=top>
<?
    echo "<ul>";

    while ($row1 = mysql_fetch_array($sql_result_info1)) {
        $isbn1 = $row1["ISBN"];
        $title1 = $row1["TITLE"];
        echo "
        <li><a href=\"shop_showbook.php?isbn=$isbn1\">$title1</a>
        ";
    }
    echo "</ul>";
?>
</td>
<td valign=top>
<?
    echo "<ul>";
    while ($row2 = mysql_fetch_array($sql_result_info2)) {
        $isbn2 = $row2["ISBN"];
        $title2 = $row2["TITLE"];
        echo "
        <li><a href=\"shop_showbook.php?isbn=$isbn2\">$title2</a>
        ";
    }
    echo "</ul>";
?>
</td>
</tr>

<tr>
<td valign=top><strong>OPERATING SYSTEMS</strong> (<?php echo "$count3"; ?>)</td>
<td valign=top><strong>PETS</strong> (<?php echo "$count4"; ?>)</td>
</tr>

<tr>
<td valign=top>
```

```
<?
    echo "<ul>";
    while ($row3 = mysql_fetch_array($sql_result_info3)) {
        $isbn3 = $row3["ISBN"];
        $title3 = $row3["TITLE"];
        echo "
        <li><a href=\"shop_showbook.php?isbn=$isbn3\">$title3</a>
        ";
    }
    echo "</ul>";
?>
</td>
<td valign=top>
<?
    echo "<ul>";
    while ($row4 = mysql_fetch_array($sql_result_info4)) {
        $isbn4 = $row4["ISBN"];
        $title4 = $row4["TITLE"];
        echo "
        <li><a href=\"shop_showbook.php?isbn=$isbn4\">$title4</a>
        ";
    }
    echo "</ul>";
?>
</td>
</tr>

<tr>
<td valign=top><strong>PROGRAMMING</strong> (<?php echo "$count5"; ?>)</td>
<td valign=top><strong>STRATEGY GUIDES</strong> (<?php echo "$count6"; ?>)</td>
</tr>

<tr>
<td valign=top>
<?
    echo "<ul>";
    while ($row5 = mysql_fetch_array($sql_result_info5)) {
        $isbn5 = $row5["ISBN"];
        $title5 = $row5["TITLE"];
        echo "
```

```
                <li><a href=\"shop_showbook.php?isbn=$isbn5\">$title5</a>
                ";
        }
    echo "</ul>";
?>
</td>
<td valign=top>
<?
    echo "<ul>";
    while ($row6 = mysql_fetch_array($sql_result_info6)) {
        $isbn6 = $row6["ISBN"];
        $title6 = $row6["TITLE"];
        echo "
        <li><a href=\"shop_showbook.php?isbn=$isbn6\">$title6</a>
        ";
    }
    echo "</ul>";
?>
</td>
</tr>

</table>
</div>

</BODY>
</HTML>
```

Save this file and place it on your Web server. Go to the main shopping menu and click on the View Products by Category link. You should see something like what is shown in Figure 8.2.

Hopefully, your categories will have more than one item in them!

The second link on the main shopping menu is the View All Products Alphabetically category. This script doesn't require any counting. In fact, it queries the database only once. Create a file called shop_viewall.php, and add the cookie code and basic MySQL connection code:

```
<?
// File name: shop_viewall.php
// set cookie if not already set
```

```
if (!isset($user_id)) {
    $token = md5(uniqid(rand()));
    setcookie("user_id",$token,time()+86400,"/",".yourcompany.com");
}
// create connection
$connection = mysql_connect("localhost","sandman","34Nhjp") or die ("Couldn't
connect to the database.");

// select database
$db = mysql_select_db("secretDB", $connection) or die ("Couldn't select database.);
```

The SQL statement is straightforward: you need only the ISBN, TITLE, and CATEGORY, so SELECT only those fields. Use ORDER BY TITLE ASC to return the results in alphabetical order:

```
// prepare SQL statement
$sql = "SELECT ISBN, TITLE, CATEGORY FROM MASTER_PRODUCTS ORDER BY TITLE ASC";
```

Query the database, and exit the script if an error occurs:

```
// execute SQL queries and exit if failure at any query
$sql_result = mysql_query($sql,$connection) or die ("Couldn't get list!");
```

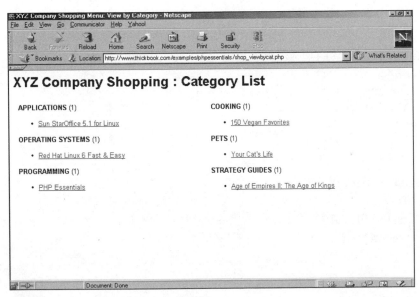

Figure 8.2   *XYZ company products listed by category*

You're out of PHP mode, so now add the basic HTML and begin a bullet list:

```
<!DOCTYPE HTML PUBLIC "-//W3C//DTD HTML 3.2//EN">
<HTML>
<HEAD>
<TITLE>XYZ Company Shopping Menu: View All Products</TITLE>
</HEAD>
<BODY>


<h1>XYZ Company Shopping : View All Products</h1>
<ul>
```

All you need to do now is create a `while` loop that steps through each row in the result set, printing the link to the product details template file, `shop_showbook.php`, along with its appropriate ISBN value as an argument within the link:

```
<?
while ($row = mysql_fetch_array($sql_result)) {
    $isbn = $row["ISBN"];
    $title = $row["TITLE"];
    $category = $row["CATEGORY"];
    echo "
    <li><a href=\"shop_showbook.php?isbn=$isbn\">$title</a> <em>($category)</em>
    ";
}
?>
```

After closing the required HTML tags, the entire script should look something like this:

```
<?
// File name: shop_viewall.php
// set cookie if not already set
if (!isset($user_id)) {
    $token = md5(uniqid(rand()));
    setcookie("user_id",$token,time()+86400,"/",".yourcompany.com");
}
// create connection
$connection = mysql_connect("localhost","sandman","34Nhjp") or die ("Couldn't
connect to the database.");

// select database
```

```
$db = mysql_select_db("secretDB", $connection) or die ("Couldn't select database.);

// prepare SQL statement
$sql = "SELECT ISBN, TITLE, CATEGORY FROM MASTER_PRODUCTS ORDER BY TITLE ASC";

// execute SQL queries and exit if failure at any query
$sql_result = mysql_query($sql,$connection) or die ("Couldn't get list!");
?>

<!DOCTYPE HTML PUBLIC "-//W3C//DTD HTML 3.2//EN">
<HTML>
<HEAD>
<TITLE>XYZ Company Shopping Menu: View All Products</TITLE>
</HEAD>
<BODY>

<h1>XYZ Company Shopping : View All Products</h1>
<ul>
<?
while ($row = mysql_fetch_array($sql_result)) {
    $isbn = $row["ISBN"];
    $title = $row["TITLE"];
    $category = $row["CATEGORY"];
    echo "
    <li><a href=\"shop_showbook.php?isbn=$isbn\">$title</a> <em>($category)</em>
    ";
}
?>

</ul>
</BODY>
</HTML>
```

Save this file and place it on your Web server. Go to the main shopping menu and click on the View All Products Alphabetically link. You should see something like what is shown in Figure 8.3.

The last step in your catalog display code is the product details template, called shop_showbook.php. Open a text file with that name, and—before you check for or set a cookie—check for the one required field: the ISBN. In this template, the ISBN is used to extract the entire product record.

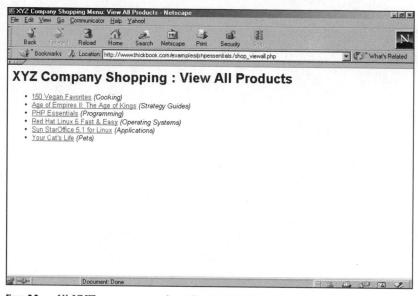

Figure 8.3   *All XYZ company products listed alphabetically*

```
<?
// File name: shop_showbook.php
    if (!($isbn)) {
        header("Location: http://www.yourcompany.com/show_menu.php");
        exit;
    }
```

Now add the usual cookie code and general connection information. The SQL statement used in this script is

```
$sql = "SELECT * FROM MASTER_PRODUCTS WHERE ISBN = \"$isbn\"";
```

Perform the query, or exit the script if an error occurs:

```
$sql_result = mysql_query($sql,$connection) or die ("Couldn't get record!");
```

Next, grab the matched row and assign meaningful variable names to the elements:

```
    $row = mysql_fetch_array($sql_result);
    $isbn = $row["ISBN"];
    $title = $row["TITLE"];
    $author = $row["AUTHOR"];
    $publisher = $row["PUBLISHER"];
    $category = $row["CATEGORY"];
    $type = $row["TYPE"];
```

```
    $info_blurb = $row["INFO_BLURB"];
    $page_num = $row["PAGE_NUM"];
    $price = $row["PRICE"];
```

You can now continue and build the HTML template, using the variable names as substitutes for values in a basic display table:

```
<h1>XYZ Company Shopping : Book Details</h1>

<h2><?php echo "$title"; ?></h2>
<P><?php echo "$info_blurb"; ?></p>

<table>
<tr>
<td><strong>Author:</strong></td>
<td><?php echo "$author"; ?></td>
</tr>

<tr>
<td><strong>Publisher:</strong></td>
<td><?php echo "$publisher"; ?></td>
</tr>

<tr>
<td><strong>ISBN:</strong></td>
<td><?php echo "$isbn"; ?></td>
</tr>

<tr>
<td><strong>Category:</strong></td>
<td><?php echo "$category"; ?></td>
</tr>

<tr>
<td><strong>Type:</strong></td>
<td><?php echo "$type"; ?></td>
</tr>

<tr>
<td><strong>Number of Pages:</strong></td>
<td><?php echo "$page_num"; ?></td>
```

```
</tr>
</table>
<h3><font color="#FF0000">Only <?php echo "$price"; ?>!</font></h3>
```

Since this is a shopping system, prepare yourself for the next lesson, and add the Add to Shopping Cart form for this item. Assume that the next script is called `shop_addtocart.php`, and use this as the form action:

```
<form method="post" action="shop_addtocart.php">
```

You'll need to track the item, item title, item price, and quantity, so create hidden fields for the values you know (ISBN, title, price) and a text field for the value completed by the user (quantity):

```
<input type="hidden" name="sel_item" value="<?php echo "$isbn"; ?>">
<input type="hidden" name="sel_item_title" value="<?php echo "$title"; ?>">
<input type="hidden" name="sel_item_price" value="<?php echo "$price"; ?>">
<em>Quantity:</em> <input type="text" name="sel_item_qty" value="1" size=3>
```

Add the submit button, and close the form:

```
<P><input type="submit" name="submit" value="Add to Shopping Cart"></p>
</form>
```

From start to finish, the product details template looks something like this:

```
<?
// File name: shop_showbook.php
    if (!($isbn)) {
        header("Location: http://www.yourcompany.com/show_menu.php");
        exit;
    }


    // set cookie if not already set
        if (!isset($user_id)) {
        $token = md5(uniqid(rand()));
        setcookie("user_id",$token,time()+86400,"/",".yourcompany.com");
    }
// create connection
$connection = mysql_connect("localhost","sandman","34Nhjp") or die ("Couldn't
connect to the database.");

// select database
```

```php
$db = mysql_select_db("secretDB", $connection) or die ("Couldn't select database.);

// prepare SQL statement
$sql = "SELECT * FROM MASTER_PRODUCTS WHERE ISBN = \"$isbn\"";

// execute SQL query and exit if failure
$sql_result = mysql_query($sql,$connection) or die ("Couldn't get record!");

    // get results and assign meaningful variable names
    $row = mysql_fetch_array($sql_result);
    $isbn = $row["ISBN"];
    $title = $row["TITLE"];
    $author = $row["AUTHOR"];
    $publisher = $row["PUBLISHER"];
    $category = $row["CATEGORY"];
    $type = $row["TYPE"];
    $info_blurb = $row["INFO_BLURB"];
    $page_num = $row["PAGE_NUM"];
    $price = $row["PRICE"];
?>


<!DOCTYPE HTML PUBLIC "-//W3C//DTD HTML 3.2//EN">
<HTML>
<HEAD>
<TITLE>XYZ Company Shopping Menu: Book Details</TITLE>
</HEAD>
<BODY>

<h1>XYZ Company Shopping : Book Details</h1>

<h2><?php echo "$title"; ?></h2>
<P><?php echo "$info_blurb"; ?></p>

<table>
<tr>
<td><strong>Author:</strong></td>
<td><?php echo "$author"; ?></td>
</tr>

<tr>
```

```
<td><strong>Publisher:</strong></td>
<td><?php echo "$publisher"; ?></td>
</tr>

<tr>
<td><strong>ISBN:</strong></td>
<td><?php echo "$isbn"; ?></td>
</tr>

<tr>
<td><strong>Category:</strong></td>
<td><?php echo "$category"; ?></td>
</tr>

<tr>
<td><strong>Type:</strong></td>
<td><?php echo "$type"; ?></td>
</tr>

<tr>
<td><strong>Number of Pages:</strong></td>
<td><?php echo "$page_num"; ?></td>
</tr>

</table>

<h3><font color="#FF0000">Only <?php echo "$price"; ?>!</font></h3>

<form method="post" action="shop_addtocart.php">
<input type="hidden" name="sel_item" value="<?php echo "$isbn"; ?>">
<input type="hidden" name="sel_item_title" value="<?php echo "$title"; ?>">
<input type="hidden" name="sel_item_price" value="<?php echo "$price"; ?>">
<em>Quantity:</em> <input type="text" name="sel_item_qty" value="1" size=3>
<P><input type="submit" name="submit" value="Add to Shopping Cart"></p>
</form>

</BODY>
</HTML>
```

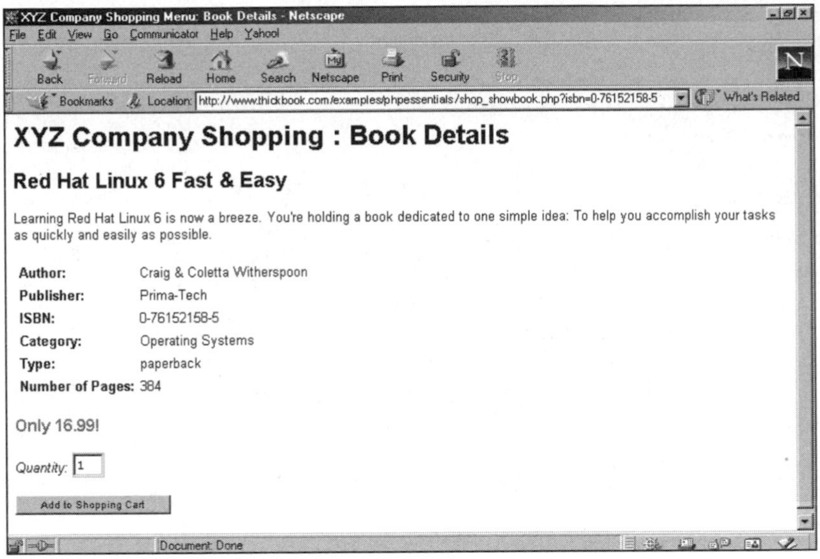

Figure 8.4 *Individual product display template*

Save this file and place it on your Web server. Go back to your shopping menu and select an individual product to view. You should see something like what is shown in Figure 8.4.

The next section details how you can hold on to the items users add to their shopping carts, ultimately resulting in numerous orders, wealth, and fame.

Tracking Your Users' Shopping Carts

To keep track of your users' shopping carts, first create a database table called something like USER_TRACK. Use the same table-creation form used to create the MASTER_PRODUCTS table earlier in this chapter. Create a seven-field table with the following field attributes:

- USER_ID varchar (100). Used to associate the entry with a user; user_id is kept in a cookie.
- SEL_ITEM varchar (25). The ISBN of the book added to the cart.
- SEL_ITEM_TITLE varchar (100). The title of the book added to the cart.
- SEL_ITEM_QTY int. The quantity the user wants to purchase.

- `SEL_ITEM_PRICE float`. The single-item price of the item the user has added to the cart.

- `SEL_ITEM_TOTALPRICE float`. The total price (single item price × quantity) of the item.

- `DATE_ADDED date`. The date the item was added to the cart.

The next PHP script you need to create is `shop_addtocart.php`, to handle user input when the user selects an item to add to his or her shopping cart.

Open your text editor and add some code to check for required fields:

```
if ((!($sel_item)) || (!($sel_item_title)) || (!($sel_item_qty)) ||
(!($sel_item_price))) {
    header("Location: http://www.yourcompany.com/show_menu.php");
    exit;
}
```

Next, add the usual cookie code and the general MySQL connectivity code. After making it through all that, do a little math. Get the total item price by multiplying the quantity and the single unit price:

```
$sel_item_totalprice = $sel_item_qty * $sel_item_price;
```

Keeping the total item price in the `USER_TRACK` table eliminates additional database queries and mathematical functions at checkout time.

Next, create a variable to hold the date, in YYYY-MM-DD format. Date-stamping an entry allows you to easily delete old shopping cart entries, should users decide not to go through the checkout process.

```
$date_added = date("Y-m-d");
```

Prepare the SQL statement for inserting the shopping cart item and execute the query:

```
$sql = "INSERT INTO USER_TRACK VALUES(\"$user_id\", \"$sel_item\",
\"$sel_item_title\", \"$sel_item_qty\", \"$sel_item_price\",
\"$sel_item_totalprice\", \"$date_added\")";
$sql_result = mysql_query($sql,$connection) or die ("Couldn't insert record!");
```

Finally, display a confirmation to the user:

```
<!DOCTYPE HTML PUBLIC "-//W3C//DTD HTML 3.2//EN">
<HTML>
<HEAD>
<TITLE>XYZ Company Shopping: Product Added to Cart</TITLE>
</HEAD>
```

```
<BODY>
<h1>XYZ Company Shopping : Product Added to Cart</h1>
<p><strong>You have added the following item to your shopping cart:</strong></p>
<P><strong>Item:</strong> <?php echo "$sel_item"; ?> <?php echo "$sel_item_title";
?><br>
<strong>Quantity:</strong> <?php echo "$sel_item_qty"; ?><br>
<strong>Single Unit Price:</strong> <?php echo "$sel_item_price"; ?><br>
<strong>Total Price:</strong> <?php echo "$sel_item_totalprice"; ?></p>
<P><a href="shop_menu.php">Continue Shopping</a></p>
</BODY>
</HTML>
```

Put it all together, and you have a script something like this:

```
<?
// File name: shop_addtocart.php
// check for required fields
    if ((!($sel_item)) || (!($sel_item_title)) || (!($sel_item_qty)) ||
(!($sel_item_price))) {
        header("Location: http://www.yourcompany.com/show_menu.php");
        exit;
    }


// set cookie if not already set
if (!isset($user_id)) {
    $token = md5(uniqid(rand()));
    setcookie("user_id",$token,time()+86400,"/",".yourcompany.com");
}


// create connection
$connection = mysql_connect("localhost","sandman","34Nhjp") or die ("Couldn't
connect to the database.");

// select database
$db = mysql_select_db("secretDB", $connection) or die ("Couldn't select database.);

// do some math!
$sel_item_totalprice = $sel_item_qty * $sel_item_price;

// format a datestamp
```

```
$date_added = date("Y-m-d");

// SQL statement to add record to track
$sql = "INSERT INTO USER_TRACK VALUES(\"$user_id\", \"$sel_item\",
\"$sel_item_title\", \"$sel_item_qty\", \"$sel_item_price\",
\"$sel_item_totalprice\", \"$date_added\")";

// execute SQL query and exit if failure
$sql_result = mysql_query($sql,$connection) or die ("Couldn't insert record!");

?>


<!DOCTYPE HTML PUBLIC "-//W3C//DTD HTML 3.2//EN">
<HTML>
<HEAD>
<TITLE>XYZ Company Shopping Menu: Product Added to Cart</TITLE>
</HEAD>
<BODY>
<h1>XYZ Company Shopping : Product Added to Cart</h1>
<p><strong>You have added the following item to your shopping cart:</strong></p>
<P><strong>Item:</strong> <?php echo "$sel_item"; ?> <?php echo "$sel_item_title";
?><br>
<strong>Quantity:</strong> <?php echo "$sel_item_qty"; ?><br>
<strong>Single Unit Price:</strong> <?php echo "$sel_item_price"; ?><br>
<strong>Total Price:</strong> <?php echo "$sel_item_totalprice"; ?></p>
<P><a href="shop_menu.php">Continue Shopping</a></p>
</BODY>
</HTML>
```

Go through the shopping menu system again, and use the Add to Shopping Cart button on an individual product page. You should see something like what is shown in Figure 8.5.

Users can now continue through your shopping site, merrily adding items. But why should you leave it up to your consumers to remember how many items they've put in their shopping carts when you have those handy SQL mathematical functions? The next section provides a short piece of code that will make your site look cool by always showing the number of items in the cart, plus you'll add in the link to the checkout form.

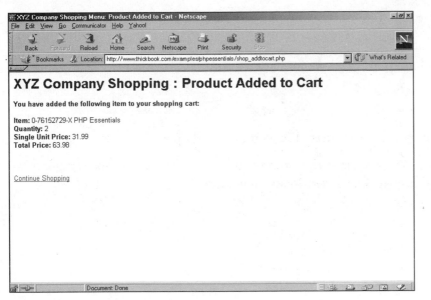

Figure 8.5   *Product added to cart: user confirmation*

Counting the Cart Items

If you plan to show the current user's shopping cart count on every page, especially after he's just added items, be sure to place the count() query after any code that adds to the cart.

The SQL statement and query functions are pretty straightforward:

```
$item_count = "SELECT SUM(SEL_ITEM_QTY) FROM USER_TRACK WHERE USER_ID =
\"$user_id\"";
$item_result = mysql_query($item_count) or die("Couldn't count!");
$item_count_total = mysql_result($item_result,0,"SUM(SEL_ITEM_QTY)");
```

Note the use of sum() instead of count(). You could use count(), but what if a user has ordered two copies of one book? Instead of showing two items in the cart, count() would return 1, since it's two copies of one item.

The hardest part is finding a space on your page to show the total number of items in the cart, but when you do, you could just say this:

```
<P>Your cart contains
<?php
if ($item_count_total == "1") {
    echo "1 item.";
} else {
    echo "$item_count_total items.";
```

```
}
?>
```

Add in a link to the checkout form, called `shop_checkout.php3`.

```
<br>
You can <a href="shop_checkout.php3">checkout</a> at any time.</p>
```

You're almost ready to collect money from your shoppers!

The `shop_addtocart.php` script from the previous section, with the shopping cart count and display code added, looks something like this:

```
<?
// File name: shop_addtocart.php
// check for required fields
    if ((!($sel_item)) || (!($sel_item_title)) || (!($sel_item_qty)) ||
(!($sel_item_price))) {
        header("Location: http://www.yourcompany.com/show_menu.php");
        exit;
    }

// set cookie if not already set
if (!isset($user_id)) {
    $token = md5(uniqid(rand()));
    setcookie("user_id",$token,time()+86400,"/",".yourcompany.com");
}

    // create connection
    $connection = mysql_connect("localhost","sandman","34Nhjp") or die
("Couldn't connect to the database.");

    // select database
    $db = mysql_select_db("secretDB", $connection) or die
("Couldn't select database.);

    // do some math!
    $sel_item_totalprice = $sel_item_qty * $sel_item_price;

    // format a datestamp
    $date_added = date("Y-m-d");

    // SQL statement to add record to track
```

```php
    $sql = "INSERT INTO USER_TRACK VALUES(\"$user_id\", \"$sel_item\",
\"$sel_item_title\", \"$sel_item_qty\", \"$sel_item_price\",
\"$sel_item_totalprice\", \"$date_added\")";

    // execute SQL query and exit if failure
    $sql_result = mysql_query($sql,$connection) or die ("Couldn't insert record!");

    //count cart items
    $item_count = "SELECT SUM(SEL_ITEM_QTY) FROM USER_TRACK WHERE USER_ID =
\"$user_id\"";
$item_result = mysql_query($item_count);
$item_count_total = mysql_result($item_result,0,"SUM(SEL_ITEM_QTY)");
?>


<!DOCTYPE HTML PUBLIC "-//W3C//DTD HTML 3.2//EN">
<HTML>
<HEAD>
<TITLE>XYZ Company Shopping Menu: Product Added to Cart</TITLE>
</HEAD>
<BODY>
<h1>XYZ Company Shopping : Product Added to Cart</h1>
<p><strong>You have added the following item to your shopping cart:</strong></p>
<P><strong>Item:</strong> <?php echo "$sel_item"; ?> <?php echo "$sel_item_title";
?><br>
<strong>Quantity:</strong> <?php echo "$sel_item_qty"; ?><br>
<strong>Single Unit Price:</strong> <?php echo "$sel_item_price"; ?><br>
<strong>Total Price:</strong> <?php echo "$sel_item_totalprice"; ?></p>
<P>Your cart contains
<?php
//display cart count
if ($item_count_total == "1") {
    echo "1 item.";
} else {
    echo "$item_count_total items.";
}
?>
<br>
You can <a href="shop_checkout.php3">checkout</a> at any time.</p>
<P><a href="shop_menu.php">Continue Shopping</a></p>
</BODY>
</HTML>
```

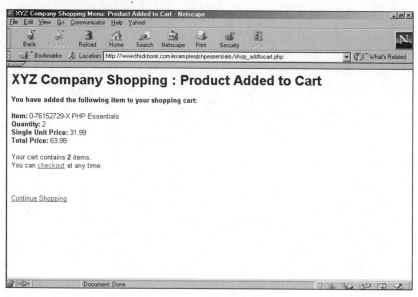

Figure 8.6 *Product added to cart: show total cart items*

Now, when you add a product to your shopping cart, the page looks something like what is shown in Figure 8.6.

If you can successfully add products to your shopping cart, there's only one more step to go before fame and fortune: checking out!

Checkout Time!

You're in the home stretch now. All that remains is creating the billing information form for users and sending the form via encrypted e-mail to your mailbox.

Create a text file called `shop_checkout.php`, and add the cookie code and basic MySQL connectivity functions. After testing the database selection, grab the data you need and do a little math. First, get the subtotal of all the items associated with this user:

```
$get_itemtot = "SELECT SUM(SEL_ITEM_TOTALPRICE) FROM USER_TRACK WHERE USER_ID =
\"$user_id\"";
$itemtot_result = mysql_query($get_itemtot) or die ("Couldn't do math!");
$itemtot = mysql_result($itemtot_result,0,"SUM(SEL_ITEM_TOTALPRICE)");
```

Next, be sure to format the results as we're used to seeing money represented—with two decimal places:

```
$fmt_itemtot = sprintf("%0.2f",$itemtot);
```

Say your store offers free shipping on any purchases over $50.00. To get an amount for shipping costs, use this simple if...else statement:

```
if ($itemtot < "50") {
    $shipping = 4.5;
} else {
    $shipping = 0;
}
```

Now format the shipping cost to two decimal places:

```
$fmt_shipping = sprintf("%0.2f",$shipping);
```

Finally, get the grand total and format the result to two decimal places:

```
$total = $itemtot + $shipping;
$fmt_total = sprintf("%0.2f",$total);
```

Next, get all the items listed in the user's cart, to display the results on the screen so that he knows what he's purchasing:

```
// get cart items
$get_cart = "SELECT SEL_ITEM, SEL_ITEM_TITLE, SEL_ITEM_QTY, SEL_ITEM_PRICE,
SEL_ITEM_TOTALPRICE FROM USER_TRACK WHERE USER_ID = \"$user_id\"";
$cart_result = mysql_query($get_cart) or die ("Couldn't get cart!");
```

Check to see that there's actually something there, and if there is, start printing the form:

```
$num_rows = mysql_numrows($cart_result);
if ($num_rows == "0") {
    echo "<P><strong>There are no items in your cart, but thanks for trying.</p>";
} else {
    echo "
        // Form goes here
```

Start creating the HTML form, using shop_sendorder.php as the form action:

```
<!DOCTYPE HTML PUBLIC \"-//W3C//DTD HTML 3.2//EN\">
<HTML>
<HEAD>
<TITLE>XYZ Company Shopping: Checkout</TITLE>
</HEAD>
<BODY>
<h1>XYZ Company Shopping : Checkout</h1>
<FORM ACTION=\"shop_sendorder.php\" METHOD=\"post\">
```

Add text fields for normal shipping and billing information: name, address, credit card information, and so on:

```
<h2>BILLING INFO</h2>
<table border=0 cellspacing=0 cellpadding=5>

<tr>
<td><strong>Full Name:</strong></td>
<td><INPUT TYPE=text NAME=\"full_name\" SIZE=30></td>
</tr>

<tr>
<td><strong>E-Mail Address:</strong></td>
<td><INPUT TYPE=text NAME=\"email\" SIZE=30></td>
</tr>

<tr>
<td><strong>Address Line 1:</strong></td>
<td><INPUT TYPE=text NAME=\"address1\" SIZE=30></td>
</tr>

<tr>
<td><strong>Address Line 2:</strong></td>
<td><INPUT TYPE=text NAME=\"address2\" SIZE=30></td>
</tr>

<tr>
<td><strong>Address Line 3:</strong></td>
<td><INPUT TYPE=text NAME=\"address3\" SIZE=30></td>
</tr>

<tr>
<td><strong>Address Line 4:</strong></td>
<td><INPUT TYPE=text NAME=\"address4\" SIZE=30></td>
</tr>

<tr>
<td><strong>Credit Card Type:</strong></td>
<td>
<SELECT NAME=\"cc_type\">
<OPTION VALUE=\"0\">-- Select One --</OPTION>
```

```
<OPTION VALUE=\"Visa\">Visa</OPTION>
<OPTION VALUE=\"MasterCard\">MasterCard</OPTION>
</SELECT>
</td>
</tr>

<tr>
<td><strong>Credit Card Number:</strong></td>
<td><INPUT TYPE=text NAME=\"cc_num\" SIZE=30></td>
</tr>

<tr>
<td><strong>Credit Card Expiration Date:</strong> </td>
<td>
<SELECT NAME=\"cc_exp_mon\">
<OPTION VALUE=\"0\">--</OPTION>
<OPTION VALUE=\"1\">01</OPTION>
<OPTION VALUE=\"2\">02</OPTION>
<OPTION VALUE=\"3\">03</OPTION>
<OPTION VALUE=\"4\">04</OPTION>
<OPTION VALUE=\"5\">05</OPTION>
<OPTION VALUE=\"6\">06</OPTION>
<OPTION VALUE=\"7\">07</OPTION>
<OPTION VALUE=\"8\">08</OPTION>
<OPTION VALUE=\"9\">09</OPTION>
<OPTION VALUE=\"10\">10</OPTION>
<OPTION VALUE=\"11\">11</OPTION>
<OPTION VALUE=\"12\">12</OPTION>
</SELECT>

 /

<SELECT NAME=\"cc_exp_yr\">
<OPTION VALUE=\"0\">--</OPTION>
<OPTION VALUE=\"1999\">1999</OPTION>
<OPTION VALUE=\"2000\">2000</OPTION>
<OPTION VALUE=\"2001\">2001</OPTION>
<OPTION VALUE=\"2002\">2002</OPTION>
<OPTION VALUE=\"2003\">2003</OPTION>
<OPTION VALUE=\"2004\">2004</OPTION>
```

```
<OPTION VALUE=\"2005\">2005</OPTION>
<OPTION VALUE=\"2006\">2006</OPTION>
<OPTION VALUE=\"2007\">2007</OPTION>
<OPTION VALUE=\"2008\">2008</OPTION>
<OPTION VALUE=\"2009\">2009</OPTION>
</SELECT>
</td>
</tr>
</table>
```

Add a heading and start a table to display the contents of the user's shopping cart:

```
<h2>CART CONTENTS</h2>
<table border=1 cellpadding=10 cellspacing=0>
<tr>
<td align=center><strong>ITEM ID</strong></td>
<td align=center><strong>TITLE</strong></td>
<td align=center><strong>QTY</strong></td>
<td align=center><strong>PRICE</strong></td>
<td align=center><strong>TOTAL</strong></td>
</tr>
";
```

Use a handy `while` loop to step through the `$cart_result` found earlier, displaying all the elements in the cart in table format:

```
while ($row = mysql_fetch_array($cart_result)) {
    // get results and assign meaningful variable names
    $sel_item = $row["SEL_ITEM"];
    $sel_item_title = $row["SEL_ITEM_TITLE"];
    $sel_item_qty = $row["SEL_ITEM_QTY"];
    $sel_item_price = $row["SEL_ITEM_PRICE"];
    $sel_item_totalprice = $row["SEL_ITEM_TOTALPRICE"];

    $fmt_item_totalprice = sprintf("%0.2f",$sel_item_totalprice);

    echo "
    <tr>
    <td>$sel_item</td>
    <td>$sel_item_title</td>
    <td align=right>$sel_item_qty</td>
    <td align=right>$ $sel_item_price</td>
```

```
                <td align=right>$ $fmt_item_totalprice</td>
                </tr>
                ";
        }
```

Pick up the table code again, adding the formatted values for the item total, shipping information, and grand total:

```
        echo "
        <tr>
        <td colspan=4 align=right><strong>Item Total:</strong></td>
        <td align=right><strong>$ $fmt_itemtot</strong></td>
        </tr>

        <tr><td colspan=4 align=right><strong>Shipping:</strong></td>
        <td align=right>
";
        if ($shipping != "0") {
            echo "<strong>$ $fmt_shipping</strong>";
        } else {
            echo "<strong>FREE!</strong>";
        }

        echo "
        </td></tr>

        <tr><td colspan=4 align=right><strong>Grand Total:</strong></td>
        <td align=right><strong>$ $fmt_total</strong></td></tr>
```

Add the Send This Order! form submission button, and close all your tags:

```
        <tr><td colspan=5 align=center><input type=\"submit\" name=\"submit\"
value=\"Send This Order!\"></td></tr>
        </table>
        </form>";
        }
?>
</BODY>
</HTML>
```

The `shop_checkout.php` script, from start to finish, looks something like this:

```
<?
// File name: shop_checkout.php
```

```php
// set cookie if not already set
if (!isset($user_id)) {
    $token = md5(uniqid(rand()));
    setcookie("user_id",$token,time()+86400,"/",".yourcompany.com");
}

    // create connection
    $connection = mysql_connect("localhost","sandman","34Nhjp") or die
("Couldn't connect to the database.");

    // select database
    $db = mysql_select_db("secretDB", $connection) or die
("Couldn't select database.);

    // get cart subtotal
    $get_itemtot = "SELECT SUM(SEL_ITEM_TOTALPRICE) FROM USER_TRACK WHERE USER_ID =
\"$user_id\"";
    $itemtot_result = mysql_query($get_itemtot) or die ("Couldn't do math!");
    $itemtot = mysql_result($itemtot_result,0,"SUM(SEL_ITEM_TOTALPRICE)");
    $fmt_itemtot = sprintf("%0.2f",$itemtot);

    if ($itemtot < "50") {
        $shipping = 4.5;
    } else {
        $shipping = 0;
    }

    $fmt_shipping = sprintf("%0.2f",$shipping);
    $total = $itemtot + $shipping;
    $fmt_total = sprintf("%0.2f",$total);

    // get cart
    $get_cart = "SELECT SEL_ITEM, SEL_ITEM_TITLE, SEL_ITEM_QTY, SEL_ITEM_PRICE,
SEL_ITEM_TOTALPRICE FROM USER_TRACK WHERE USER_ID = \"$user_id\"";
    $cart_result = mysql_query($get_cart) or die ("Couldn't get cart!");

    $num_rows = mysql_numrows($cart_result);

    if ($num_rows == "0") {
```

```
        echo "<P><strong>There are no items in your cart, but thanks for trying.</p>";
    } else {
echo "
<!DOCTYPE HTML PUBLIC \"-//W3C//DTD HTML 3.2//EN\">
<HTML>
<HEAD>
<TITLE>XYZ Company Shopping: Checkout</TITLE>
</HEAD>
<BODY>
<h1>XYZ Company Shopping : Checkout</h1>
<FORM ACTION=\"shop_sendorder.php\" METHOD=\"post\">
<h2>BILLING INFO</h2>
<table border=0 cellspacing=0 cellpadding=5>

<tr>
<td><strong>Full Name:</strong></td>
<td><INPUT TYPE=text NAME=\"full_name\" SIZE=30></td>
</tr>

<tr>
<td><strong>E-Mail Address:</strong></td>
<td><INPUT TYPE=text NAME=\"email\" SIZE=30></td>
</tr>

<tr>
<td><strong>Address Line 1:</strong></td>
<td><INPUT TYPE=text NAME=\"address1\" SIZE=30></td>
</tr>

<tr>
<td><strong>Address Line 2:</strong></td>
<td><INPUT TYPE=text NAME=\"address2\" SIZE=30></td>
</tr>

<tr>
<td><strong>Address Line 3:</strong></td>
<td><INPUT TYPE=text NAME=\"address3\" SIZE=30></td>
</tr>

<tr>
```

```
<td><strong>Address Line 4:</strong></td>
<td><INPUT TYPE=text NAME=\"address4\" SIZE=30></td>
</tr>

<tr>
<td><strong>Credit Card Type:</strong></td>
<td>
<SELECT NAME=\"cc_type\">
<OPTION VALUE=\"0\">-- Select One --</OPTION>
<OPTION VALUE=\"Visa\">Visa</OPTION>
<OPTION VALUE=\"MasterCard\">MasterCard</OPTION>
</SELECT>
</td>
</tr>

<tr>
<td><strong>Credit Card Number:</strong></td>
<td><INPUT TYPE=text NAME=\"cc_num\" SIZE=30></td>
</tr>

<tr>
<td><strong>Credit Card Expiration Date:</strong> </td>
<td>
<SELECT NAME=\"cc_exp_mon\">
<OPTION VALUE=\"0\">--</OPTION>
<OPTION VALUE=\"1\">01</OPTION>
<OPTION VALUE=\"2\">02</OPTION>
<OPTION VALUE=\"3\">03</OPTION>
<OPTION VALUE=\"4\">04</OPTION>
<OPTION VALUE=\"5\">05</OPTION>
<OPTION VALUE=\"6\">06</OPTION>
<OPTION VALUE=\"7\">07</OPTION>
<OPTION VALUE=\"8\">08</OPTION>
<OPTION VALUE=\"9\">09</OPTION>
<OPTION VALUE=\"10\">10</OPTION>
<OPTION VALUE=\"11\">11</OPTION>
<OPTION VALUE=\"12\">12</OPTION>
```

```
</SELECT>

 /

<SELECT NAME=\"cc_exp_yr\">
<OPTION VALUE=\"0\">--</OPTION>
<OPTION VALUE=\"1999\">1999</OPTION> .
<OPTION VALUE=\"2000\">2000</OPTION>
<OPTION VALUE=\"2001\">2001</OPTION>
<OPTION VALUE=\"2002\">2002</OPTION>
<OPTION VALUE=\"2003\">2003</OPTION>
<OPTION VALUE=\"2004\">2004</OPTION>
<OPTION VALUE=\"2005\">2005</OPTION>
<OPTION VALUE=\"2006\">2006</OPTION>
<OPTION VALUE=\"2007\">2007</OPTION>
<OPTION VALUE=\"2008\">2008</OPTION>
<OPTION VALUE=\"2009\">2009</OPTION>
</SELECT>
</td>
</tr>
</table>

<h2>CART CONTENTS</h2>

<table border=1 cellpadding=10 cellspacing=0>

<tr>
<td align=center><strong>ITEM ID</strong></td>
<td align=center><strong>TITLE</strong></td>
<td align=center><strong>QTY</strong></td>
<td align=center><strong>PRICE</strong></td>
<td align=center><strong>TOTAL</strong></td>
</tr>
";

while ($row = mysql_fetch_array($cart_result)) {
    // get results and assign meaningful variable names
```

```php
        $sel_item = $row["SEL_ITEM"];
        $sel_item_title = $row["SEL_ITEM_TITLE"];
        $sel_item_qty = $row["SEL_ITEM_QTY"];
        $sel_item_price = $row["SEL_ITEM_PRICE"];
        $sel_item_totalprice = $row["SEL_ITEM_TOTALPRICE"];


        $fmt_item_totalprice = sprintf("%0.2f",$sel_item_totalprice);

        echo "
        <tr>
        <td>$sel_item</td>
        <td>$sel_item_title</td>
        <td align=right>$sel_item_qty</td>
        <td align=right>$ $sel_item_price</td>
        <td align=right>$ $fmt_item_totalprice</td>
        </tr>
        ";
    }


    echo "
    <tr>
    <td colspan=4 align=right><strong>Item Total:</strong></td>
    <td align=right><strong>$ $fmt_itemtot</strong></td></tr>

    <tr><td colspan=4 align=right><strong>Shipping:</strong></td>
    <td align=right>";

        if ($shipping != "0") {
            echo "<strong>$ $fmt_shipping</strong>";
        } else {
            echo "<strong>FREE!</strong>";
        }

    echo "
    </td></tr>

    <tr><td colspan=4 align=right><strong>Grand Total:</strong></td>
    <td align=right><strong>$ $fmt_total</strong></td></tr>
    <tr><td colspan=5 align=center><input type=\"submit\" name=\"submit\"
```

```
value=\"Send This Order!\"></td></tr>
    </table>
    </form>";
    }
?>
</BODY>
</HTML>
```

Go back to any page that has the checkout link, and follow that link. You should now see a form and a cart displayed, as shown in Figure 8.7.

There is one final step: sending the encrypted form and clearing out the cart items!

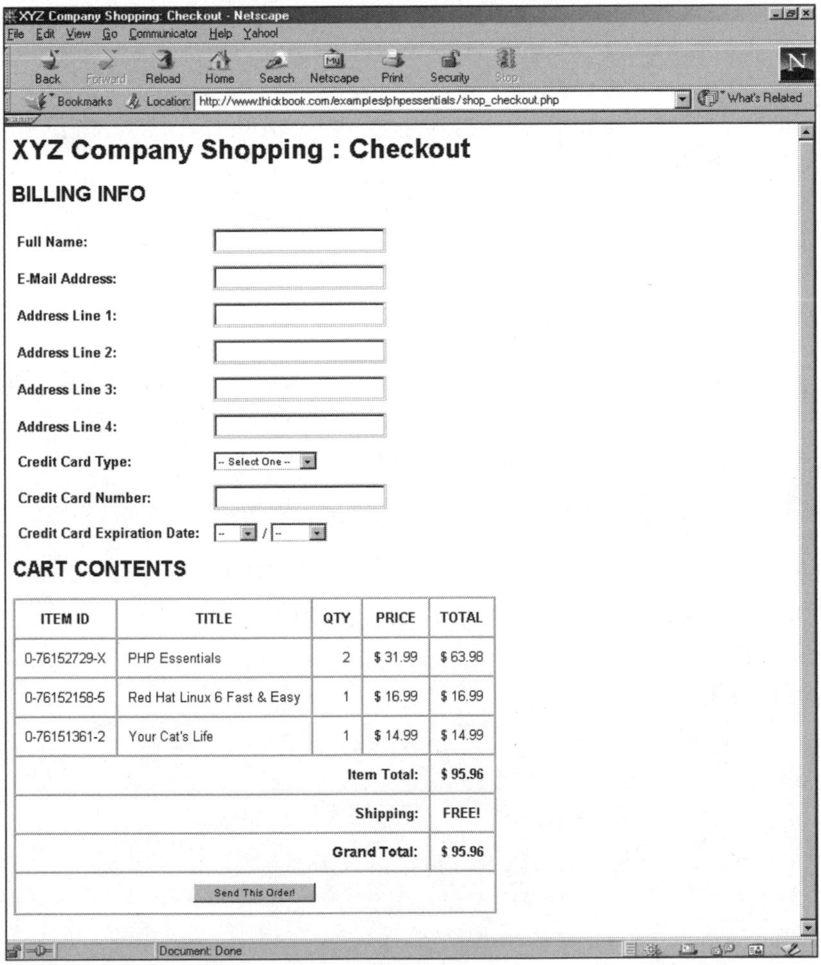

Figure 8.7 *Checkout form and cart contents displayed*

Sending Secure Orders Via E-Mail

This is it: the moment of truth. This final step will take the contents of the checkout form and send them to you via encrypted e-mail, as you learned at the beginning of this chapter. The PHP script for this step, `shop_sendorder.php`, is nearly identical to `shop_checkout.php`, so make a copy of the latter, and I'll walk you through the changes.

First, check for required fields. There are a bunch, so be prepared for a big `if` statement!

```
// check for required fields
if ((!($full_name)) || (!($email)) || (!($address1)) || (!($cc_type)) ||
(!($cc_num)) || (!($cc_exp_mon)) || (!($cc_exp_yr))) {
    header("Location: http://www.yourcompany.com/show_checkout.php");
    exit;
}
```

The next change is to remove the form elements and print the values of the variables as text, as a confirmation to the user. For example, within the `echo` statement, display the user's full name like this:

```
<tr>
<td><strong>Full Name:</strong></td>
<td>$full_name</td>
</tr>
```

Continue the process for the other fields from the checkout form. The next modification is part of the `while` loop that displays the cart items to the user. Keep the original echo statement within that loop, but add this after it:

```
$items .= "$sel_item_qty $sel_item ($sel_item_title) at $sel_item_price each\n";
```

This adds the elements to a string called `$items`, which we'll use in a moment.

Everything else remains the same until after all the HTML has been displayed. Now it's time to build the e-mail. Start by creating a `$msg` variable, and then concatenate to your heart's delight:

```
$msg = "XYZ COMPANY ORDER FORM\n";
$msg .= "-------------------------------------------\n\n";
$msg .= "CUSTOMER INFORMATION\n";
$msg .= "Full Name:         $full_name\n";
$msg .= "E-mail:            $email\n";
$msg .= "Address Line 1:    $address1\n";
```

```
$msg .= "Address Line 2:      $address2\n";
$msg .= "Address Line 3:      $address3\n";
$msg .= "Address Line 4:      $address4\n";
$msg .= "Credit Card Type:    $cc_type\n";
$msg .= "Credit Card Number:  $cc_num\n";
$msg .= "Expiration Date:     $cc_exp_mon / $cc_exp_yr\n\n";
$msg .= "ITEMS ORDERED\n";
```

Now add the `$items` string that you created earlier as part of the `while` loop:

```
$msg .= "$items\n\n";
```

Keep going, finishing by adding the totals to the message string:

```
$msg .= "TOTALS\n";
$msg .= "Item Total:          $fmt_itemtot\n";
```

Use an `if...else` statement to add the proper shipping amount to the message string:

```
    if ($shipping != "0") {
        $msg .= "Shipping:            $fmt_itemtot\n";
    } else {
        $msg .= "Shipping:            FREE\n";
    }
$msg .= "Grand Total:         $fmt_total\n";
```

Next, issue a SQL statement to clear the items from the shopping cart so that they don't take up any space:

```
$rm_item_sql = "DELETE FROM USER_TRACK WHERE USER_ID = \"$user_id\"";
mysql_query($rm_item_sql);
```

It's time to encrypt the e-mail. Follow the same process that you used at the beginning of this chapter. This example uses PGP encryption, but you can substitute GNUPG encryption.

```
// set the environment variable for PGPPATH
putenv("PGPPATH=/homedir/of/PHP/user/.pgp");

// Create a file for writing temporary data.
// Put contents of message string into the file
// created above, then close the file.
$fp = fopen("/path/to/temp/input/data", "w+");
fputs($fp, $msg);
```

```
fclose($fp);

// Invoke PGP to encrypt data and output to new file.
system("/usr/local/bin/pgpe -r \"Julie Meloni <julie@thickbook.com>\" -o /path/to/
temp/output/data -a /path/to/temp/input/data");

// remove unencrypted file from system
unlink("/path/to/temp/input/data");

// Assign the value of the encrypted data path to a
// variable called $crypted.
$crypted = "/path/to/temp/output/data";

// Open encrypted file for reading, put entire
// contents of encrypted file into variable
// called $mail_cont, then close file.
$fd = fopen($crypted, "r");
$mail_cont = fread($fd, filesize($crypted));
fclose($fd);

// Remove encrypted file from system.
unlink("$crypted");

// Build mail message and send it to target recipient.
$recipient = "julie@thickbook.com";
$subject = "XYZ Company Order Form";
$mailheaders = "From: XYZ Company Web Site\n";
$mailheaders .= "Reply-To: $email\n\n";

mail("$recipient", "$subject", $mail_cont, $mailheaders);
```

Amazingly enough, that's all there is to it. The entire `shop_sendorder.php` script looks something like this:

```
<?php
// File name: shop_sendorder.php
// set cookie if not already set
if (!isset($user_id)) {
    $token = md5(uniqid(rand()));
```

```
        setcookie("user_id",$token,time()+86400,"/",".yourcompany.com");
}


// create connection
$connection = mysql_connect("localhost","sandman","34Nhjp") or die ("Couldn't
connect to the database.");

// select database
$db = mysql_select_db("secretDB", $connection) or die ("Couldn't select database.);

    // get cart subtotal
    $get_itemtot = "SELECT SUM(SEL_ITEM_TOTALPRICE) FROM USER_TRACK WHERE USER_ID =
\"$user_id\"";
    $itemtot_result = mysql_query($get_itemtot) or die("Couldn't do math!");
    $itemtot = mysql_result($itemtot_result,0,"SUM(SEL_ITEM_TOTALPRICE)");
    $fmt_itemtot = sprintf("%0.2f",$itemtot);

    if ($itemtot < "50") {
        $shipping = 4.5;
    } else {
        $shipping = 0;
    }

    $fmt_shipping = sprintf("%0.2f",$shipping);
    $total = $itemtot + $shipping;
    $fmt_total = sprintf("%0.2f",$subtotal);

    // get cart
    $get_cart = "SELECT SEL_ITEM, SEL_ITEM_TITLE, SEL_ITEM_QTY, SEL_ITEM_PRICE,
SEL_ITEM_TOTALPRICE FROM USER_TRACK WHERE USER_ID = \"$user_id\"";
    $cart_result = mysql_query($get_cart) or die("Couldn't get cart!");
    $num_rows = mysql_numrows($cart_result);

    if ($num_rows == "0") {
    echo "<P><strong>There are no items in your cart, but thanks for trying.</p>";

    } else {

echo "
```

```
<!DOCTYPE HTML PUBLIC \"-//W3C//DTD HTML 3.2//EN\">
<HTML>
<HEAD>
<TITLE>XYZ Company Shopping: Order Sent!</TITLE>
</HEAD>
<BODY>
<h1>XYZ Company Shopping : Order Sent!</h1>

<h2>BILLING INFO</h2>
<table border=0 cellspacing=0 cellpadding=5>

<tr>
<td><strong>Full Name:</strong></td>
<td>$full_name</td>
</tr>

<tr>
<td><strong>E-Mail Address:</strong></td>
<td>$email</td>
</tr>

<tr>
<td><strong>Address Line 1:</strong></td>
<td>$address1</td>
</tr>

<tr>
<td><strong>Address Line 2:</strong></td>
<td>$address2</td>
</tr>

<tr>
<td><strong>Address Line 3:</strong></td>
<td>$address3</td>
</tr>

<tr>
<td><strong>Address Line 4:</strong></td>
```

```
<td>$address4</td>
</tr>

<tr>
<td><strong>Credit Card Type:</strong></td>
<td>$cc_type</td>
</tr>

<tr>
<td><strong>Credit Card Number:</strong></td>
<td>$cc_num</td>
</tr>

<tr>
<td><strong>Credit Card Expiration Date:</strong> </td>
<td>$cc_exp_mon  / $cc_exp_yr  </td>
</tr>
</table>

<h2>CART CONTENTS</h2>

<table border=1 cellpadding=10 cellspacing=0>
<tr>
<td align=center><strong>ITEM ID</strong></td>
<td align=center><strong>TITLE</strong></td>
<td align=center><strong>QTY</strong></td>
<td align=center><strong>PRICE</strong></td>
<td align=center><strong>TOTAL</strong></td>
</tr>
";

while ($row = mysql_fetch_array($cart_result)) {
    // get results and assign meaningful variable names
    $sel_item = $row["SEL_ITEM"];
    $sel_item_title = $row["SEL_ITEM_TITLE"];
    $sel_item_qty = $row["SEL_ITEM_QTY"];
    $sel_item_price = $row["SEL_ITEM_PRICE"];
```

```php
    $sel_item_totalprice = $row["SEL_ITEM_TOTALPRICE"];

    $fmt_item_totalprice = sprintf("%0.2f",$sel_item_totalprice);

    echo "
    <tr>
    <td>$sel_item</td>
    <td>$sel_item_title</td>
    <td align=right>$sel_item_qty</td>
    <td align=right>$ $sel_item_price</td>
    <td align=right>$ $fmt_item_totalprice</td>
    </tr>
    ";

    $items .= "$sel_item_qty $sel_item ($sel_item_title) at $sel_item_price
each\n";
}

    echo "
    <tr>
    <td colspan=4 align=right><strong>Item Total:</strong></td>
    <td align=right><strong>$ $fmt_itemtot</strong></td></tr>

    <tr><td colspan=4 align=right><strong>Shipping:</strong></td>
    <td align=right>";

        if ($shipping != "0") {
            echo "<strong>$ $fmt_shipping</strong>";
        } else {
            echo "<strong>FREE!</strong>";
        }

    echo "
    </td></tr>

    <tr><td colspan=4 align=right><strong>Grand Total:</strong></td>
    <td align=right><strong>$ $fmt_total</strong></td></tr>

    <tr><td colspan=5 align=center><strong>THANK YOU FOR YOUR ORDER!</strong></
```

```
td></tr>

    </table>
    </form>
</body>
</html>
";

    // start building mail

    $msg = "XYZ COMPANY ORDER FORM\n";
    $msg .= "----------------------------------------\n\n";
    $msg .= "CUSTOMER INFORMATION\n";
    $msg .= "Full Name:          $full_name\n";
    $msg .= "E-mail:             $email\n";
    $msg .= "Address Line 1:     $address1\n";
    $msg .= "Address Line 2:     $address2\n";
    $msg .= "Address Line 3:     $address3\n";
    $msg .= "Address Line 4:     $address4\n";
    $msg .= "Credit Card Type:   $cc_type\n";
    $msg .= "Credit Card Number: $cc_num\n";
    $msg .= "Expiration Date:    $cc_exp_mon / $cc_exp_yr\n\n";
    $msg .= "ITEMS ORDERED\n";
    $msg .= "$items\n\n";
    $msg .= "TOTALS\n";
    $msg .= "Item Total:         $fmt_itemtot\n";


        if ($shipping != "0") {
            $msg .= "Shipping:           $fmt_itemtot\n";
        } else {
            $msg .= "Shipping:           FREE\n";
        }

    $msg .= "Grand Total:        $fmt_total\n";

    // remove items from cart
    $rm_item_sql = "DELETE FROM USER_TRACK WHERE USER_ID = \"$user_id\"";
```

```php
        mysql_query($rm_item_sql) or die("Couldn't delete items.");

// set the environment variable for PGPPATH
putenv("PGPPATH=/homedir/of/PHP/user/.pgp");

// Create a file for writing temporary data.
// Put contents of message string into the file
// created above, then close the file.
$fp = fopen("/path/to/temp/input/data", "w+");
fputs($fp, $msg);
fclose($fp);

// Invoke PGP to encrypt data and output to new file.
system("/usr/local/bin/pgpe -r \"Julie Meloni <julie@thickbook.com>\" -o /path/to/
temp/output/data -a /path/to/temp/input/data");

// remove unencrypted file from system
unlink("/path/to/temp/input/data");

// Assign the value of the encrypted data path to a
// variable called $crypted.
$crypted = "/path/to/temp/output/data";

// Open encrypted file for reading, put entire
// contents of encrypted file into variable
// called $mail_cont, then close file.
$fd = fopen($crypted, "r");
$mail_cont = fread($fd, filesize($crypted));
fclose($fd);

// Remove encrypted file from system.
unlink("$crypted");

// Build mail message and send it to target recipient.
$recipient = "julie@thickbook.com";
$subject = "XYZ Company Order Form";
$mailheaders = "From: XYZ Company Web Site\n";
```

```
$mailheaders .= "Reply-To: $email\n\n";


mail("$recipient", "$subject", $mail_cont, $mailheaders);


?>
```

Go ahead and place an order—it's your store, after all! I sent a test order like the one shown in Figure 8.8, and the screen displayed results similar to those shown in Figure 8.9.

Figure 8.8 *Completed checkout form*

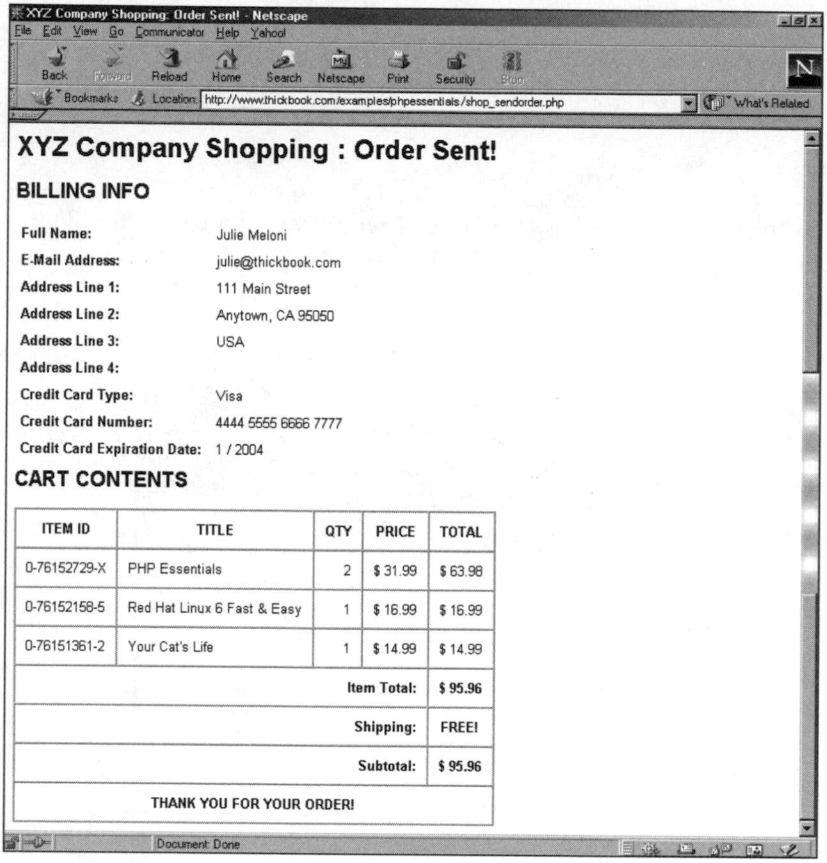

Figure 8.9   *Order sent!*

Then, check your mailbox for an encrypted e-mail using something like this:

----BEGIN PGP MESSAGE----

Version: PGP for Personal Privacy 5.0

MessageID: W8X3uX6pCu7bELmJf4uslEseKZK6s3K0

9dwd84bzK+qWhf5sPNnjgS7ji5eVU8GYJ74/jqgYxvhiD3VlMf+i6Erm93fZes6y

xMKK87hPat8Ge7hBo3MPdymdM52A/XGAEf0ncCpgHU0uW4qNhISbo5/LnFRa4L3D

L0bv+iwixpvoTe4XN+dn+PbWz5okonY3xir5lU2l0Qm8WSU1or+smxzLANDWhY6M

z0JVBXk5TV3txksJRpnQvRdYQBkOap7AkswvEZfEsiuLAWblvmMZUGdRwLzcnRJf

zHoGYotoZNwNpCh0K007P6VfVlAL/2E/+4EXgl5JDLLL/xqgJexZgC44KNCDrmfL

V8mjjrAAauDXF58tmrKP9epRpG52MPcHtP/OXM6cdHYv5JxxKIvz0/GUNSTudLxX

OquF0FMxuvLtvSCNmvVmvQ8Jd9nizRNYl1YwdSDnXGCKn99xml9oWISPG2R/DjLq

DM3qx5X5GnXmxjw9zIj1uZJXtHDI2X/Eem+zUwK0HBH+Zs8MqDYV602x5vaCd4Dc

48856EbHDBPmhdegcpDGuBobjo4McS7Z/CZGTTtLAVyTOQ3mhc2GZ1myWpTjr4hh

lRWUnr9rJ2KHYOypfN6/XNF7/RJKTxkqisKAMJ8njU2BoMfQHFQKeHHg3O4Bok9M

oxfZGZWzB+71MaN8EPgRKODqens28A2swzcFjfb2BnztovR8Ik3CTsvWBfzr3H+o

JufNdUKbVwM40j88jMVz+SPjRpcQoaNCsCY4SFEbxt0+/KYHcdQEyMYxFsTjrwWE

+hU8tNuSkjxJFRZAJflc9kB1wzUJg8nA0Fnp+lYfhxIRwtyj6t76dBLkMeHR+p5r

vIwBdRcZte3wntoeDBqnNpVcgDeFkGuKQ7U8C/W7PlK5/YFULI2nj8Hb+JUgQNSn

Grz6xX7ba6k+og5KPh+AbZbA46e48rWQOxH3uo7kCW1l4Hfm3OtCEV7Y+ZMQbn/G

UMcMSVXsaBqGi4CwjSM93SVsOyj9+r1FCAAxHOIp3juOIHTpSR5iFuOS4gQnvVXH

----END PGP MESSAGE----

Once you get that message, you're in business!

More Advanced Techniques

PHP is much more than saving product information in a database and creating a shopping cart count. For example, with additional libraries, you can create images and PDF files on-the-fly and use additional data encryption techniques. Using built-in IMAP functions, you can create Web-based e-mail applications. You can even create Web-based calendar applications using the built-in MCAL functions.

I could easily write a longer book on all of these features, but the goal of this book is to form a solid foundation with the basic concepts of PHP and leave the large books for another day. At http://www.thickbook.com/, you can find tutorials that I've written that are outside the scope of this book. Hopefully, these tutorials will help you as you get more involved with developing applications in PHP. Please feel free to leave feedback at thickbook.com, to let me know about the advanced PHP techniques you'd like to learn more about.

Appendix A: Essential PHP Language Reference

PHP Syntax

Variables

Operators

Control Structures

Built-In Functions

T his appendix is by no means a copy of the PHP Manual (found at http://www.php.net/manual/), which contains user-submitted comments and code samples. Instead, this appendix serves as an "essential" reference—it contains the elements of PHP which (in my opinion) you can't live without. The PHP Development Team and all of the documentation contributors have done a wonderful job with the entire PHP Manual, and there's no need to reinvent the wheel. However, since this appendix touches on only a small percentage of all there is to know about PHP, check the PHP Manual before asking a question on one of the PHP mailing lists.

PHP Syntax

To combine PHP code with HTML, the PHP code must be *escaped*, or set apart, from the HTML. The PHP engine will consider anything within the tag pairs shown in Table A.1 as PHP code.

Table A.1   Basic PHP Syntax

Opening Tag	Closing Tag
`<?php`	`?>`
`<?`	`?>`
`<script language="php">`	`</script>`

Here's an example that uses all three in the same script, called `tagtest.php`:

```
<!DOCTYPE HTML PUBLIC "-//W3C//DTD HTML 3.2//EN">
<HTML>
<HEAD>
<TITLE>Tag Test</TITLE>
</HEAD>
<BODY>
<?php echo "I am using the first tag pair type.<br>"; ?>
```

```
<? echo "I am using the second tag pair type.<br>"; ?>

<script language="php">
echo "I am using the third tag pair type.<br>";
</script>
</BODY>
</HTML>
```

When accessed, the script displays this:

> I am using the first tag pair type.
>
> I am using the second tag pair type.
>
> I am using the third tag pair type.

When you create PHP scripts, you're creating a series of instructions that are sent to the PHP engine. Each instruction must end with a semicolon (;), also known as an instruction separator.

These are examples of properly terminated instructions:

```
<?php
    echo "<P>Hello World!  I'm using PHP!</P>\n";
    echo "<P>This is another message.</P>";
?>
```

One of these instructions is missing a semicolon:

```
<?php
    echo "<P>Hello World!  I'm using PHP!</p>\n"
    echo "<P>This is another message.</p>";
?>
```

so it will produce a nasty error, such as this:

```
Parse error: parse error, expecting "," or ";" in /path/to/script on line 9
```

The last important bit of PHP syntax is the method of commenting inside code. Use double forward slashes (//) to indicate a comment:

```
<?php
    // The next statement prints a line of text
    echo "<P>Hello World!  I'm using PHP!</P>\n";
?>
```

The comment "The next statement prints a line of text" is visible in your source code but is not printed in your HTML output.

For multiline comments, you can surround your text with /* and */, like this:

```php
<?php
    /* This is a really long comment that
    will run onto multiple lines */
?>
```

Commenting code is a good habit to have, because it helps other programmers figure out what you're trying to do with a piece of code if they have to make changes or if they're trying to learn from your work.

Variables

You create variables to represent data. For instance, the following variable holds a value for sales tax:

```php
$sales_tax = 0.0875;
```

This variable holds an SQL statement:

```php
$sql = "SELECT * FROM MY_TABLE";
```

You can refer to the value of other variables when determining the value of a new variable:

```php
$tax_total = $sales_tax * $sub_total;
```

The following are true of variable names:

- They begin with a dollar sign ($).
- They cannot begin with a numeric character.
- They can contain numbers and the underscore character (_).
- They are case-sensitive.

Here are some common variable types:

- arrays
- floats
- integers
- strings

These types are determined by PHP, based on the context in which they appear.

Arrays

In the following example, $fave_colors is an array that contains strings represent-ing array elements. In this case, the array elements (0 to 3) are names of colors.

```
$fave_colors[0] = "red";
$fave_colors[1] = "blue";
$fave_colors[2] = "black";
$fave_colors[3] = "white";
```

Array elements are counted with 0 as the first position.

Floats

Each of the following variables is a float, or floating-point number. Floats are also known as "numbers with decimal points."

```
$a = 1.552;
$b = 0.964;
$sales_tax = 0.875;
```

Integers

Integers are positive or negative whole numbers, or "numbers without decimal points." Each of the following variables is an integer.

```
$a = 15;
$b = -521;
```

Strings

A series of characters grouped within double quotes is considered a string:

```
$a = "I am a string.";
$b = "<P>This book is <strong>cool</strong>!";
```

You can also reference other variables within your string, which will be replaced when your script is executed. For example:

```
$num = 57; // an integer
$my_string = "I read this book $num times!"; // a string
```

When you run the script, $my_string will become "I read this book 57 times!".

Variables from HTML Forms

Depending on the method of your HTML form (GET or POST), the variables will be part of the $HTTP_POST_VARS or $HTTP_GET_VARS global associative array. The name of the input field will become the name of the variable. For example, the following input field produces the variable $first_name:

```
<input type="text" name="first_name" size="20">
```

If the method of this form were POST, this variable could also be referenced as $HTTP_POST_VARS["first_name"]. If the method were GET, you could also use $HTTP_GET_VARS["first_name"].

Variables from Cookies

Like variables from forms, variables from cookies are kept in a global associative array called $HTTP_COOKIE_VARS. If you set a cookie called "user" with a value of "Joe Smith," like so:

```
SetCookie ("user", "Joe Smith", time()+3600);
```

a variable called $user will have been placed in $HTTP_COOKIE_VARS, with a value of "Joe Smith." You can refer to $user or $HTTP_COOKIE_VARS['user'] to get that value.

Environment Variables

When a Web browser makes a request of a Web server, it sends along with the request a list of extra variables called *environment variables*. They can be very useful for displaying dynamic content or authorizing users.

By default, environment variables are available to PHP scripts as $VAR_NAME. However, to be absolutely sure that you're reading the correct value, you can use the getenv() function to assign a value to a variable of your choice. Following are some common environment variables:

REMOTE_ADDR gets the IP address of the machine making the request. For example:

```
<?php
    $remote_address = getenv("REMOTE_ADDR");
    echo "Your IP address is $remote_address.";
?>
```

HTTP_USER_AGENT gets the browser type, browser version, language encoding, and platform. For example:

```
<?php
    $browser_type = getenv("HTTP_USER_AGENT");
```

```
        echo "You are using $browser_type.";
?>
```

For a list of HTTP environment variables and their descriptions, visit http://hoohoo.ncsa.uiuc.edu/cgi/env.html.

Operators

An operator is a symbol that represents a specific action. For example, the + arithmetic operator adds two values, and the = assignment operator assigns a value to a variable.

Arithmetic Operators

Arithmetic operators bear a striking resemblance to simple math, as shown in Table A.2. In the examples, `$a = 5` and `$b = 4`.

Table A.2 Arithmetic Operators

Operator	Name	Example	
+	addition	$c = $a + $b;	// $c = 9
-	subtraction	$c = $a - $b;	// $c = 1
*	multiplication	$c = $a * $b;	// $c = 20
/	division	$c = $a / $b;	// $c = 1.25
%	modulus, or "remainder"	$c = $a % $b;	// $c = 1

Assignment Operators

The = is the basic assignment operator:

```
$a = 124; // the value of $a is 124
```

Other assignment operators include +=, -=, and .=.

```
$ex += 1;    // Assigns the value of ($ex + 1) to $ex.
             // If $ex = 2, then the value of ($ex += 1) is 3.
$ex -= 1;    // Assigns the value of ($ex - 1) to $ex.
             // If $ex = 2, then the value of ($ex -= 1) is 1.
$ex .= "coffee";    // Concatenates (adds to) a string. If $ex = "I like "
                    // then the value of ($ex .= "coffee") is "I like coffee".
```

Comparison Operators

It should come as no surprise that comparison operators compare two values. A value of TRUE or FALSE is returned by the comparison, as shown in Table A.3.

Table A.3   Comparison Operators

Operator	Name	Example	Result (T/F)
==	equal to	$a == $b	TRUE if $a is equal to $b
!=	not equal to	$a != $b	TRUE if $a is not equal to $b
>	greater than	$a > $b	TRUE if $a is greater than $b
<	less than	$a < $b	TRUE if $a is less than $b
>=	greater than or equal to	$a >= $b	TRUE if $a is greater than or equal to $b
<=	less than or equal to	$a <= $b	TRUE if $a is less than or equal to $b

Increment/Decrement Operators

The increment/decrement operators do just what their name implies: add or subtract from a variable (see Table A.4).

Table A.4   Increment/Decrement Operators

Name	Usage	Result
Pre-increment	++$a	Increments by 1 and returns $a
Post-increment	$a++	Returns $a and then increments $a by 1
Pre-decrement	--$a	Decrements by 1 and returns $a
Post-decrement	$a--	Returns $a and then decrements $a by 1

Logical Operators

Logical operators allow your script to determine the status of conditions and, in the context of your if...else or while statements, execute certain code based on which conditions are true and which are false (see Table A.5).

Table A.5   Logical Operators

Operator	Name	Example	Result (T/F)
!	not	!$a	TRUE if $a is not true
&&	and	$a && $b	TRUE if both $a and $b are true
||	or	$a || $b	TRUE if either $a or $b is true

Control Structures

Programs are essentially a series of statements. Control structures, as their name implies, control how those statements are executed. Control structures are usually built around a series of conditions, such as "If the sky is blue, go outside and play." In this example, the condition is "If the sky is blue" and the statement is "go outside and play."

Control structures utilize curly braces ({ and }) to separate the groups of statements from the remainder of the program. Examples of common control structures follow; memorizing these will make your life much easier.

if . . . elseif . . . else

The `if…elseif…else` construct executes a statement based on the value of the expression being tested. In the following sample `if` statement, the expression being tested is "$a is equal to 10."

```
if ($a == "10") {
    // execute some code
}
```

After $a is evaluated, if it is found to have a value of 10 (that is, if the condition is TRUE), the code inside the curly braces will execute. If $a is found to be something other than 10 (if the condition is FALSE), the code will be ignored, and the program will continue.

To offer an alternative series of statements, should $a not have a value of 10, add an `else` statement to the structure to execute a section of code when the condition is FALSE:

```
if ($a == "10") {
    echo "a equals 10";
```

```
} else {
    echo "a does not equal 10";
}
```

The `elseif` statement can be added to the structure to evaluate an alternative expression before heading to the final else statement. For example, the following structure first evaluates whether $a is equal to 10. If that condition is FALSE, the `elseif` statement is evaluated. If it is found to be TRUE, the code within its curly braces executes. Otherwise, the program continues to the final else statement:

```
if ($a == "10") {
    echo "a equals 10";
} elseif ($b == "8") {
    echo "b equals 8";
} else {
    echo "a does not equal 10 and b does not equal 8.";
}
```

You can use `if` statements alone or as part of an `if...else` or `if...elseif...else` statement. Whichever you choose, you will find this structure to be an invaluable element in your programs!

while

Unlike the `if...elseif...else` structure, in which each expression is evaluated once and an action is performed based on its value of TRUE or FALSE, the `while` statement continues to loop until an expression is FALSE. In other words, the `while` loop continues while the expression is TRUE.

For example, in the following `while` loop, the value of $a is printed on the screen and is incremented by 1 as long as the value of $a is less than or equal to 5.

```
$a = 0 // set a starting point
while ($a <= "5") {
    echo "a equals $a<br>";
    $a++;
}
```

Here is the output of this loop:

    a equals 0
    a equals 1

a equals 2

a equals 3

a equals 4

a equals 5

for

Like `while` loops, `for` loops evaluate the set of conditional expressions at the beginning of each loop. Here is the syntax of the `for` loop:

```
for (expr1; expr2; expr3) {
    // code to execute
}
```

At the beginning of each loop, the first expression is evaluated, followed by the second expression. If the second expression is TRUE, the loop continues by executing the code and then evaluating the third expression. If the second expression is FALSE, the loop does not continue, and the third expression is never evaluated.

Take the counting example used in the `while` loop, and rewrite it using a `for` loop:

```
for ($a = 0; $a <= "5"; $a++) {
    echo "a equals $a<br>";
}
```

The output is the same as the `while` loop:

a equals 0

a equals 1

a equals 2

a equals 3

a equals 4

a equals 5

Built-In Functions

Numerous PHP functions are available for use with arrays. Only a few are noted here—those that I find absolutely essential, and those that form a foundation of knowledge for working with arrays. The new array functions in PHP4 are indicated as such, and do make working with arrays so much easier!

array()

The `array()` function allows you to manually assign values to an array. Here is the syntax of the `array()` function:

```
$array_name = array("val1", "val2", "val3", …);
```

For example, to create an array called `$colors`, containing the values "blue," "black," "red," and "green," use the following:

```
$colors = array("blue", "black", "red", "green");
```

array_push()

New Feature

The `array_push()` function allows you to add one or more elements to the end of an existing array.

The syntax of the `array_push()` function is:

```
array_push(array_name, "element 1", "element 2", …);
```

For example, say you have an array that contains the elements "1" and "2" and you want to add the elements "3", "4", "5" and "cool" to it. You would use this snippet of code:

```
$sample = array(1, 2);
array_push($sample, 3, 4, 5, "cool");
```

You can use the example script below to print the "Before" and "After" versions of the `$sample` array:

```
<?php
// print before
$sample = array(1, 2);

echo "BEFORE:<br>";
while (list($key,$value) = each($sample)) {
    echo "$key : $value<br>";
}
// reset array pointer to first position
reset($sample);

// add to end of an existing array
array_push($sample, 3, 4, 5, "cool");

// print after
echo "<br>AFTER:<br>";

while (list($key,$value) = each($sample)) {
    echo "$key : $value<br>";
```

```
}
?>
```

The above script will print:

> BEFORE:
>
> 0 : 1
>
> 1 : 2
>
> AFTER:
>
> 0 : 1
>
> 1 : 2
>
> 2 : 3
>
> 3 : 4
>
> 4 : 5
>
> 5 : cool

array_pop()

The syntax of the `array_pop()` function is:

```
array_pop(array_name);
```

For example, say you have an array that contains the elements "1", "2", "3", "4", "5" and "cool", and you want to pop off the "cool" element. You would use this snippet of code:

```
$sample = array(1, 2, 3, 4, 5, "cool");
$last = array_pop($sample);
```

You can use the example script below to print the "Before" and "After" versions of the `$sample` array and the value of `$last`:

```php
<?php
// print before
$sample = array(1, 2, 3, 4, 5, "cool");

echo "BEFORE:<br>";
while (list($key,$value) = each($sample)) {
    echo "$key : $value<br>";
}

// reset array pointer to first position
```

New Feature

The `array_pop()` function allows you to take (pop) off the last element of an existing array.

```
reset($sample);

// pop off end of an existing array
$last = array_pop($sample);

// print after
echo "<br>AFTER:<br>";

while (list($key,$value) = each($sample)) {
    echo "$key : $value<br>";
}
echo "<br>and finally, in \$last: $last";
?>
```

The above script will print:

BEFORE:

0 : 1

1 : 2

2 : 3

3 : 4

4 : 5

5 : cool

AFTER:

0 : 1

1 : 2

2 : 3

3 : 4

4 : 5

and finally, in $last: cool

array_unshift()

New Feature

The `array_unshift()` function allows you to add elements to the beginning of an existing array.

The syntax of the `array_unshift()` function is:

```
array_unshift(array_name, "element 1", "element 2", …);
```

For example, say you have an array that contains the elements "1" and "2", and you want to add the elements "3", "4", "5" and "cool". You would use this snippet of code:

```
$sample = array(1, 2);
array_unshift($sample, 3, 4, 5, "cool");
```

You can use the example script below to print the "Before" and "After" versions of the $sample array:

```
<?php
// print before
$sample = array(1, 2);

echo "BEFORE:<br>";
while (list($key,$value) = each($sample)) {
    echo "$key : $value<br>";
}
// reset array pointer to first position
reset($sample);

// push onto beginning of existing array
array_unshift($sample, 3, 4, 5, "cool");

// print after
echo "<br>AFTER:<br>";

while (list($key,$value) = each($sample)) {
    echo "$key : $value<br>";
}
?>
```

The above script will print:

> BEFORE:
> 0 : 1
> 1 : 2
> AFTER:
> 0 : 3
> 1 : 4
> 2 : 5
> 3 : cool
> 4 : 1
> 5 : 2

New Feature

The array_shift()
function allows
you to take (pop)
off the first ele-
ment of an
existing array.

array_shift()

The syntax of the `array_shift()` function is:

```
array_shift(array_name);
```

For example, say you have an array that contains the elements "1", "2", "3", "4", "5" and "cool", and you want to pop off the "1" element. You would use this snippet of code:

```
$sample = array(1, 2, 3, 4, 5, "cool");
$first = array_shift($sample);
```

You can use the example script below to print the "Before" and "After" versions of the $sample array and the value of $first:

```php
<?php
// print before
$sample = array(1, 2, 3, 4, 5, "cool");

echo "BEFORE:<br>";
while (list($key,$value) = each($sample)) {
    echo "$key : $value<br>";
}

// reset array pointer to first position
reset($sample);

// pop off beginning of an existing array
$first = array_shift($sample);

// print after
echo "<br>AFTER:<br>";
echo "in \$first: $first<br>";

while (list($key,$value) = each($sample)) {
    echo "$key : $value<br>";
}
?>
```

The above script will print:

    BEFORE:
    0 : 1
    1 : 2

2 : 3

3 : 4

4 : 5

5 : cool

AFTER:

in $first: 1

0 : 2

1 : 3

2 : 4

3 : 5

4 : cool

array_slice()

The syntax of the `array_slice()` function is:

```
array_slice(array_name, start_position, offset, length);
```

For example, say you have an array that contains the elements "1", "2", "3", "4", "5" and "cool", and you want to extract some portions of this array. Some examples are:

```
$sample = array(1, 2, 3, 4, 5, "cool");

// start at 2nd position
$slice1 = array_slice($sample, 1);

// start at 2nd position, go to next to last
$slice2 = array_slice($sample, 1, -1);

// start at 5th position
$slice3 = array_slice($sample, 4);

// start at 1st position, take 3 elements
$slice4 = array_slice($sample, 0, 3);
```

You can use the example script below to print the "Before" version of the $sample array and the value of the various "slices":

```
<?php
// print before
```

New Feature

The `array_slice()` function allows you to extract a chunk of an existing array.

```php
$sample = array(1, 2, 3, 4, 5, "cool");

echo "BEFORE:<br>";
while (list($key,$value) = each($sample)) {
    echo "$key : $value<br>";
}

// reset array pointer to first position
reset($sample);

// extract slices of existing array
$slice1 = array_slice($sample, 1);
$slice2 = array_slice($sample, 1, -1);
$slice3 = array_slice($sample, 4);
$slice4 = array_slice($sample, 0, 3);

// echo slice1
echo "<br>slice1 (start at 2nd position) looks like:<br>";
while (list($key,$value) = each($slice1)) {
    echo "$key : $value<br>";
}

// echo slice2
echo "<br>slice2 (start at 2nd pos, go to next to last) looks like:<br>";
while (list($key,$value) = each($slice2)) {
    echo "$key : $value<br>";
}

// echo slice3
echo "<br>slice3 (start at 5th pos) looks like:<br>";
while (list($key,$value) = each($slice3)) {
    echo "$key : $value<br>";
}

// echo slice4
echo "<br>slice4 (start at 1st pos, print 3 elements) looks like:<br>";
while (list($key,$value) = each($slice4)) {
```

```
        echo "$key : $value<br>";
    }
?>
```

The above script will print:

BEFORE:

0 : 1

1 : 2

2 : 3

3 : 4

4 : 5

5 : cool

slice1 (start at 2nd position) looks like:

0 : 2

1 : 3

2 : 4

3 : 5

4 : cool

slice2 (start at 2nd pos, go to next to last) looks like:

0 : 2

1 : 3

2 : 4

3 : 5

slice3 (start at 5th pos) looks like:

0 : 5

1 : cool

slice4 (start at 1st pos, print 3 elements) looks like:

0 : 1

1 : 2

2 : 3

New Feature

The array_merge() function allows you to combine two or more existing arrays.

array_merge()

The syntax of the `array_merge()` function is:

```
array_merge(array1, array2, …);
```

For example, say you have an array that contains the elements "1", "2", "3", "4", "5" and "cool", and another array that contains the elements "a", "b", "c", "d", "e" and "cooler", and you want to combine the two. You would use this snippet of code:

```
$sample1 = array(1, 2, 3, 4, 5, "cool");
$sample2 = array(a, b, c, d, e, "cooler");
$merged = array_merge($sample1, $sample2);
```

You can use the example script below to print the "Before" and "After" versions of the arrays:

```
<?php
// print samples before
$sample1 = array(1, 2, 3, 4, 5, "cool");

echo "BEFORE - SAMPLE1:<br>";
while (list($key,$value) = each($sample1)) {
    echo "$key : $value<br>";
}

reset($sample1);

$sample2 = array(a, b, c, d, e, "cooler");

echo "<br>BEFORE - SAMPLE2:<br>";
while (list($key,$value) = each($sample2)) {
    echo "$key : $value<br>";
}

reset($sample2);

// merge $sample1 and $sample2
$merged = array_merge($sample1, $sample2);

// print after
echo "<br>AFTER:<br>";

while (list($key,$value) = each($merged)) {
```

```
        echo "$key : $value<br>";
}


?>
```

The above script will print:

BEFORE - SAMPLE1:

0 : 1

1 : 2

2 : 3

3 : 4

4 : 5

5 : cool

BEFORE - SAMPLE2:

0 : a

1 : b

2 : c

3 : d

4 : e

5 : cooler

AFTER:

0 : 1

1 : 2

2 : 3

3 : 4

4 : 5

5 : cool

6 : a

7 : b

8 : c

9 : d

10 : e

11 : cooler

New Feature

The array_keys() function will return an array of all the key names in an existing array.

array_keys()

The syntax of the array_keys() function is:

```
array_keys(array_name);
```

Suppose you have an array that looks like this:

```
$sample = array("key0" => "1", "key1" => "2", "key2" => "3", "key3" => "4", "key4"
=> "5", "key6" => "cool");
```

You can use the example script below to print all the keys in $sample:

```php
<?php
$sample = array("key0" => "1", "key1" => "2", "key2" => "3", "key3" => "4", "key4"
=> "5", "key6" => "cool");

// print $sample array
echo "SAMPLE ARRAY:<br>";
while (list($key,$value) = each($sample)) {
    echo "$key : $value<br>";
}

// print keys in $sample array
$keys = array_keys($sample);
echo "<br>KEYS IN SAMPLE ARRAY:<br>";
while (list($key,$value) = each($keys)) {
    echo "$key : $value<br>";
}
?>
```

The above script will print:

> SAMPLE ARRAY:
>
> key0 : 1
>
> key1 : 2
>
> key2 : 3
>
> key3 : 4
>
> key4 : 5
>
> key6 : cool
>
> KEYS IN SAMPLE ARRAY:
>
> 0 : key0

1 : key1

2 : key2

3 : key3

4 : key4

5 : key6

array_values()

The syntax of the `array_values()` function is:

```
array_values(array_name);
```

Suppose you have an array that looks like this:

```
$sample = array("key0" => "1", "key1" => "2", "key2" => "3", "key3" => "4", "key4"
=> "5", "key6" => "cool");
```

You can use the example script below to print all the values in `$sample`:

```php
<?php
$sample = array("key0" => "1", "key1" => "2", "key2" => "3", "key3" => "4", "key4"
=> "5", "key6" => "cool");

// print $sample array
echo "SAMPLE ARRAY:<br>";
while (list($key,$value) = each($sample)) {
    echo "$key : $value<br>";
}

// print values in $sample array
$values = array_values($sample);

echo "<br>VALUES IN SAMPLE ARRAY:<br>";
while (list($key,$value) = each($values)) {
    echo "$key : $value<br>";
}
?>
```

The above script will print:

SAMPLE ARRAY:

key0 : 1

key1 : 2

New Feature

The `array_values()` function will return an array of all the values in an existing array.

key2 : 3

key3 : 4

key4 : 5

key6 : cool

VALUES IN SAMPLE ARRAY:

0 : 1

1 : 2

2 : 3

3 : 4

4 : 5

5 : cool

count()

The `count()` function counts the number of elements in a variable. It's usually used to count the number of elements in an array, because any variable that is not an array will have only one element—itself.

In the following example, `$a` is assigned a value equal to the number of elements in the `$colors` array:

```
$a = count($colors);
```

If `$colors` contains the values "blue," "black," "red," and "green," `$a` will be assigned a value of 4.

You can create a `for` loop that will loop through an array and print its elements, using the result of the `count()` function as the second expression in the loop. For example:

```
$colors = array("blue", "black", "red", "green");
for ($i = 0; $i < count($colors); $i++) {
    echo "The current color is $colors[$i].<br>";
}
```

produces this result:

The current color is blue.

The current color is black.

The current color is red.

The current color is green.

In this example, the value of the count() function is used as the stopping point for the loop; the statement $i < count($colors) in this case is the equivalent of $i < 4.

each() and list()

The each() and list() functions usually appear together, in the context of stepping through an array and returning its keys and values. Here is the syntax for these functions:

```
each(arrayname);
list(val1, val2, val3, …);
```

For example, when you submit an HTML form via the GET method, each key/ value pair is placed in the global variable $HTTP_GET_VARS. If your form input fields are named first_name and last_name and the user enters values of Joe and Smith, the key/value pairs are first_name/Joe and last_name/Smith. In the $HTTP_GET_VARS array, these variables are represented as the following:

```
$HTTP_GET_VARS["first_name"] // value is "Joe"
$HTTP_GET_VARS["last_name"]  // value is "Smith"
```

You can use the each() and list() functions to step through the array in this fashion, printing the key and value for each element in the array:

```
while (list($key, $val) = each($HTTP_GET_VARS)) {
   echo "$key has a value of $val<br>";
}
```

Continuing the example, this would produce the following results:

> first_name has a value of Joe.
>
> last_name has a value of Smith.

reset()

The reset() function rewinds the pointer to the beginning of the array. The syntax of the reset() function is:

```
reset(array_name);
```

shuffle()

The shuffle() function will randomize the elements of a given array. The syntax of the shuffle() function is:

```
shuffle(array_name);
```

For example, say you have an array that contains the numbers "1" through "10" and you want to randomize the elements. You can use the example script below to print the "Before" and "After" versions of the $sample array:

```php
<?php
// print samples before
$sample = array(1, 2, 3, 4, 5, 6, 7, 8, 9, 10);
echo "BEFORE:<br>";

while (list($key,$value) = each($sample)) {
    echo "$key : $value<br>";
}

reset($sample);

// seed the randomizer
srand(time());

// shuffle $sample
shuffle($sample);

// print after
echo "<br>AFTER:<br>";

while (list($key,$value) = each($sample)) {
    echo "$key : $value<br>";
}
?>
```

The above script could print:

BEFORE:

0 : 1

1 : 2

2 : 3

3 : 4

4 : 5

5 : 6

6 : 7

7 : 8

8 : 9

9 : 10

AFTER:

0 : 6

1 : 8

2 : 1

3 : 3

4 : 5

5 : 2

6 : 4

7 : 10

8 : 9

9 : 7

sizeof()

The sizeof() function counts the number of elements in an array. In the following example, $a is assigned a value equal to the number of elements in the $colors array:

```
$a = sizeof(colors);
```

If $colors contains the values "blue," "black," "red," and "green," $a is assigned a value of 4.

You can create a for loop that will loop through an array and print its elements, using the sizeof() function as the second expression in the loop. For example:

```
$colors = array("blue", "black", "red", "green");
for ($i = 0; $i < sizeof($colors); $i++) {
    echo "The current color is $colors[$i].<br>";
}
```

Here is the result:

> The current color is blue.
>
> The current color is black.
>
> The current color is red.
>
> The current color is green.

In this example, the value of the sizeof() function is used as the stopping point for the loop; the statement $i < sizeof($colors) in this case is the equivalent of $i < 4.

Database Connectivity Functions

Database connectivity functions in PHP tend to follow the same patterns: connect to database, get results, close connection, and so on. However, several specific database types have their own set of functions, taking into consideration the nuances of the software. The following sections show the basic syntax of the database functions for common database types. Extended examples for each database can be found in Chapter 3, "Working with Databases."

Informix Functions

There are numerous PHP functions for connecting to and querying Informix databases. Following are some basic functions and their syntax. See the PHP Manual at http://www.php.net/manual/ for a complete listing of Informix functions.

ifx_connect()

Opens a connection to the Informix database. Requires a database name, server name, username, and password.

```
$connection = ifx_connect("dbname@SERVERNAME", "username", "password");
```

ifx_query()

Issues the SQL statement. Requires an open connection to the database.

```
$sql_result = ifx_query("SELECT * FROM SOMETABLE",$connection);
```

ifx_htmltbl_result()

Automatically formats query results into an HTML table. Requires a query result and can optionally include HTML table attributes.

```
ifx_htmltbl_result($sql_result,"border=1");
```

ifx_free_result()

Frees the memory resources used by a database query.

```
ifx_free_result($sql_result);
```

ifx_close()

Explicitly closes a database connection.

```
ifx_close($connection);
```

Microsoft SQL Server Functions

There are numerous PHP functions for connecting to and querying Microsoft SQL Server. Following are some basic functions and their syntax. See the PHP Manual at http://www.php.net/manual/ for a complete listing of Microsoft SQL Server functions.

mssql_connect()

This function opens a connection to the Microsoft SQL Server; it requires a server name, username, and password.

```
$connection = mssql_connect("servername","username","password");
```

mssql_select_db()

This function selects a database on the Microsoft SQL Server for use by subsequent queries; it requires that a valid connection has been established.

```
$db = mssql_select_db("myDB", $connection);
```

mssql_query()

This function issues the SQL statement; it requires an open connection to the database.

```
$sql_result = mssql_query("SELECT * FROM SOMETABLE",$connection);
```

mssql_fetch_array()

This function automatically places the SQL statement result row into an array.

```
$row = mssql_fetch_array($sql_result)
```

mssql_free_result()

This function frees the memory resources used by a database query.

```
mssql_free_result($sql_result);
```

mssql_close()

This function explicitly closes a database connection.

```
mssql_close($connection);
```

mSQL Functions

Numerous PHP functions exist for connecting to and querying an mSQL server. Following are some basic functions and their syntax. See the PHP Manual at http://www.php.net/manual/ for a complete listing of mSQL functions.

msql_connect()

This function opens a connection to the mSQL server; it requires a server name.

```
$connection = msql_connect("servername");
```

msql_select_db()

This function selects a database on the mSQL server for use by subsequent queries; it requires that a valid connection has been established.

```
$db = msql_select_db("myDB", $connection);
```

msql_query()

This function issues the SQL statement; it requires an open connection to the database.

```
$sql_result = msql_query("SELECT * FROM SOMETABLE",$connection);
```

msql_fetch_array()

This function automatically places the SQL statement result row into an array.

```
$row = msql_fetch_array($sql_result)
```

msql_free_result()

This function frees the memory resources used by a database query.

```
msql_free_result($sql_result);
```

msql_close()

This function explicitly closes a database connection.

```
msql_close($connection);
```

MySQL Functions

Numerous PHP functions exist for connecting to and querying a MySQL server. Following are some basic functions and their syntax. See the PHP Manual at http://www.php.net/manual/ for a complete listing of MySQL functions.

mysql_connect()

This function opens a connection to MySQL. Requires a server name, username, and password.

```
$connection = mysql_connect("servername","username","password");
```

mysql_select_db()

This function selects a database on the MySQL server for use by subsequent queries; it requires that a valid connection has been established.

```
$db = mysql_select_db("myDB", $connection);
```

mysql_query()

This function issues the SQL statement; it requires an open connection to the database.

```
$sql_result = mysql_query("SELECT * FROM SOMETABLE",$connection);
```

mysql_fetch_array()

This function automatically places the SQL statement result row into an array.

```
$row = mysql_fetch_array($sql_result)
```

mysql_free_result()

This function frees the memory resources used by a database query.

```
mysql_free_result($sql_result);
```

mysql_close()

This function explicitly closes a database connection.

```
mysql_close($connection);
```

ODBC Functions

PHP contains functions for making generic ODBC connections, should your database type not have an explicit set of functions. Following are some basic functions and their syntax. See the PHP Manual at http://www.php.net/manual/ for a complete listing of ODBC functions.

odbc_connect()

This function opens an ODBC connection; it requires a server name, username, and password.

```
$connection = odbc_connect("YourDataSourceName","username","password");
```

odbc_prepare()

This function readies a SQL statement for execution by the ODBC datasource.

```
$sql_result = odbc_prepare($connection,"SELECT * FROM TABLENAME");
```

odbc_execute()

This function executes a prepared SQL statement.

```
odbc_execute($sql_result);
```

odbc_result_all()

This function automatically formats query results into an HTML table; it requires a query result and can optionally include HTML table attributes.

```
odbc_result_all($sql_result,"border=1");
```

odbc_free_result()

This function frees the memory resources used by a database query.

```
odbc_free_result($sql_result);
```

odbc_close()

This function explicitly closes a database connection.

```
odbc_close($connection);
```

Oracle Functions

Numerous PHP functions exist for connecting to and querying an Oracle 7 or Oracle 8 Server. Following are some basic functions and their syntax. See the PHP Manual at http://www.php.net/manual/ for a complete listing of Oracle functions.

OCILogon()

This function opens a connection to Oracle; it requires that the environment variable `ORACLE_SID` has been set and that you have a valid username and password.

```
$connection = OCILogon("username","password");
```

OCIParse()

This function parses a SQL statement; it requires an open database connection.

```
$sql_statement = OCIParse($connection,"SELECT * FROM TABLENAME");
```

OCIExecute()

This function executes a prepared SQL statement.

```
OCIExecute($sql_statement);
```

OCIFetch()

This function gets the next row in the result of a SQL statement and places it in a results buffer; it requires a valid result set.

```
OCIFetch($sql_statement);
```

OCIResult()

This function gets the value of the named column in the current result row; it requires a valid result set.

```
OCIResult($sql_statement,"COLUMN")
```

OCIFreeStatement()

This function frees the resources in use by the current statement.

```
OCIFreeStatement($sql_result);
```

OCILogoff()

This function explicitly closes a database connection.

```
OCILogoff($connection);
```

PostgreSQL Functions

Numerous PHP functions exist for connecting to and querying a PostgreSQL Server. Following are some basic functions and their syntax. See the PHP Manual at http://www.php.net/manual/ for a complete listing of PostgreSQL functions.

pg_connect()

This function opens a connection to a PostgreSQL database; it requires a hostname, database name, username, and password.

```
$connection = pg_connect("host=YourHostname dbname=YourDBName user=YourUsername
password=YourPassword");
```

pg_exec()

This function issues the SQL statement; it requires an open connection to the database.

```
$sql_result = pg_exec($connection,$sql);
```

pg_fetch_array()

This function automatically places the SQL statement result row into an array.

```
pg_fetch_array($sql_result, [row]);
```

pg_freeresult()

This function frees the memory resources used by a database query.

```
pg_freeresult($sql_result);
```

pg_close()

This function explicitly closes a database connection.

```
pg_close($connection);
```

Sybase Functions

Numerous PHP functions exist for connecting to and querying a Sybase database. Following are some basic functions and their syntax. See the PHP Manual at http://www.php.net/manual/ for a complete listing of Sybase functions.

sybase_connect()

This function opens a connection to Sybase; it requires a server name, username, and password.

```
$connection = sybase_connect("servername","username","password");
```

sybase_select_db()

This function selects a database on the Sybase server for use by subsequent queries; it requires that a valid connection has been established.

```
$db = sybase_select_db("myDB", $connection);
```

sybase_query()

This function issues the SQL statement; it requires an open connection to the database.

```
$sql_result = sybase_query("SELECT * FROM SOMETABLE",$connection);
```

sybase_fetch_array()

This function automatically places the SQL statement result row into an array.

```
$row = sybase_fetch_array($sql_result)
```

sybase_free_result()

This function frees the memory resources used by a database query.

```
sybase_free_result($sql_result);
```

sybase_close()

This function explicitly closes a database connection.

```
sybase_close($connection);
```

Date and Time Functions

The basic PHP date and time functions let you easily format timestamps for use in database queries and calendar functions, as well as simply printing the date on an order form receipt.

date()

The date() function returns the current server timestamp, formatted according to a given a set of parameters. Here is the syntax of the date() function:

```
date(format, [timestamp]);
```

If the timestamp parameter is not provided, the current timestamp is assumed. Table A.6 shows the available formats.

Table A.6   date() Function Formats

Character	Meaning
a	prints "am" or "pm"
A	prints "AM" or "PM"
h	hour, 12-hour format (01 to 12)
H	hour, 24-hour format (00 to 23)
g	hour, 12-hour format without leading zero (1 to 12)
G	hour, 24-hour format without leading zero (0 to 23)
i	minutes (00 to 59)
s	seconds (00 to 59)
Z	time zone offset in seconds (-43200 to 43200)
U	seconds since the Epoch (January 1, 1970 00:00:00 GMT)
d	day of month, two digits (01 to 31)
j	day of month, two digits without leading zero (1 to 31)
D	day of week, text (Mon to Sun)
l	day of week, long text (Monday to Sunday)
w	day of week, numeric, Sunday to Saturday (0 to 6)
F	month, long text (January to December)
m	month, two digits (01 to 12)
n	month, two digits without leading zero (1 to 12)
M	month, three-letter text (Jan to Dec)
Y	year, four digits (2000)
y	year, two digits (00)
z	day of the year (0 to 365)
t	number of days in the given month (28 to 31)
S	English ordinal suffix (th, nd, st)

For example, the following will print the current date in this format: January 10th 2000, 08:08AM.

```
echo date ("F jS Y, h:iA.");
```

checkdate()

The `checkdate()` function validates a given date. Successful validation means that the year is between 0 and 32767, the month is between 1 and 12, and the proper number of days are in each month (leap years are accounted for). Here's the syntax of `checkdate()`:

```
checkdate(month, day, year);
```

For example, if you have a date such as "12/30/1973" (which happens to be my birthday so I'm pretty sure it's valid), you can use the following code to break apart the date and validate it, returning a response to the user:

```php
<?php
$orig_date = "12/30/1973";
$date = explode("/", "$orig_date");

$month = $date[0];
$day = $date[1];
$year = $date[2];

$res = checkdate($month, $day, $year);

if ($res == 1) {
    echo "$orig_date is a valid date!";
} else {
    echo "$orig_date is not valid.";
}
?>
```

The output of this script is

    12/30/1973 is a valid date!

mktime()

The `mktime()` function returns the UNIX timestamp as a long integer (in the format of seconds since the Epoch) for a given date. Thus, the primary use of `mktime()` is to format dates in preparation for mathematical functions and date validation. Here's the syntax of `mktime()`:

```
mktime(hour, minute, second, month, day, year);
```

For example, if the month is January (1), the day of the month is 10, and the year is 2000:

```
echo mktime(0,0,0,1,10,2000);
```

the result is 947480400.

time() and microtime()

The `time()` function returns the current system time, measured in seconds since the Epoch. The syntax of `time()` is simply

```
time();
```

For example, to print the current system timestamp, use

```
echo time();
```

You could get a result such as 951255198. Well actually you couldn't, because that moment has already passed, about 15 seconds before I wrote this sentence!

Using `microtime()` adds a count of microseconds, so instead of just 951255198, I got 0.28305600 951255198 at the exact moment I asked for the time since the Epoch in both seconds and microseconds.

Filesystem Functions

The built-in filesystem functions can be very powerful tools—or weapons, if used incorrectly. Be very careful when using filesystem functions, especially if you have PHP configured to run as root or some other system-wide user. For example, using a PHP script to issue an `rm -R` command while at the root level of your directory would be a very bad thing.

chmod(), chgrp(), and chown()

Like the shell commands of the same name, the `chmod()`, `chgrp()`, and `chown()` functions will modify the permissions, group, and owner of a directory or file. The syntax of these functions is

```
chmod("filename", mode);
chgrp("filename", newgroup);
chown("filename", newowner);
```

For example, to change the permissions on a file called `index.html` in your home directory, use

```
chmod("/home/username/index.html", 0755);
```

To change to a new group, called users:

```
chgrp("/home/username/index.html", users);
```

To change to a new owner, called joe:

```
chown("/home/username/index.html", joe);
```

In order to change permissions, groups and owners, the PHP user must be the owner of the file, or the permissions must already be set to allow such changes by that user.

copy()

The `copy()` function works much like the `cp` shell command: it needs a file name and a destination in order to copy a file. The syntax of `copy()` is

```
copy("source filename", "destination");
```

For example, to make a backup copy of the file `index.html` in your home directory, use

```
copy("/home/username/index.html", "/home/username/index.html.bak");
```

The PHP user must have permission to write into the destination directory, or the copy function will fail.

diskfreespace()

The `diskfreespace()` function returns the total free space for a given directory, in bytes. The syntax of `diskfreespace()` is

```
diskfreespace(directory);
```

For example, to see the available space on your UNIX machine, use

```
$space = diskfreespace("/");
echo "$space";
```

On your Windows machine, you can use

```
$space = diskfreespace("C:\\");
echo "$space";
```

fopen()

The `fopen()` function opens a specified file or URL for reading and/or writing. The syntax of `fopen()` is

```
fopen("filename", "mode")
```

To open a URL, use `http://` or `ftp://` at the beginning of the file name string.

If the file name begins with anything else, the file is opened from the filesystem, and a file pointer to the opened file is returned. Otherwise, the file is assumed to reside on the local filesystem.

The specified mode determines whether the file is opened for reading, writing, or both. Table A.7 lists the valid modes.

Table A.7   fopen() Function Modes

Mode	Description
r	Read-only. The file pointer is at the beginning of the file.
r+	Reading and writing. The file pointer is at the beginning of the file.
w	Write-only. The file pointer is at the beginning of the file, and the file is truncated to zero length. If the file does not exist, attempt to create it.
w+	Reading and writing. The file pointer is at the beginning of the file, and the file is truncated to zero length. If the file does not exist, attempt to create it.
a	Write-only. The file pointer is at the end of the file (it appends content to the file). If the file does not exist, attempt to create it.
a+	Reading and writing. The file pointer is at the end of the file (it appends content to the file). If the file does not exist, attempt to create it.

For example, to open the file `index.html` in your home directory for reading only, use

```php
$fp = fopen("/home/username/index.html", "r");
```

To open a nonexistent file called `temp.txt` in your home directory, use

```php
$fp = fopen("/home/username/temp.txt", "w+");
```

fread()

Use the `fread()` function to read a specified number of bytes from an open file pointer. The syntax of `fread()` is

```php
fread(filepointer, length);
```

For example, to read the first 1024 bytes of a file and assign the string as a value of a variable called `$content`, use this code:

```
$fp = fopen("/home/username/temp.txt", "r"); // open the file pointer
$content = fread($fp, 1024);  // read 1024 bytes into a variable
```

fputs()

The fputs() function writes to an open file pointer. The syntax of fputs() is

```
fputs(filepointer, content, [length]);
```

The file pointer must be open in order to write to the file. The length parameter is optional. If it isn't specified, all specified content is written to the file.

For example, to write "I love PHP" to an open file pointer, use

```
fputs($filepointer, "I love PHP");
```

Alternatively, you can place the content in a variable and then reference only the variable:

```
$content = "I love PHP";
fputs($filepointer, $content);
```

fclose()

Use the fclose() function to close an open file pointer. The syntax of fclose() is

```
fclose(filepointer);
```

For example, if you used the fopen() function to open a file pointer called $new_file, you would use the following code to close the file pointer:

```
fclose($new_file);
```

file_exists()

The file_exists() function checks to see if a file of the specified name already exists. The syntax of file_exists() is

```
file_exists("filename");
```

For example, the following code checks to see if the file index.html exists in a directory and then prints a message depending on the results:

```
if (!file_exists("/home/username/index.html")) {
    echo "The file index.html does not exist.";
} else {
    echo "Success!  index.html exists.";
}
```

mkdir()

Like the mkdir shell command, the mkdir() function creates a new directory on the filesystem. The syntax of mkdir() is

```
mkdir("pathname", mode);
```

For example, to create a directory called public_html in your home directory, use

```
mkdir("/home/username/public_html", 0755);
```

The PHP user must have write permission in the specified directory.

rename()

As its name suggests, the rename() function attempts to give a new name to an existing file. The syntax of rename() is

```
rename("oldname", "newname");
```

For example, to rename a file in your home directory from index.html to temp1.html, use

```
rename("/home/username/index.html", "/home/username/temp1.html");
```

The PHP user must have permission to modify the file.

rmdir()

Like the rmdir shell command, the rmdir() function removes a directory from the filesystem. The syntax of rmdir() is

```
rmdir("pathname");
```

For example, to remove the directory public_html from your home directory, use

```
rmdir("/home/username/public_html");
```

The PHP user must have write permission in the specified directory.

symlink()

The symlink() function creates a symbolic link from an existing file or directory on the filesystem to a specified link name. The syntax of symlink() is

```
symlink("targetname", "linkname");
```

For example, to create a symbolic link called index.html to an existing file called index.html, use

```
symlink("index.html", "index.phtml");
```

unlink()

The `unlink()` function deletes a file from the filesystem. The syntax of `unlink()` is

```
unlink("filename");
```

For example, to delete a file called `index.html` in your home directory, use

```
unlink("/home/username/index.html");
```

The PHP user must have write permission for this file.

HTTP Functions

The built-in functions for sending specific HTTP headers and cookie data are crucial aspects of developing large Web-based applications in PHP. Luckily, the syntax for these functions is quite easy to understand and implement.

header()

The `header()` function outputs an HTTP header string, such as a location redirection. This output must occur before any other data is sent to the browser, including HTML tags.

> This information bears repeating over and over again: Do not attempt to send information of any sort to the browser before sending a `header()`. You can perform any sort of database manipulations or other calculations before the `header()`, but just cannot print anything to the screen, not even a new line character.

For example, to use the `header()` function to redirect a user to a new location, use this code:

```
header("Location: http://www.newlocation.com");
exit;    // Follow a header statement with the exit command.
         // This ensures that the code does not continue to execute.
```

setcookie()

The `setcookie()` function sends a cookie to the user. Cookies must be sent before any other header information is sent to the Web browser. The syntax for `setcookie()` is

```
setcookie("name", "value", "expire", "path", "domain", "secure");
```

For example, you would use the following code to send a cookie called username with a value of joe that is valid for one hour within all directories on the testcompany.com domain:

```
setcookie("username","joe", time()+3600, "/", ".testcompany.com");
```

Mail Function

The PHP mail function makes the interface between your HTML forms and your server's mail program a snap!

mail()

If your server has access to `sendmail` or an SNMP gateway, the `mail()` function sends mail to a specified recipient. The syntax of `mail()` is

```
mail("recipient", "subject", "message", "mail headers");
```

For example, the following code sends mail to `julie@thickbook.com`, with a subject of "I'm sending mail!" and a message body saying "PHP is cool!" The "From:" line is part of the additional mail headers:

```
mail("julie@thickbook.com", "I'm sending mail!", "PHP is cool!", "From:
youremail@yourdomain.com\n");
```

Mathematical Functions

Since I have very little aptitude for mathematics, I find PHP's built-in mathematical functions to be of utmost importance! In addition to all the functions, the value of pi (3.14159265358979323846) is already defined as a constant in PHP (M_PI).

ceil()

The `ceil()` function rounds a fraction up to the next higher integer. The syntax of `ceil()` is

```
ceil(number);
```

For example:

```
ceil(2.56); // result is "3";
ceil(1.22); // result is "2";
```

decbin() and bindec()

The `decbin()` and `bindec()` functions convert decimal numbers to binary numbers, and binary numbers to decimal numbers, respectively. The syntax of these functions is

```
decbin(number);
bindec(number);
```

For example, the following code takes a decimal number, converts it to binary, and converts it back to decimal.

```php
<?php
$orig_dec = 66251125;

$dec2bin = decbin($orig_dec);
$bin2dec = bindec($dec2bin);

echo "original decimal number: $orig_dec <br>";
echo "new binary number: $dec2bin <br>";
echo "back to decimal: $bin2dec <br>";
?>
```

The output of this script is

> original decimal number: 66251125
> new binary number: 11111100101110100101110101
> back to decimal: 66251125

dechex() and hexdec()

The `dechex()` and `hexdec()` functions convert decimal numbers to hexadecimal numbers, and hexadecimal numbers to decimal numbers, respectively. The syntax of these functions is

```
dechex(number);
hexdec(number);
```

For example, the following code takes a decimal number, converts it to hexadecimal, and converts it back to decimal.

```php
<?php
$orig_dec = 255;

$dec2hex = dechex($orig_dec);
```

```
$hex2dec = hexdec($dec2hex);

echo "original decimal number: $orig_dec <br>";
echo "new hexadecimal number: $dec2hex <br>";
echo "back to decimal: $hex2dec <br>";
?>
```

The output of this script is

> original decimal number: 255
>
> new hexadecimal number: ff
>
> back to decimal: 255

decoct() and octdec()

The decoct() and octdec() functions convert decimal numbers to octal numbers, and octal numbers to decimal numbers, respectively. The syntax of these functions is

```
decoct(number);
octdec(number);
```

For example, the following code takes a decimal number, converts it to octal, and converts it back to decimal.

```
<?php
$orig_dec = 34672;

$dec2oct = decoct($orig_dec);
$oct2dec = octdec($dec2oct);

echo "original decimal number: $orig_dec <br>";
echo "new octal number: $dec2oct <br>";
echo "back to decimal: $oct2dec <br>";
?>
```

The output of this script is

> original decimal number: 34672
>
> new octal number: 103560
>
> back to decimal: 34672

floor()

The `floor()` function rounds a fraction down to the next lower integer. The syntax of `floor()` is

```
floor(number);
```

For example:

```
floor(2.56); // result is "2";
floor(1.22); // result is "1";
```

number_format()

The `number_format()` function returns the formatted version of a specified number. The syntax of `number_format()` is

```
number_format("number", "decimals", "dec_point", "thousands_sep");
```

For example, to return a formatted version of the number 12156688, with two decimal places and a comma separating each group of thousands, use

```
echo number_format("12156688","2",".",",");
```

The result is 12,156,688.00.

If only a number is provided, the default formatting does not use a decimal point and has a comma between every group of thousands.

pow()

The `pow()` function returns the value of a given number, raised to the power of a given exponent. The syntax of `pow()` is

```
pow(number, exponent);
```

For example, this code raises 19 to the fifth power:

```
echo pow(19, 5);
```

The result is 2476099.

rand()

The `rand()` function generates a random value from a specific range of numbers. The syntax of `rand()` is

```
rand(min, max);
```

For example, to return a random value between 0 and 576, use

```
echo rand(0,576);
```

round()

The `round()` function rounds a fraction to the next higher or next lower integer. The syntax of the `round()` function is

```
round(number);
```

For example:

```
round(2.56);    // returns "3"
round(1.22);    // returns "1"
round(55.22);    // returns "55"
```

sqrt()

The `sqrt()` function returns the square root of a given number. The syntax of `sqrt()` is

```
sqrt(number);
```

For example, to find the square root of 5561, use

```
echo sqrt(5561);
```

The result is 74.572112750009.

srand()

The `srand()` function provides the random number generator with a set of possible values. The syntax of `srand()` is

```
srand(seed);
```

A common practice is to seed the random number generator by using a number of microseconds:

```
srand((double)microtime()*1000000);
```

Miscellaneous Functions

The `die()` and `exit` functions provide useful control over the execution of your script, offering an "escape route" for programming errors.

die()

The `die()` function outputs a given message and terminates the script when a returned value is FALSE. The syntax of `die()` is

```
die("message");
```

For example, you would use the following code to print a message and stop the execution of your script upon failure to connect to your database:

```
$connection = mysql_connect("servername", "username", "password") or die ("Can't
connect to database.");
```

exit

The `exit` function terminates the execution of the current script at the point where the `exit` function is called.

For example, to exit the script after a location redirection header has been sent, use

```
header("Location: http://www.newlocation.com/");
exit;
```

sleep() and usleep()

The `sleep()` and `usleep()` functions put a pause, or a delay, at a given point in the execution of your PHP code. The syntax of these functions is

```
sleep(seconds);
usleep(microseconds);
```

The only difference between `sleep()` and `unsleep()` is that the given wait period for `sleep()` is in seconds, and the wait period for `unsleep()` is in microseconds.

uniqid()

The `uniqid()` function generates a unique identifier, with a prefix if you so desire. The basic syntax of `uniqid()` is

```
uniqid("prefix");
```

That's boring, though. Suppose you want a unique ID with a prefix of "phpuser", so you use

```
$id = uniqid("phpuser");
echo "$id";
```

and get something like phpuser38b320a6b5482.

But if you use something really cool like

```
$id = md5(uniqid(rand()));
echo "$id";
```

Then you get an ID like 999d8971461bedfc7caadcab33e65866.

Network Functions

There are several network functions available, some for opening and reading from sockets, some FTP functions, but the two network functions that I use most often are the IP and name resolution functions.

gethostbyaddr() and gethostbyname()

The `gethostbyaddr()` and `gethostbyname()` functions will return the IP address or hostname of a given machine, respectively. The syntax of these commands is

```
gethostbyaddr(IP);
gethostbyname(hostname);
```

The sample code below shows both of these functions in action:

```
<?php
// assign some variables
$ip = "204.71.200.75";
$host = "www.yahoo.com";

$verify_ip = gethostbyaddr($ip);
$verify_name = gethostbyname($host);

echo "$ip resolves to $verify_ip<br>";
echo "$host resolves to $verify_name<br>";
?>
```

The output of the script above is:

> 204.71.200.75 resolves to www10.yahoo.com
>
> www.yahoo.com resolves to 204.71.200.74

PHP Version and Related Information

Sometimes you'll need to get a quick snapshot of your operating environment, especially if you're like me and can't remember what you've loaded on which Web server! PHP has a few functions that make environment information very easy to discover and modify.

phpinfo()

Calling the `phpinfo()` function will output a template containing PHP version information, extensions information, and numerous other environment variables. Simply create a file with one line in it:

```
<? phpinfo(); ?>
```

Access that file with your Web browser. You'll see more information than you ever needed to know!

phpversion()

If `phpinfo()` provides more information than you want, you can use the `phpversion()` function to return just the version number currently in use. For example, on one of my systems, this snippet of code

```
echo "Current version is: ".phpversion();
```

shows:

Current version is: 4.0b3

Program Execution Functions

You can use PHP's built-in program execution functions to use programs residing on your system, such as encryption programs, third-party image manipulation programs, and so forth. For all program execution functions, the PHP user must have permission to execute the given program.

exec()

The `exec()` function executes an external program. The syntax of `exec()` is

```
exec(command, [array], [return_var]);
```

If an array is specified, the output of the `exec()` function will append to the array. If a `return_var` is specified, it will be assigned a value of the program's return status.

For example, you would use the following code to perform a "ping" of a server five times and print the output:

```
$command = "ping -c5 www.thickbook.com";
exec($command, $result, $rval);
```

```
for ($i = 0; $i < sizeof($result); $i++) {
    echo "$result[$i]<br>";
}
```

passthru()

Like the `exec()` function, the `passthru()` function executes an external program. The difference between the two is that `passthru()` returns the raw output of the action. The syntax of `passthru()` is

```
passthru(command, return_var);
```

If a `return_var` is specified, it will be assigned a value of the program's return status.

system()

The `system()` function executes an external program and displays output as the command is being executed. The syntax of `system()` is

```
system(command, [return_var]);
```

If a `return_var` is specified, it will be assigned a value of the program's return status.

For example, you would use the following code to perform a "ping" of a server five times and print the raw output:

```
$command = "ping -c5 www.thickbook.com";
system($command);
```

Regular Expression Functions
ereg_replace() and eregi_replace()

The `ereg_replace()` and `eregi_replace()` functions replace instances of a pattern within a string and return the new string. The `ereg_replace()` function performs a case-sensitive match, and `eregi_replace()` performs a case-insensitive match. Here is the syntax for both functions:

```
ereg_replace(pattern, replacement, string);
eregi_replace(pattern, replacement, string);
```

For example, you would use the following code to replace "ASP" with "PHP" in the string "I really love programming in ASP!":

```
$old_string = "I really love programming in ASP!";
$new_string = ereg_replace("ASP", "PHP", $old_string);
echo "$new_string";
```

If "ASP" is mixed case, such as "aSp", use the `eregi_replace()` function:

```
$old_string = "I really love programming in aSp!";
$new_string = eregi_replace("ASP", "PHP", $old_string);
echo "$new_string";
```

split()

The `split()` function splits a string into an array using a certain separator (comma, colon, semicolon, and so on). The syntax of `split()` is

```
split(pattern, string, [limit]);
```

If a limit is specified, the `split()` function stops at the named position—for example, at the tenth value in a comma-delimited list.

For example, you would use the following code to place the first 10 elements in a comma-delimited list called `$comma_list` into an array called `$new_array`:

```
$new_array = split(",", $comma_list, 10);
```

Session Handling Functions

Added to PHP4, session handling is a way of holding on to data as a user navigates throughout your Web site. Data can be variables or entire objects.

session_start()

The `session_start()` function starts a session if one has not already been started, or resumes a session if the session ID is present for the user. This function takes no arguments and is called simply by placing the following at the beginning of your code:

```
session_start();
```

session_register()

The `session_register()` function registers a variable within the current session. In other words, if you want to keep track of the value of a variable called `$username` within a user's session, you must first register `$username` as a session variable. The syntax of `session_register()` is

```
session_register("variable_name");
```

For example, to register `$username` as a global session variable, use

```
session_register("username");
```

session_unregister()

The `session_unregister()` function unregisters, or "forgets" a variable within the current session. The syntax of `session_unregister()` is

```
session_unregister("variable_name");
```

For example, to forget about the global session variable called `$username`, use

```
session_unregister("username");
```

session_destroy()

The `session_destroy()` function effectively destroys all the variables and values registered for the current session. This function takes no arguments and is called simply by placing the following in your code:

```
session_destroy();
```

String Functions

This section only scratches the surface of PHP's built-in string manipulation functions, but if you understand these common functions, your programming life will be quite a bit easier!

addslashes() and stripslashes()

The `addslashes()` and `stripslashes()` functions are very important when inserting and retrieving data from a database. Often, text inserted into a database will contain special characters (single quotes, double quotes, backslashes, NULL) that must be "escaped" before being inserted. The `addslashes()` function does just that, using the syntax:

```
addslashes(string);
```

Similarly, the `stripslashes()` function will return a string with the slashes taken away, using the syntax:

```
stripslashes(string);
```

chop(), ltrim() and trim()

All three of these functions remove errant whitespace from a string. The `chop()` function removes whitespace from the end of a string, while `ltrim()` removes whitespace from the beginning of a string. The `trim()` function removes both leading and trailing whitespace from a string. The syntax of these functions is

```
chop(string);
ltrim(string);
trim(string);
```

echo()

The `echo()` function returns output. The syntax of `echo()` is

```
echo (parameter1, parameter2, …)
```

For example:

```
echo "I'm using PHP!";     // output is: I'm using PHP!
echo 2+6;                  // output is: 8
```

The parentheses are not required when using echo.

explode() and implode()

The `explode()` function splits a string using a given separator and returns the values in an array. The syntax of `explode()` is

```
explode("separator", "string");
```

For example, the following code takes a string called `$color_list`, containing a comma-separated list of colors, and places each color into an array called `$my_colors`:

```
$color_list = "blue,black,red,green,yellow,orange";
$mycolors = explode(",", $color_list);
```

Conversely, the `implode()` function takes an array and makes it into a string, using a given separator. The syntax of `implode()` is

```
implode("separator", "string");
```

For example, the following code takes an array called `$color_list`, then creates a string called `$mycolors`, containing the values of the `$color_list` array, separated by commas:

```
$mycolors = implode(",", $color_list);
```

htmlspecialchars() and htmlentities()

The `htmlspecialchars()` and `htmlentities()` functions convert special characters and HTML entities within strings into their acceptable entity representations.

The `htmlspecialchars()` function only converts the less-than sign (< becomes <), greater-than sign (> becomes >), double quotes ("" becomes "), and the ampersand (& becomes &). The `htmlentities()` function will convert the characters in the ISO-8859-1 character set to the proper HTML entity. The syntax of these functions is

```
htmlspecialchars(string);
htmlentities(string);
```

nl2br()

The `nl2br()` function will replace all ASCII newlines with the HTML line break (`<BR>`). The syntax of the `nl2br()` function is

```
nl2br(string);
```

sprintf()

The `sprintf()` function returns a string that has been formatted according to a set of directives. The syntax of `sprintf()` is

```
sprintf(directives, string);
```

Table A.8 lists the formatting directives.

Table A.8   sprintf() Function Formatting Directives

Directive	Result
%	Adds a percent sign.
b	Considers the string an integer and formats it as a binary number.
c	Considers the string an integer and formats it with that ASCII value.
d	Considers the string an integer and formats it as a decimal number.
f	Considers the string a double and formats it as a floating-point number.
o	Considers the string an integer and formats it as an octal number.
s	Considers and formats the string as a string.
x	Considers the string an integer and formats it as a hexadecimal number (lowercase letters).
X	Considers the string an integer and formats it as a hexadecimal number (uppercase letters).

For example, to format currency using `sprintf()`, use this code:

```
$tax = 1.06;
$subtotal = 10.94;
$total = $tax + $subtotal;
$fmt_total = sprintf ("%0.2f", $total);
echo "$fmt_total";
```

The value of `$fmt_total` is 12.00 instead of simply 12.

strlen()

The `strlen()` function returns the length of a given string. The syntax of the `strlen()` function is

```
strlen(string);
```

strtolower()

The `strtolower()` function returns a given string with all alphabetic characters in lowercase. The syntax of `strtolower()` is

```
strtolower(str);
```

For example, to return ABGH 10023 as lowercase, use

```
echo strtolower("ABGH 10023");
```

The result is abgh 10023.

strtoupper()

The `strtoupper()` function returns a given string with all alphabetic characters in uppercase. The syntax of `strtoupper()` is

```
strtoupper (str);
```

For example, to return abgh 10023 as uppercase, use

```
echo strtoupper ("abgh 10023");
```

The result is ABGH 10023.

substr()

The `substr()` function returns a portion of a string, given a starting position and optional ultimate length. The syntax of `substr()` is

```
substr(string, start, [length]);
```

If the start position is a positive number, the starting position is counted from the beginning of the string. If the start position is negative, the starting position is counted from the end of the string.

Similarly, if the optional length parameter is used and is a positive number, the length is counted from the beginning of the string. If the length parameter is used and is a negative number, the length is counted from the end of the string.

For example:

```
$new_string = substr("PHP is great!", 1); // returns "HP is great!"
$new_string = substr("PHP is great!", 0, 7); // returns "PHP is"
$new_string = substr("PHP is great!", -1); // returns "!"
$new_string = substr("PHP is great!", -6, 5); // returns "great"
```

ucfirst()

The `ucfirst()` function changes the first alphabetic character in a string to an uppercase character. The syntax of `ucfirst()` is

```
ucfirst(string);
```

For example, if your string is "i love PHP", the following code returns "I love PHP":

```
ucfirst("i love PHP");
```

ucwords()

The `ucwords()` function changes the first letter of each word in a string to uppercase. The syntax of `ucwords()` is

```
ucwords(string);
```

For example, if your string is "i love PHP", the following code will return "I Love PHP":

```
ucwords("i love PHP");
```

Variable Functions

The two basic variable functions, `isset()` and `unset()`, help you manage your variables within the scope of an application.

isset() and unset()

The `isset()` function determines whether a variable exists. The `unset()` function explicitly destroys the named variable. Here is the syntax of each:

```
isset(var);
unset(var);
```

The `isset()` function returns TRUE if the variable exists and FALSE if it does not. For example, if you have a variable called `$foo`, with a value of "bar", the following returns TRUE:

```
$foo = "bar";
echo isset($foo);
```

Now, if you use the `unset()` function on `$foo`, like this:

```
unset($foo);
```

The value of `isset($foo)` will now be false:

```
echo isset($foo); // FALSE!
```

Appendix B: Getting Support

Web Sites

Mailing Lists

One of the greatest aspects of the Open Source community is that people are eager to help you learn as much as you can, so that you can become an advocate as well. However, you probably should attempt to find answers to your questions before posing them to the community at large. Doing so includes reading available manuals and FAQs, searching through mailing list archives, and visiting PHP-related Web sites. Chances are good that someone else has had the same question you have.

Web Sites

The Web sites listed below are only a sampling of the sites that are out there for PHP developers. The majority of these sites are maintained by people on their own time, so if you use any of their resources, try to give back to the community by helping others out with their questions, when you can, and contributing code snippets to code repositories and so forth.

www.php.net

Simply start at the home of PHP; the on-line manual is here, as well as links to ISPs that offer access to PHP, the PHP FAQ, news articles, and much more!

www.thickbook.com

I created this Web site as a supplement to this book. You will find links to other Web sites, additional code samples and tutorials, code fixes for examples in this book, every piece of code used in this book (downloadable so you don't have to type), and a feedback section where you can tell me what you want to see in the next version of the book (or what you want me to cut!).

www.zend.com

Zend Technologies, the folks behind the Zend engine of PHP4, have created a portal site for PHP developers. This personalized site not only showcases how you can build a high-traffic, dynamic site using PHP, it provides pointers, resources, and lessons on how to maximize the potential of PHP in all your on-line applications.

Webmonkey (hotwired.lycos.com/webmonkey/)

The company that brings us Wired Magazine also brings us HotWired, which spawned Webmonkey, a developer's resource site with a section devoted to PHP. Don't limit yourself just to the PHP section of Webmonkey, for there's much information to be had in other sections as well. A favorite of mine, not only because I write for them, but because they're smart folks.

WeberDev (www.weberdev.com)

A long-time favorite of PHP developers, this site contains development tricks and tips for many programming languages (just to be fair) as well as a content management system for everyone to add their own code snippets, tutorials, and more! Great weekly newsletter, and high traffic. Go contribute!

PHPBuilder (www.phpbuilder.com)

A very good tutorial site for intermediate and advanced PHP developers, containing weekly "How To" columns for real-world applications, such as "Building Dynamic Pages With Search Engines in Mind," "Generating Pronounceable Passwords" and tons more. Highly recommended!

DevShed (www.devshed.com)

Many user-submitted tutorials, news articles, interviews and competitive analyses of server-side programming languages. Covers PHP as well as many other topics of interest to developers, such as servers and databases.

px.sklar.com

A bare-bones code repository, but who needs graphics when all you're looking for are code snippets? Borrowing from the "take a penny, leave a penny" mentality, grab a code snippet to start with, then add your own when you feel confident in sharing.

AlbaSoftware PHP Resources (www.albasoftware.com)

This PHP portal is designed for all levels of PHP developers, and contains general information and articles/tutorials for developers. You can also find information on contributing to open source projects started by AlbaSoftware.

www.php-center-de and www.dynamic-webpages.de

Two German-language PHP portals, containing FAQs, tutorials, links, code samples—everything portal sites should be!

www.phpindex.com

Quite like the German PHP portals, PHP Index is a wonderful PHP portal – entirely in French.

Mailing Lists

There are several high-traffic mailing lists available for PHP discussion. Please remember your netiquette when asking a question: be polite, offer as many examples you can (if you're describing a problem), provide your system information (if looking for a solution), and did I mention to say please and thank you?

You can always find mailing list subscription information in the "Support" section at http://www.php.net/, but here are some addresses for the general lists:

- To subscribe to the General PHP Mailing List (English), send an email to `php3-digest-subscribe@lists.php.net`
- To subscribe to the French PHP Mailing List, send an email to `php3-france-subscribe@onelist.com`
- To subscribe to the German PHP Mailing List, send an email to `php@infosoc.uni-koeln.de`
- To subscribe to the Italian PHP Mailing List, send an email to `php3-it-request@michel.enter.it`
- To subscribe to the Portuguese PHP Mailing List, send an email to `php-pt-subscribe@eGroups.com`
- To subscribe to the Spanish PHP Mailing List, send an email to `php-subscribe@listserver.iwcc.com.ar`

The English PHP mailing lists are archived and available for searching at http://marc.theaimsgroup.com/. Just look for the PHP-related lists under the "WWW" heading. An invaluable resource, which archives the MySQL mailing list as well as quite a few others!

A

Add to Shopping Cart form, 252
addition (+) operator, 37
addslashes() string function, 340
admin_addrecord1.php, 170, 173, 176–179
admin_addrecord2.php file, 173, 179–185
admin_delrecord1.php, 170, 208–210
admin_delrecord2.php file, 210–215
admin_delrecord3.php file, 215–217
admin_modrecord1.php, 170, 186, 189–191
admin_modrecord2.php file, 187, 191, 197–203
admin_modrecord3.php file, 205–207
administration menu
    adding records to a product catalog, 172–186
    deleting product catalog records, 208–217
    modifying product catalog records, 186–208
    user authentication, 169–172
angle < and > brackets, HTML tags, 26
ANSI (American National Standards Institute), SQL standards, 74
Apache
    htpasswd program, 135–136
    HTTP authentication configuration, 135–139
    httpd.conf file directives, 136–137
    Open Source software example, 5
    UNIX system installation process, 7–11
    UNIX system/PHP3 configuration, 19
    user/group file creation, 135–136
    Windows system installation process, 6–7
    Windows system/PHP3 configuration, 16–17
arithmetic operators, described, 37–38, 293
array() function, 298
array_keys() function, 308–309
array_merge() function, 306–307
array_pop() function, 299–300
array_push() function, 298–299
array_shift() function, 302–303
array_slice() function, 303–305
array_unshift() function, 300–301
array_values() function, 309–310
arrays
    described, 39
    double brace[] characters, 112
    variables, 291

ASP (Active Server Pages), scripting language, 4
assignment operators, 293
    described, 37
    equal sign (=) character, 37
asterisk (*) character, multiplication operator, 37
attributes, HTML tags, 27
authentication
    database-driven, 139–146
    HTTP, 134–139
    limit by IP address, 146–147
authentication-enabled Web server, HTTP authentication element, 134
authorize1.php file, 137–138
authorize2.php file, 138–139
authorize3.php file, 140–141

B

backslash (\) character, delineating a dollar sign ($) character, 42
BIND, Open Source software example, 5
bindec() mathematical function, 331
blob data type, 75
block-level tags, HTML, 27–28
browser_match.php file, 55–58
browser_type.php file, 51
browser-specific code, displaying, 55–58
built-in functions, See functions.

C

calc01.php file, 39–41
calc02.php file, 42–43
calculation script, calc01.php file, 39–41
ceil() mathematical function, 330
CGI extension, versus module, 15
challenge/response scheme, HTTP authentication, 134–139
char data type, 75
check out, shopping system, 262–273
checkboxes, HTML form input element, 31–32
checkdate() function, 323
chgrp() filesystem function, 324–325

chmod() filesystem function, 324
chop() string function, 340–341
chown() filesystem function, 324–325
client-side code execution, described, 34
code execution, client-side versus server-side, 34
ColdFusion, scripting language, 4
comma (,) character, field definition separator, 116
commands
  ALTER, SQL, 74–76
  CREATE, SQL, 74–75
  DELETE, 215–217
  DELETE, SQL, 74, 79–80
  DROP, SQL, 74, 76
  echo, 35
  INSERT, SQL, 74, 76–77
  REPLACE, 204
  SELECT, SQL, 74, 78–79
  semicolon (;) instruction terminator, 35
  SQL, 74
  UPDATE, SQL, 74, 77–78
comments, HTML, 33
comparison operators, described, 38, 294
control statements
  comparison operator uses, 38
  logical operator uses, 39
control structures
  described, 295
  for, 297
  if...elseif...else, 295–296
  while, 296–297
cookies
  described, 150
  PHPSESSID, 155, 164
  reading, 152–154
  setting, 151–152
  user_id, 236
cookies variable, 292
copy() filesystem function, 325
count variable, session handling, 155–156
count() function, 259, 310–311
count_me.php file, 158–159
cryptography, public-key, 221

D

data
  display techniques, 128–132
  selection techniques, 128–132
  table entry techniques, 121–128

data encryption
  development history, 220–221
  GNUPG, 229–235
  OpenPGP standard, 221
  PGP (Pretty Good Privacy), 221–228
  public-key cryptography, 221
data files
  reading, 66–68
  writing, 64–66
data types, described, 75
database connectivity function, 314–321
database tables, product catalog, 167–169
database-driven authentication
  described, 139
  HMTL form for user validation, 141–146
  PHP authentication variables, 139–141
databases
  adding records to a table, 121–128
  data selection/display techniques, 128–132
  field definitions, 110–115
  field naming conventions, 70
  Informix connectivity functions, 81–83
  installation process, 21–23
  Microsoft SQL Server connectivity functions, 83–86
  mSQL connectivity functions, 86–90
  MySQL database connectivity functions, 21–23, 90–93
  ODBC connectivity functions, 103–105
  Oracle connectivity functions, 93–97
  PHP3 support issues, 2, 21
  PostgreSQL connectivity functions, 97–100
  relationships, 72–74
  structural elements, 70
  supported data types, 75
  Sybase connectivity functions, 100–103
  table data entry techniques, 121–128
  table definition, 108–110
  unique identifier importance, 71–72
date and time functions
  checkdate(), 323
  date(), 321–322
  microtime(), 324
  mktime(), 323–324
  time(), 324
date data type, 75
date() function, 321–322
datetime data type, 75
decbin() mathematical function, 331
dechex() mathematical function, 331–332
decoct() mathematical function, 332

decrement operators, 294
DELETE command, deleting product
    catalog records, 215–217
die() function, 81, 335
diskfreespace() filesystem function, 325
display_products.php file, 129–130
division (/) operator, 37
do_addrecord.php file, 121–127
do_calculate.php file, 45–49
do_createtable.php file, 111, 115–119
do_redirect.php file, 52–54
do_sendfeedback.php file, 59–62
do_sendsecret.php file, 223–228, 230–235
do_showfielddef.php file, 109–110, 113–115
docalc.php file, 43
documents
    HTML creation process, 28–33
    Web browser request process, 34
dollar sign ($) character, printing, 42
double brace [] characters, array indicator, 112
double data type, 75
double equal sign (==) characters, described, 37
drop-down list boxes
    HTML form input element, 32
    if...else statement uses, 196
dynamic content
    displaying, 51–58
    displaying browser-specific code, 55–58
    redirecting a user to a new location, 51–55

E

each() function, 311
echo() string function, 341
e-commerce
    cookie uses, 150–154
    data encryption, 220–235
e-mail
    feedback forms, 58–64
    sending, 58–64
    sending data files, 67
    sending secure orders, 274–285
encryption, development history, 220–221
environment variables, 292–293
    described, 49
    HTTP_USER_AGENT, 50–51
    REMOTE_ADDR, 50
    viewing, 50
equal sign (=) character
    assignment operator, 37
    variables, 36

ereg_replace() regular expression function, 338
eregi_replace() regular expression function,
    338–339
error messages, die() function uses, 81, 83, 87
escaped code, described, 34
exec() program execution function, 337
exit() function, 335
explode() string function, 341

F

fclose() function, 65, 327
feedback forms
    creating, 58–64
    show_feedback.html file, 58–60
field definitions, comma (,) character as
    separator, 116
fields
    defining, 110–115
    naming conventions, 70
    product catalog, 167–168
    shopping cart tracking table, 255–256
file name argument, fopen() function uses, 64
file pointer, described, 64
file_exists() filesystem function, 327
files
    admin_addrecord1.php, 170, 173, 176–179
    admin_addrecord2.php, 173, 179–185
    admin_delrecord1.php, 170, 208–210
    admin_delrecord2.php, 210–215
    admin_delrecord3.php, 215–217
    admin_modrecord1.php, 170, 186, 189–191
    admin_modrecord2.php, 187, 191, 197–203
    admin_modrecord3.php, 205–207
    authorize1.php, 137–138
    authorize2.php, 138–139
    authorize3.php, 140–141
    browser_match.php, 55–58
    browser_type.php, 51
    calc01.php, 39–41
    calc02.php, 42–43
    count_me.php, 158–159
    display_products.php, 129–130
    do_addrecord.php, 121–127
    do_calculate.php, 45–49
    do_createtable.php, 111, 115–119
    do_redirect.php, 52–54
    do_sendfeedback.php, 59–62
    do_sendsecret.php, 223–228, 230–235
    do_showfielddef.php, 109–110, 113–115
    docalc.php, 43

files (continued)

first.php, 34–35

goform.php, 44

group, 135–136

httpd.conf, 136–137

limitbyIP.php, 146–147

login.html, 141–142

login.php, 142–143

login_form.inc, 143

login2.php, 144–145

phpinfo.php, 49–50

read_data.php, 66–67

remote_address.php, 50

secret_form.html, 223, 230

session1.php, 157

session2.php, 161–164

shop_addtocart.php, 252, 256–258, 260–261

shop_checkout.php, 262–273

shop_checkout.php3, 260

shop_menu.php, 236–237

shop_sendorder.php, 263, 274–285

shop_showbook.php, 249–255

shop_viewall.php, 236, 246–249

shop_viewbycat.php, 236–246

show_addrecord.html, 121–123

show_calculate.html, 45–46

show_createtable.html, 167–169

show_createtable1.html, 108–109

show_feedback.html, 58–60

show_menu.html, 52–54

user, 135–136

write_data.php, 65

filesize() function, reading a complete file, 66

filesystem functions

chgrp(), 324–325

chmod(), 324

chown(), 324–325

copy(), 325

diskfreespace(), 325

fclose(), 327

file_exists(), 327

fopen(), 325–326

fputs(), 327

fread(), 326–327

mkdir(), 328

rename(), 328

rmdir(), 328

symlink(), 328

unlink(), 329

first.php file, 34–35

floating-point numbers, variable value type, 36

floats variables, 291

floor() mathematical function, 333

fopen() filesystem function, 64–65, 325–326

for control structure, 297

forms

Add to Shopping Cart, 252

feedback, 58–64

HTML, 30–33

user preference, 158–168

user validation, 141–146

validation techniques, 62

fputs() filesystem function, 65, 327

fread() filesystem function, 66, 326–327

functions

array(), 298

array_keys(), 308–309

array_merge(), 306–307

array_pop(), 299–300

array_push(), 298–299

array_shift(), 302–303

array_slice(), 303–305

array_unshift(), 300–301

array_values(), 309–310

count(), 259, 310–311

database connectivity, 314–321

date and time, 321–324

die(), 81, 83, 87, 335

each(), 311

exit(), 335

sleep(), 335

uniqui(), 335–336

unsleep(), 335

fclose(), 65

filesize(), 66

Filesystem, 324–329

fopen(), 64

fputs(), 65

fread(), 66

fwrite(), 65

header(), 137–139

HTTP, 329–330

ifx_close(), 81–82

ifx_connect(), 81

ifx_free_result(), 81–82

ifx_htmltbl_result(), 81–82

ifx_query(), 81–82

include(), 143–145

Informix, 81–83, 314

list(), 311

mail(), 58, 330

mathematical, 330–334

Microsoft SQL Server, 83–86, 315
mSQL, 86–90, 316
msql_close(), 83, 85, 89
msql_connect(), 83, 87
msql_fetch_array(), 83–84, 87
msql_free_result(), 83, 85, 89
msql_query(), 83–84, 87
msql_select_db(), 83–84, 87
MySQL 90–93, 317
mysql_close(), 90, 92
mysql_connect(), 90
mysql_fetch_array(), 90–91
mysql_free_result(), 90, 92
mysql_query(), 90–91
mysql_select_db(), 90
Network function, 336
OCIExecute(), 93–94
OCIFetch(), 93, 95
OCIFreeStatement(), 93, 96–97
OCILogoff(), 93, 96–97
OCILogon(), 93–94
OCINumCols(), 93, 95
OCIParse(), 93–94
OCIResult(), 93
ODBC, 103–105, 317–318
odbc_close(), 103–104
odbc_connect(), 103–104
odbc_execute(), 103–104
odbc_free_result(), 103–104
odbc_prepare(), 103–104
odbc_result_all(), 103–104
Oracle, 318–**319**
Oracle database connections, 93–97
pg_close(), 97, 99
pg_connect(), 97
pg_fetch_array(), 97–98
pg_freeresult(), 97, 99
pgexec(), 97–98
PHP 336–337
phpinfo(), 49
PostgreSQL, 319–320
PostgreSQl connectivity, 97–100
preg_match(), 55
program execution, 337–338
regular expression, 338–339
reset(), 311
session handling, 339–340
setcookie(), 152
shuffle(), 311–313
sizeof(), 313
sleep(), 335

uniqui(), 335–336
unsleep(), 335
sprintf(), 42
string 340–344
Sybase, 100–103, 320–321
sybase_close(), 100, 102
sybase_connect(), 100
sybase_fetch_array(), 100–101
sybase_free_result(), 100, 102
sybase_query(), 100–101
sybase_select_db(), 100
system(), 225, 232
time(), 225, 232
uniqui(), 335–336
unsleep(), 335
variable, 344–345
fwrite() function, described, 65

G

GET method
  PHPSESSID cookie, 164
  sending HTML forms, 31
gethostbyaddr() network function, 336
gethostbyname() network function, 336
GNUPG
  data encryption process, 230–235
  described, 229
  public key addition, 229
goform.php file, 44
group files, HTTP authentication creation,
  135–136
Gutmans, Andi, PHP3 developer, 2

H

header() function, HTTP authentication
  variables, 137–139, 329
headers, HTTP, 52–55
hexdec() mathematical function, 331–332
hits, described, 150
HTML (Hypertext Markup Language)
  angle < and > brackets, 26
  block-level tags, 27–28
  comments, 33
  described, 26
  document creation process, 28–33
  opening/closing tag conventions, 26–27
  paired tags, 26–27
  PHP code coexistence, 34
  tag attributes, 27
  text-level tags, 28

HTML forms
checkboxes, 31–32
drop-down list boxes, 32
element types, 43
input elements, 31–32
interactive coffee bean calculator, 45–49
internal elements, 30–33
list boxes, 32
password fields, 31
radio buttons, 31
sending methods, 31
show_calculate.html file, 45–46
submit buttons, 32–33
text areas, 32
text fields, 31
variable passing, 44
variables, 43–49
HTML forms variable, 292
HTML tables, structuring, 29–30
htmlentities() string function, 341–342
htmlspecialchars() string function, 341–342
htpasswd program, Apache Web server user/group file creation, 135–136
HTTP authentication
Apache Web server configuration, 135–139
challenge/response scheme, 134
described, 134–135
PHP authentication variables, 137–139
required elements, 134
user/group file creation process, 135–136
HTTP, environment variables, 49–51
HTTP functions
header(), 329
setcookie(), 329–330
HTTP headers, sending from a PHP script, 52–55
HTTP_COOKIE_VARS variable, 153
HTTP_USER_AGENT environment variable, described, 50–51
httpd.conf file, Apache/HTTP authentication configuration, 136–137

I

IBM, SQL development history, 74
identifiers, database tables, 71–72
if...else statements, drop-down list box uses, 196
if...elseif...else control structure, 295–296
ifx_close() function, Informix database connections, 81–82, 314

ifx_connect() function, Informix database connections, 81, 341
ifx_free_result() function, Informix database connections, 81–82, 314
ifx_htmltbl_result() function, Informix database connections, 81–82, 314
ifx_query() function, Informix database connections, 81–82, 314
IMAP (Internet Message Access Protocol), PHP3 support, 2
implode() string function, 341
include() function, database-driven authentication, 143–145
increment operators, 294
Informix functions
database connection, 81–83
ifx_close(), 314
ifx_connect(), 314
ifx_free_result(), 314
ifx_htmltbl_result(), 314
ifx_query(), 314
installation
Apache Web server/UNIX system, 7–11
Apache Web server/Windows system, 6–7
databases, 21–23
Microsoft IIS, 14
MySQL database, 22–23
PHP3/Windows system, 15–18
testing, 20–21
WebTen server/Macintosh system, 14–15
Xitami server/UNIX system, 13
Xitami server/Windows system, 11–12
instruction terminator (;) character, PHP code, 35
int data type, 75
integers variable, 291
integers, variable value type, 36
interactive coffee bean calculator form, 45–49
IP address, user authentication method, 146–147
isset() variable function, 345

J

JavaScript, client-side code execution, 34
JSP (Java Server Pages), scripting language, 4

K

keys, database fields, 72

L

Lerdorf, Rasmus, PHP/FI developer, 2
limit by IP address authentication,
    described, 146
limitbyIP.php file, 146–147
Linux, Open Source software example, 5
list boxes, HTML form input element, 32
list() function, 311
logical operators, 39, 294–295
login.html file, user validation form, 141–142
login.php file, 142–143
login_form.inc file, 143
login2.php file, 144–145
loops, if...else statements, 196
ltrim() string function, 340–341

M

Macintosh, WebTen server installation, 14–15
Mail functions, mail(), 330
mail() function, arguments, 58
mailing lists, PHP, 21, 350
mathematical functions
    bindec(), 331
    ceil(), 330
    decbin(), 331
    dechex(), 331–332
    decoct(), 332
    floor(), 333
    hexdec(), 331–332
    number_format(), 333
    octdec(), 332
    pow(), 333
    rand(), 333–334
    round(), 334
    sqrt(), 334
    srand(), 334
Microsoft IIS (Internet Information Server)
    installation process, 14
    PHP3 configuration, 17–18
Microsoft SQL Server functions
    connectivity, 83–86
    described, 315
    mssql_close(), 315
    mssql_connect(), 315
    mssql_fetch_array(), 315
    mssql_free_result(), 315
    mssql_query(), 315
    mssql_select_db(), 315

microtime() function, 324
minus sign (-) character, subtraction
    operator, 37
miscellaneous functions
    die(), 335
    exit(), 335
    sleep(), 335
    uniqui(), 335–336
    unsleep(), 335
mkdir() filesystem function, 328
mktime() function, 323–324
mode argument, fopen() function uses, 64
module, versus CGI extension, 15
modulus (%) operator, 37
mSQL functions
    msql_close(), 83, 85, 89, 316
    msql_connect(), 83, 87, 316
    msql_fetch_array(), 83–84, 87, 316
    msql_free_result(), 83, 85, 89, 316
    msql_query(), 83–84, 316
    msql_select_db(), 83–84, 87, 316
msql_close() mSQL function, 83, 85, 89, 316
msql_connect() mSQL function, 83, 87, 316
msql_fetch_array() mSQL function, 83–84,
    87, 316
msql_free_result() mSQL function, 83, 85,
    89, 316
msql_query() mSQL function, 83–84, 316
msql_select_db() mSQL function, 83–84,
    87, 316
mssql_close() Microsoft SQL Server
    function, 315
mssql_connect() Microsoft SQL Server
    function, 315
mssql_fetch_array() Microsoft SQL Server
    function, 315
mssql_free_result() Microsoft SQL Server
    function, 315
mssql_query() Microsoft SQL Server
    function, 315
mssql_select_db() Microsoft SQL Server
    function, 315
multiplication (+) operator, 37
MySQL
    connectivity functions, 90–93
    data selection/display techniques,
      128–132
    database table creation process, 115–120
    database-driven authentication, 139–146
    licensing information, 22

MySQL (continued)
product catalog database table creation, 167–169
reading/setting cookies, 152–154
table data entry techniques, 121–128
UNIX system installation/configuration, 22–23
Windows system installation/configuration, 22

MySQL functions
mysql_close(), 90, 92, 317
mysql_connect(), 90, 317
mysql_fetch_array(), 90–91, 317
mysql_free_result(), 90, 92, 317
mysql_query(), 90–91, 317
mysql_select_db(), 90, 317

mysql_close() mySQL functions, 90, 92, 317
mysql_connect() mySQL functions, 90, 317
mysql_fetch_array() mySQL functions, 90–91, 317
mysql_free_result() nySQL functions, 90, 92, 317
mysql_query() mySQL functions, 90–91, 317
mysql_select_db() mySQL functions, 90, 317

N

network functions
gethostbyaddr(), 336
gethostbyname(), 336
newline (\n) character, PHP code, 35
nl2br() string function, 342
number_format() mathematical function, 333

O

objects, session, 155
OCIExecute() function, 93–94, 319
OCIFetch() function, 93, 95, 319
OCIFreeStatement() function, 93, 96–97, 319
OCILogoff() function, 93, 96–97, 319
OCILogon() function, 93–94, 319
OCINumCols() function, 93, 95
OCIParse() function, 93–94, 319
OCIResult() function, 93, 319
octdec() mathematical function, 332
ODBC (Open Database Connectivity)
connectivity functions, 103–105
described, 103
ODBC functions
odbc_close(), 103–104, 318

odbc_connect(), 103–104, 318
odbc_execute(), 103–104, 318
odbc_free_result(), 103–104
odbc_prepare(), 103–104, 318
odbc_result_all(), 103–104, 318
odbc_close() function, 103–104, 318
odbc_connect() function, 103–104, 318
odbc_execute() function, 103–104, 318
odbc_prepare() function, 103–104, 318
odbc_result_all() function, 103–104, 318
Open Source software, criteria, 4–5
operators
arithmetic, 37–38, 293
assignment, 37, 293
comparison, 38, 294
decrement, 294
described, 293
increment, 294
logical, 39, 294–295
Oracle functions
OCIExecute(), 93–94, 319
OCIFetch(), 93, 95, 319
OCIFreeStatement(), 93, 96–97, 319
OCILogoff(), 93, 96–97, 319
OCILogon(), 93–94, 319
OCIParse(), 93–94, 319
OCIResult(), 93, 319

P

passthru() program execution function, 338
password fields, HTML form input element, 31
passwords, HTTP authentication element, 134
percent sign (%) character, modulus operator, 37
Perl, scripting language, 4
pg_close() PostgreSQL function, 97, 99, 320
pg_connect() PostgreSQL function, 97, 320
pg_exec() PostgreSQL function, 97–98, 320
pg_fetch_array() PostgreSQL function, 97–98, 320
pg_freeresult() PostgreSQL function, 97, 99, 320
PGP (Pretty Good Privacy)
data encryption process, 223–228
development history, 221
public key addition, 222–223
PHP functions
phppinfo(), 337
phpversion(), 337

PHP syntax, 288–290
PHP3 (Personal Home Page Tools)
  Apache Web server/UNIX system
    configuration, 19
  Apache Web server/Windows system
    configuration, 16–17
  common uses, 3
  database support issues, 21
  development history, 2–3
  future expectations, 3–4
  HTML code coexistence, 34
  image creation uses, 285
  installation testing, 20–21
  Microsoft IIS configuration, 17–18
  module versus CGI extension, 15
  Open Source software, 4–5
  UNIX system installation process, 18–19
  when to use, 4
  Windows system installation process, 15–18
  Xitami Web server/UNIX system
    configuration, 20
  Xitami Web server/Windows system
    configuration, 17
PHP4
  backward-compatibility, 3
  beta download/installation process, 23
  registering session variables, 156–157
  Server Abstraction Layer, 4
  session handling techniques, 154–164
  session variable types, 155–156
  user preference forms, 158–164
  Zend engine, 3–5
phpinfo.php file, 49–40
phppinfo() PHP function, 49, 337
PHPSESSID cookie
  GET method use, 164
  session variables, 155
phpversion() PHP function, 337
plus sign (+) character, addition operator, 37
POST method, sending HTML forms, 31
PostgreSQL functions
  pg_close(), 97, 99, 320
  pg_connect(), 97, 320
  pg_exec(), 97–98, 320
  pg_fetch_array(), 97–98, 320
  pg_freeresult(), 97, 99, 320
pow() mathematical function, 333
preg_match() function, described, 55
printing, dollar sign ($) character, 42
product catalog
  adding records to, 172–186

  administration menu elements, 169–217
  database table creation, 167–169
  deleting records from, 208–217
  display techniques, 236–255
  fields, 167–168
  information types, 166–167
  modifying records, 186–208
product details template, shopping system,
  249–255
program execution functions
  exec(), 337
  passthru(), 338
  system(), 338
public key cryptography
  adding to PHP user's public key ring
    w/GNUPG, 229
  adding to PHP user's public key ring
    w/PGP, 222–223
  described, 221

R

radio buttons, HTML form input
    element, 31
rand() mathematical function, 333–334
read_data.php file, 66–67
realm, described, 135
records
  adding to a database table, 121–128
  adding to a product catalog, 172–186
  deleting, 79–80
  deleting from a product catalog, 208–217
  inserting, 76–77
  modifying product catalog, 186–208
  selection techniques, 78–79
  updating, 77–78
redirection scripts, creating, 52–54
regular expression functions
  ereg_replace(), 338
  eregi_replace(), 338–339
  split(), 339
relational databases, described, 72
relationships, database, 72–74
REMOTE_ADDR environment variable,
    described, 50
remote_address.php file, 50
rename() filesystem function, 328
REPLACE command, inserting a record, 204
reset() function, 311
rmdir() filesystem function, 328
round() mathematical function, 334

S

scalar variables, described, 36
scripts
  admin_addrecord1.php, 170, 173, 176–179
  admin_addrecord2.php, 173, 179–185
  admin_delrecord1.php, 170, 208–210
  admin_delrecord2.php, 210–215
  admin_delrecord3.php, 215–217
  admin_modrecord1.php, 170, 186, 189–191
  admin_modrecord2.php, 187, 191, 197–203
  admin_modrecord3.php, 205–207
  authorize1.php, 137–138
  authorize2.php, 138–139
  authorize3.php, 140–141
  browser_match.php, 55–58
  browser_type.php, 51
  calc01.php file, 39–41
  calc02.php file, 42–43
  count_me.php, 158–159
  display_products.php, 129–130
  do_addrecord.php, 121–127
  do_calculate.php file, 45–49
  do_createtable.php, 111, 115–119
  do_redirect.php, 52–54
  do_sendfeedback.php, 59–62
  do_sendsecret.php, 223–228, 230–235
  do_showfielddef.php, 109–110, 113–115
  docalc.php, 43
  enabling variable tracking, 44
  first.php file, 34–35
  goform.php, 44
  limitbyIP.php, 146–147
  login.php, 142–143
  login2.php, 144–145
  PHP opening/closing tags, 34
  phpinfo.php file, 49–50
  read_data.php, 66–67
  remote_address.php, 50
  sending HTTP headers, 52–55
  session1.php, 157
  session2.php, 161–164
  shop_addtocart.php, 252, 256–258, 260–261
  shop_checkout.php, 262–273
  shop_checkout.php3, 260
  shop_menu.php, 236–237
  shop_sendorder.php, 263, 274–285
  shop_showbook.php, 249–255
  shop_viewall.php, 236, 246–249
  shop_viewbycat.php, 236–246
  write_data.php, 65

secret_form.html file, 223, 230
security
  GNUPG data encryption, 229–235
  PGP data encryption, 220–228
semicolon (;) character, instruction
  terminator, 35
Sendmail, Open Source software example, 5
Server Abstraction Layer, PHP4 feature, 4
servers, Web, 5–15
server-side code execution, described, 34
session, described, 155
session handling
  PHP4 techniques, 154–164
  registering session variables, 156–157
  starting a session, 156–157
  user preference forms, 158–164
  user preference management, 157–164
  variable types, 155–156
session handling functions
  session_destroy(), 340
  session_register(), 339
  session_start(), 339
  session_unregister(), 340
session object, described, 155
session variables, registering, 155–157
session_destroy() session handling
  function, 340
session_register() session handling
  function, 339
session_start() session handling function, 339
session_unregister() session handling
  function, 340
session1.php file, 157
session2.php file, 161–164
setcookie() HTTP function, 152, 329–330
shop_addtocart.php file, 252, 256–258, 260–261
shop_checkout.php file, 262–273
shop_checkout.php3 file, 260
shop_menu.php file, 236–237
shop_sendorder.php file, 263, 274–285
shop_showbook.php file, 249–255
shop_viewall.php file, 236, 246–249
shop_viewbycat.php file, 236–246
shopping carts
  counting items, 259–262
  tracking, 255–259
shopping system
  Add to Shopping Cart form, 252
  checking out, 262–273
  counting shopping cart items, 259–262
  creating, 235–285

product catalog display techniques, 236–255
product details template, 249–255
sending secure orders via e-mail, 274–285
shopping cart tracking, 255–259
View All Products Alphabetically page, 246–249
View Products by Category page, 238–246
show_addrecord.html, 121–123
show_calculate.html file, 45–46
show_createtable.html file, 167–169
show_createtable1.html file, 108–109
show_feedback.html file, 58–60
show_menu.html file, 52–54
shuffle() function, 311–313
sizeof() function, 313
slash (/) character, division operator, 37
sleep() function, 335
**SNMP (Simple Network Management
    Protocol), PHP3 support,** 2
software, Open Source criteria, 4–5
split() regular expression function, 339
sprintf() string function, 342–343
SQL (Structured Query Language)
    ALTER command, 74–76
    CREATE command, 74–75
    DELETE command, 74, 79–80
    described, 74
    development history, 74
    DROP command, 74, 76
    INSERT command, 74, 76–77
    proprietary enhancements, 74
    SELECT command, 74, 78–79
    UPDATE command, 74, 77–78
sqrt() mathematical function, 334
srand() mathematical function, 334
Stephenson, Neal, Cryptonomicon, 220
string functions
    addslashes(), 340
    chop(), 340–341
    echo(), 341
    explode(), 341
    htmlentities(), 341–342
    htmlspecialchars(), 341–342
    implode(), 341
    ltrim(), 340–341
    nl2br(), 342
    sprintf(), 342–343
    stripslashes(), 340
    strlen(), 343
    strtolower(), 343
    strtoupper(), 343
    substr(), 343–344

trim(), 340–341
ucfirst(), 344
ucwords(), 344
strings variable, 36, 291
stripslashes() string function, 340
strlen() string function, 343
strtolower() string function, 343
strtoupper() string function, 343
submit button, HTML form element, 32–33
substr() string function, 343–344
subtraction (-) operator, 37
Suraski, Zeev, PHP3 developer, 2
Sybase functions
    sybase_close(), 100, 102, 321
    sybase_connect(), 100, 320
    sybase_fetch_array(), 100–101, 321
    sybase_free_result(), 100, 102, 321
    sybase_query(), 100–101, 321
    sybase_select_db(), 100, 321
sybase_close() Sybase function, 100, 102, 321
sybase_connect() Sybase function, 100, 320
sybase_fetch_array() Sybase function,
    100–101, 321
sybase_free_result() Sybase function, 100,
    102, 321
sybase_query() Sybase function, 100–101, 321
sybase_select_db() Sybase function, 100, 321
symlink() filesystem function, 328
syntax, PHP, 288–290
system() function
    invoking GNUPG, 232
    invoking PGP, 225
    program execution function, 338

T

tables
    creating, 74–75
    data display techniques, 128–132
    data entry techniques, 121–128
    data selection techniques, 128–132
    defining, 108–110
    deleting, 76
    field definitions, 110–115
    HTML, 29–30
    inserting records, 76–77
    modifying, 75–76
    record addition, 121–128
    relationships, 72–74
    shopping cart tracking fields, 255–256
    unique identifier importance, 71–72

text areas, HTML form input element, 32
text data type, 75
text fields, HTML form input element, 31
text-level tags, HTML, 28
time data type, 75
time() function, 225, 235, 324
trim() string function, 340–341

U

ucfirst() string function, 344
ucwords() string function, 344
uniqui() function, 335–336
UNIX
    Apache Web server installation, 7–11
    MySQL installation/configuration, 22
    PHP3 installation process, 18–19
unlink() filesystem function, 329
unset() variable function, 345
unsleep() function, 335
user authentication
    database-driven, 139–146
    described, 134
    HTTP, 134–139
    limit by IP address, 146–147
    product catalog administration, 169–172
    types, 134
user files, HTTP authentication creation, 135–136
user ID, PGP requirement, 225
user preferences
    HTML form, 158–164
    managing with sessions, 157–164
user tracking
    cookies, 150–154
    hit logs, 150
    shopping carts, 255–259
user validation form, database-driven authentication, 141–146
user_id cookie, described, 236
usernames, HTTP authentication element, 134

V

valid variable, session handling, 155–156
varchar data type, 75
variable functions
    isset(), 345
    unset(), 345

variable tracking, enabling, 44
variables
    arithmetic operators, 37–38
    arrays, 291
    assignment operators, 37
    calculation script, 39–41
    comparison operators, 38
    cookies, 292
    count, 155–156
    described, 36, 290
    enabling variable tracking in a script, 44
    environment, 49–51, 292–293
    equal sign (=) character, 36
    floating-point numbers, 36
    floats, 291
    HTML form, 43–49, 292
    HTTP_COOKIE_VARS, 153
    integers, 36, 291
    logical operators 39
    naming conventions, 36
    operators, 37–39
    scalar versus array, 39
    session handling types, 155–156
    strings, 36, 291
    types, 36
    valid, 155–156
View All Products Alphabetically page, shopping system, 246–249
View Products by Category page, shopping system, 238–246

W

Web browsers
    Browser War, 55
    displaying browser-specific code, 55–58
    document request process, 34
Web servers
    Apache, 6–11, 16–17, 19, 135–139
    Microsoft IIS, 14, 17–18
    module versus CGI extension w/PHP3, 15
    PHP3 support, 2
    WebTen installation, 14–15
    Xitami, 11–13, 17, 20
Web sites
    AlbaSoftware PHP resources, 349
    Apache, 6
    author's thickbook.com, 20
    book supplement, 348
    code snippets, 349

Devshed, 349
French PHP portals, 350
German language PHP portals, 350
GNUPG, 229
HotWired, 55
HTTP 1.1 specification, 52
HTTP environment variable descriptions, 50
mailing lists, 350
Microsoft IIS (Internet Information
    Server), 14
MySQL, 21–22
Netscape's cookie specification, 152
Open Source, 4
PGP, 222
PHP FAQ, 21
PHP home page, 348
PHP mailing list archives, 21
PHP Manual, 15, 80, 108
PHP3 Funding page, 5
PHP4, 23
PHPOBuilder, 349
RSA Labs Crypto FAQ, 221
ServerWatch, 5
WeberDev, 349
Webmonkey, 349
WebTen/Tenon Intersystems, 14
Xitami, 11
Zend Technologies, 4, 348

Web-based database administration
    described, 166
    product catalog planning, 166–217
WebTen, Macintosh installation process,
    14–15
while control structure, 296–297
white space, described, 75
Windows
    Apache Web server installation, 6–7
    MySQL installation/configuration, 22
    PHP3 installation process, 15–18
Windows NT, Microsoft IIS (Internet
    Information Server) installation, 14
write_data.php file, 65

X

Xitami
    UNIX system installation process, 13
    UNIX system/PHP3 configuration, 20
    Windows system installation process, 11–12
    Windows system/PHP3 configuration, 17

Z

Zend Technologies, PHP4/Zend engine, 3–5
Zimmerman, Phil, PGP (Pretty Good
    Privacy) developer, 221